WHERE SHE DANCED

ALFRED A. KNOPF

NEW YORK

1979

WHERE SHE DANCED

BY ELIZABETH KENDALL

THIS IS A BORZOI BOOK

PUBLISHED BY ALFRED A. KNOPF, INC.

Portions of this book originally appeared in
Ballet Review in slightly different form.

Photographic credits appear on pages ix–x.

Library of Congress Cataloging in Publication Data
Kendall, Elizabeth.
Where she danced.   Bibliography: p.   Includes index.
1.   Dancing—United States—History.
2.   Dancers—United States—Biography.   I.   Title.
GV1623.K46   793.3'1973   78–20544
ISBN 0–394–40029–1

MANUFACTURED IN THE
UNITED STATES OF AMERICA
FIRST EDITION

To my grandmother
Elizabeth Bemis Conant

and to Ann, Claire, and Don

Though it be as perfect in outline and ornament as classic taste can make it, as simple and serviceable as the most energetic worker can desire, a costume has not business to exist, is, indeed, an embodied crime, if it deforms or weakens or tortures the body it pretends to serve. For that should be sacred: it is God's handiwork. He made it as he wished it to be; capable, by wonderful mechanisms, of swift and easy motion; shaped in contours which artists despair of reproducing; and so responsive to our will, so varied in its capacities, so lightly moved from place to place by its own powers, that in its perfect state the soul which inhabits it is almost unconscious of its existence, and knows it only as a source of help and pleasure.

—FROM *Dress Reform,*
EDITED BY ABBA GOOLD WOOLSON,
BOSTON, 1874

Contents

Illustrations

All of the photographs, with the exception of those for the Prologue and Chapters 2 and 8, are reproduced courtesy of the Dance Collection: The New York Public Library at Lincoln Center; Astor, Lenox, and Tilden Foundations.

Acknowledgments

I would like to thank these people:

Dancers and actresses who trusted me with their stories, pictures, and explanations: Dorothy Bird, Bonnie Bird, Carol Dempster, Lillian Gish, Blanche Sweet, Lillian Powell, Nina Ness, Ann Douglas Doucet, Virginia Sheffield Burridge, Amelia and April Gilmore, Valeria Ladd of the Florence Fleming Noyes School, Virginia Lee of Ballet Arts Studio, Julia Levien, Hortense Kooluris, and Anita Zahn of the various Duncan schools (Isadora's and Elizabeth's);

Santa Barbara residents who described their community circa 1913: Hazel Dewling, John Northrup, Mildred Dawes, and especially my dear friend Pauline Finley;

Miss Genevieve Oswald and her staff at the Dance Collection of the Performing Arts Research Center of the New York Public Library, who were constantly helpful;

Charles Silver and Emily Sieger in the Film Study Center of the Museum of Modern Art; Eileen Bowser, Curator of the Film Department, for all she has done to preserve the oeuvre of D. W. Griffith;

Lydia Brontë and the Rockefeller Foundation's Humanities Department, for a generous grant to research this book;

Concerned friends Elliott Sirkin, David Vaughan, Grey Poole, Richard Hayes;

And especially Arlene Croce, Ann Douglas, Anne Hollander, Gemze de Lappe, and Don Daniels, who by their own work and thinking helped me immeasurably;

Maxine Groffsky, my agent, who was always there;

Carole Frankel, Neal Jones, Holly McNeely, and Ellen McNeilly at Knopf;

And Bob Gottlieb, my editor, who believed in this book from the beginning.

Preface

A kind of dancing that looks quaint to us now used to be the newest and freshest dancing in the world. It was called aesthetic or interpretive (or free-form or barefoot or "figure") dance; it emerged from the nineteenth-century romantic revival of the antique, and it inaugurated a modern, twentieth-century way to see motion.

The new dance of the turn of the century and the teens offered the audience what it craved: human images of great beauty. In a world obsessed and troubled by the newness of speed—by airplanes, automobiles, telephones—dancing was speed that refreshed its watchers. It belonged to light and water and moving air and the shifting chiaroscuro of surfaces. The excitement of it so penetrated the culture that even today we seem to know what Vaslav Nijinsky looked like in his *fantaisie* garb of faun or rose-creature, or Isadora Duncan in her Botticellian tunics. They embodied a change in the very perception of a human figure; after them human beauty was no longer pictured in portraits or theatrical postures but in flashes, glimpses of something vulnerable and alive and caught in a musical motion.

Although Europe was the milieu where the new dancing flourished, the dancers came from the two vast lands on the edges of European culture: Russia and America. In Russia great innovations could have been predicted, since Russia contained a tradition of theater dance that was rich and alive: the ballet. But America had no theater-dance tradition. Our aesthetic dancing was an original art, born of a strange blend of naïveté and expertise. Several young women invented it; they were definitely trained in theatrical skills, also in some feminist attitudes—but absolutely untamed in the imagination. Nevertheless, the isolated imaginations of these girls conjured up a theatrical image so basic to us now that we forget its original impact on audiences: the solo human figure in space. They put themselves alone on stage, and being accomplished performers they held an audience as they tried out wordless and rhapsodic ways to behave. It must not be forgotten how well they knew the theater of their time and how clearly the audience saw their intentions. American aesthetic dancing, this blend of skill and presumption, brought forth certain qualities that seem now to have been born with the art: speed, drama, abandon.

Where She Danced is the story of two generations of American dancers: how they were educated, what gave them the courage, the insight, the foolhardiness to say they had found a new art form, and what gave them the drive to insist on its ultimate seriousness.

WHERE SHE DANCED

Prologue

One hundred years ago a kind of entertainment called spectacle-extravaganza flourished, and it was there that theatrical dancing as an art survived, no matter how tenuously, in this country. The dancing was called ballet, although it was a very different ballet from today's. Popular dancing of that time—square dancing, jigs, reels, vaudeville soft-shoe—was not considered art, not until it began to borrow some of the fancy ballet look of the spectacle-extravaganzas that were not plays or operas or musicals or ballets but blends of all these forms inside a loose fantastical pantomime plot geared to the display of theatrical marvels.

Every country in the Western world produced spectacle-extravaganzas, with variations according to nationality. Some of the classics of the genre have survived in the repertories of modern ballet companies because of their splendid music scores—Delibes' *Coppélia* (France, 1870), Tchaikovsky's *Sleeping Beauty* and *The Nutcracker* (Russia, 1890 and 1892). No American spectacle is extant, because this country's productions tended to be even more loosely structured and, in modern terms, far-fetched, than Europe's. They were vast tableaux with processions, displays of empires or of fairy kingdoms, featuring the latest theater technology—but they did not really represent a theatrical form with its roots in American culture the way the same spectacles in Europe recalled the old court masques and the pomp and hierarchical display of monarchies.

American spectacles with dancing are thought to date from the first production of *The Black Crook* (1866), a lavish show whose dance emphasis came about by chance. When the manager of a popular New York theater, Niblo's Garden, inserted into his theater's current melodrama a whole foreign corps de ballet he had just bought, the resulting hybrid was a monumental hit. The "crook" in the title was a learned hunchback, Herzog, who made a pact with the devil about the fate of three other characters, Aminta (whom he loved), Rudolfo (whom she loved), and Count Wolfenstein. It was a familiar Faustian tale, with plenty of occasion for theatrical wonders to appear and disappear: flying scenery, clouds of golden mist, magic glades, gilded chariots, and the like—and, thanks to the manager, a stunning array of diminutive foreign ballerinas in gauze costumes and satin toeshoes.

America was dimly familiar with the look of ballet dancing from the tours of Europe's solo Romantic ballerinas of the 1840s—the most memorable of whom was Fanny Elssler with her famous *Cracovienne* and her *La Tarentule*. When Elssler and her counterparts came from Europe in the forties, their highly articulate art was almost nowhere taught in America, and Mlle. Elssler's ballet master, James Sylvain, had a desperate time trying to find girls just to fill the stage and stand correctly for her corps de ballet. This remained the general condition until twenty years later, when *The Black Crook* encouraged some teaching of ballet decorum: the original production and its many revivals required a corps of 150 girls along with demi-soloists and soloists (soloists in the first production, Marie Bonfanti and Rita Sangalli, were artists and set high standards from the beginning). No one in the American audiences, though, quite realized there was a *system* involved in this kind of dancing, and a highly exacting mode of study; that the ballerinas advertised from La Scala or from San Carlo had emerged from academies far stricter and more disciplined than any convent school for girls. Instead, for a good many years, they were seen as wildly exotic curiosities. During this time, scores and scores of new soloists and corps de ballet girls populated the countless *Black Crook* revivals and imitations. Indeed, the reason *The Black Crook* seems to have fascinated the public for so long was not merely the display of legs but the un-Americanness of the whole thing. Watching *The Black Crook* was to most people a form of ogling foreigners in their most exotic plumage. The importance of ballet and also its peculiarly nonsensical aura in America can be recognized in advertisements for subsequent spectacles, like this one for *Enchantment* (1879):

An Entirely New Grand Spectacle of 4 Acts and 20 Tableaux

First appearance in America of the renowned Terpsichorean
artists: Mlles Casati, Conalba and E. Capelini
(Europe's greatest premier danseuses assolutas
from The Theater La Scala, Milan, and San Carlo,
Naples, and the Grand Opera House, Paris)

Also appearances of Mlles Sallio, Camis, Ortoli (Theater
National, Bucharest), Mlles R. Carpelini, Pasta and
Ciappa, together with extensive Corps of Coryphées

Miss Rose Lee (from the Covent Garden Theater, London)
Miss Jessie Greville (of the Alhambra, London)
Miss Eugenie Nicholson (from the Crystal Palace,
Southampton)
Mr. C. T. Campbell (of the Opera Comique, London)
Les Vantoches Vallotte, Human Automatons
Molva, most graceful of all gymnasts,

La Troupe Rajade, Comic Eccentrics
& Occarinistes, who play upon an entirely new instrument

The featured ballet dancers—Italian, French, English (the Russians hadn't come out of their dark continent yet)—might as well have been creatures from the moon for all the public knew or cared—they seemed more like contortionists than actresses (and actresses were foreign enough). At any rate, if they were viewed as people, as women, at all, they were condemned as absolutely outside the pale of normal American social intercourse. It is fascinating to think how many of them must have been crisscrossing America in the 1880s and 90s in spectacle after touring spectacle—*La Surprise* (after *Lucia di Lammermoor*), *La Nymphe de Diane* (after *Sylvia*), *Ali Baba, Aladdin's Lamp, The Black Venus, Excelsior, Columbus and the Discovery of America, Railroads on Parade, Turco the Terrible*—to name only a few.

While the soloists toured, the corps de ballet never travelled from city to city; instead it was assembled in each new territory by an advance ballet master. He drew on collections of American girls of the humblest social order, country girls just come to the city, factory girls, runaway girls who read in a newspaper that a corps of 150 was needed. They called at the stage door and were fitted into tutus and drilled in lines to stand obediently, or walk or turn as coryphées, without having the least idea of what ballet dancing was about. This race of girls did not give ballet a very high standing—and in fact ballet was considered synonymous with the leg shows that also featured ranks of girls in tights. One was a San Francisco production of the late 1860s called *The Female Forty Thieves, or, The Golden Legion of the Fairy Region*. The San Francisco *Bulletin*'s comment about it could have served for many leg shows and the spectacle-extravaganzas:

> The bountiful display of Amazonian limbs, and the number of revolving tableaux introduced without any particular reason, pleased the spectators.

The American "pick-up" ballet girls, even the high-class ones with some training, were if anything more suspect than the incomprehensible foreigners—they couldn't dance as well *and* they had presumably chosen to throw away all respectability and a normal life. Whether or not it was true, all were assumed to be at the disposal of gentlemen who hired them for club celebrations and bachelor dinners. A former ballet girl could not enter domestic service or work in a shop once she had been in that sort of theater work. The only way for her to advance in her profession was laterally, over to a vaudeville solo spot or from show to show. Many girls did go to vaudeville, starting in the 1890s as solo acts came to prominence, and a whole new genre—skirt dancing, a cross between jigs and clogs and the formal pseudo-ballet steps of spectacles—arose for girl solo dancers. Those who were chorines, ballet girls, and skirt dancers of the late-nineteenth century are mostly invisible to us now: they rarely wrote their memoirs. But by searching old magazines and programs it is possible to follow a few of them from show to show and to learn what training they had, if any.

In New York at least, some training was available. All along, certain of the foreign ballerinas in those American spectacles married in this country or simply retired, and taught privately in their homes —usually girls already in the theater. Gradually by the 1890s a relaxation of moral standards for women meant that these Mesdames attracted more pupils, amateur *and* professional, and could afford studios —especially when some of the smart ones added dance fads such as physical culture exercises, aesthetic posing, or risqué serpentine motions to the classical techniques they had been taught and were still trying to propagate. The Metropolitan Opera didn't open a ballet school until 1909, but earlier, Marie Bonfanti, original star of *The Black Crook*, maintained a studio near Union Square and then one next to the Palace Theater on Broadway. Léon Espinosa and members of his family taught dancing at Madison Square Garden after he was appointed ballet master there in 1890. Mme. Elizabetta Menzeli, former Berlin colleague of Marie Taglioni, also trained in Paris, St. Petersburg, and Vienna, had a professional school on East 16th Street in the 1880s and 90s, the Conservatoire de Chorégraph Classique. There she taught a few girls with serious dance ambitions and coached many amateur ladies for "all kinds of acts, plays, sketches, etc."

The existence of these schools was one reason for the rise in the late 1890s of the first generation of American solo dancers whose names are remembered today—Loie Fuller, La Belle Dazié, Gertrude Hoffman, Bessie Clayton, Isadora Duncan, Ruth St. Denis. All of them began as ballet girls, but they are remembered now because they came out of the corps de ballet to become soloists, on vaudeville stages or musical comedy stages or on various art stages of their own devising. All of them were strong-minded, original young women who were not happy in a corps de ballet of a spectacle, nor were they willing to accept the age-old taint of the American ballet girl, which had nothing to do with their dreams and ambitions. They were of their time, a time that saw the birth of a new social being, the Modern American Woman. They, the dancers, would become one of her prime symbols. The New Woman emerged as America emerged into world politics. She happened after decades of reformers' and feminists' trying to free women's bodies and minds through spiritual and physical panaceas: dress reform, open air, aesthetic exercise, artistic pursuits. Physical culture and art came into vogue at the same time, in the 1890s, and occupied women in a country where women had more time, more money, more space to be individuals than in any other country at any other time. In fact, "the physical" and "the artistic" were the two realms where American women's new capacities for self-expression were exercised. Dancing was the synthesis of those two realms.

If there was a new American woman, it was not exactly clear what was correct for her to do. Henry James, that constant observer of women, said the American woman was the one in the world who was the least afraid, "the most confidently grown, the most freely en-couraged plant in our democratic garden." Yet he thought this kind of encouragement interfered with women's learning true femininity in the age-old sense of that term. James lived in Europe. By 1907, when he wrote two articles for *Harper's Bazaar* on the speech and manners of American women following a long return visit to America, he saw that women here were ignoring, had always ignored, the feminine qualities that he most admired in European women, which consisted of "definite conceptions of duty, activity, influence; of a possible grace, of a possible sweetness, a possible power to soothe, to please and above all to exemplify."

In Europe a woman was trained to be a private being within a complex social fabric. A European woman could shun wifehood and motherhood and choose the life of nun, courtesan, artist, ballerina, joining a parochial feminine hierarchy whose values were understood and needed by the whole society. An American woman was trained for a cruder and more public purpose. Very little true artistic discipline was offered her in the nineteenth century. Girls were taught to sew and read and play the piano, even to perform quadrilles and other social dances, insofar as these things helped them to be valuable members of families, wives and mothers and citizens of the Democracy. Even such staunch feminists as Catharine Esther Beecher, eldest daughter of the famous Calvinist Lyman Beecher and sister of Harriet Beecher Stowe, did not believe a woman should cultivate her personality for her own sake but for a larger, more selfless purpose. She described this in an 1871 address to the Christian Women of America:

Women's great mission is to train immature, weak and ignorant creatures, to obey the laws of God; the physical, the intellectual, the social and the moral—first in the family, then in the school, then in the neighbourhood, then in the nation, then in the world—the great family of God whom the Master came to teach and to save.

There were a few examples in nineteenth-century America of unconventional educations producing women with bold minds of their own. Margaret Fuller, the sole female among the cabal of Transcendentalist writers in Concord and Boston, was one of these. She was specially tutored by her father in the "masculine" disciplines of logic, Latin, law, and oratory—but she did not learn the arts. She did not, for instance, study ballet, which was a discipline as articulate and civilized as logic or law, only in another realm, an artistic and wordless one that was not available to upstanding American women. To have seriously taught Margaret Fuller theatrical dancing or any art would have been more subversive than to discipline her mind—for it would have permitted her a private cultivation of her spirit, an artist's intense dialogue with self which in fact Margaret Fuller sought painfully all her life. An artist, a woman alone with a vigorous, disciplined imagination that she listened to over and above her husband, children, or neighbors, was *not* part of the American design. A woman like Margaret Fuller, over-trained in a consciousness of public morality, was.

Contemporary with Margaret Fuller lived several non-intellectual, seemingly immoral, Bohemian heroines who put *themselves* outside of the American design—*they* were supposed to be the artists. Lola Montez, the Irish dancer-courtesan who almost became a Californian, was a woman like this, or Adah Isaacs Menken, the Jewess from New Orleans, proclaimer of free verse and frequent star of the old pantomime *Mazeppa* (in which she always made her entrance costumed as a prince, "en travestie," in tights, strapped to the back of a white stallion who galloped down several runways to deposit his rider in the center of the drama). These women, unlike the fine and strictly professional actresses of nineteenth-century America, used the theater to advertise their personalities. They were in fact "artistes," poseurs instead of real artists, for they suffered from the opposite malady from Margaret Fuller's—they had no discipline instead of too much; wild ideas, without any experience of artistic skill or structure. Adah Menken never could learn her dramatic lines, nor did she see the reason to—for her instincts in gesture and costume (a "one-piece yellow-silk garment" sometimes replaced the tights) kept her audience captive. Although Adah Menken may be considered the first American spectacle-extravaganza star, she had no effect on the genre itself. She was an isolated legend. Her only real skill was equestrian. (She herself rode the horse onstage in *Mazeppa*, instead of the cardboard dummy that was standard for this galloping entrance.)

Extravagant and uncultivated "artistic" impulses troubled Henry James in his countrywomen fifty years after Adah Menken's career had peaked. And now these impulses were in style; they cropped up in numbers of high-spirited modern girls who came of age in the 1880s and 90s. There was money to indulge an artistic bent, yet no one knew quite how to do this in a society where wives and mothers were still the only feminine models of good behavior. Only by going abroad could an American girl encounter the artistic discipline to guide her new-found instincts. Back home, professional training only occurred in exceptional cases in the theater and music or literature (a fine writer like Kate Chopin—*The Awakening*, 1899—was allowed to imitate modern French literature in her Catholic and cosmopolitan education in St. Louis). But dancing, the art that was scorned and misunderstood, the art that wasn't even an art, provided discipline.

American artistic dance was born of some American dancers' extravagant desires for self-expression, guided, no matter how unconsciously, by disciplines they had absorbed from the theater. An old-fashioned corps de ballet, casual though that institution was in America, provided the only secular example of a disciplined feminine hierarchy based on Henry James's "conceptions of duty" and "a possible grace." These new dancers had been physically trained in these conceptions of duty; their bodies had learned to move to the rhythm, and to be still. Their minds raged against the confinement of a corps de ballet, yet their bodies had been taught harmony. They were ballet girls possessed of those "unballetic" qualities of the new American woman—her "great fund of life," her self-absorption, her fearlessness, her unbounded imagination, and her often monstrous daring. It was the combination of the ballet girl's body with the American untamed spirit that produced our first solo dancers and our first native art form.

The unskilled American ballet chorine did not disappear with the advent of a new dance; she was more than ever present in the expanded theater activity at the turn of the century. She was needed in large numbers for the choruses of the musical comedies that were replacing the old spectacles as the most popular theatrical genre. Her story has been told in uncanny detail in Theodore Dreiser's great novel of 1900, *Sister Carrie*. But it is not Dreiser's silent, helpless, and strangely elegant Carrie who concerns us in the story of American art-dance, nor is it Henry James's high-strung but undisciplined heroines of the leisure class who never thought of the theater as an arena for themselves—but a rarer kind of girl somewhere between those two.

A sort of pattern emerges, even from the strongly individual stories of these first dancers. They were usually of genteel background but poor; they turned to the theater first for money and then for adventure. Gertrude Hoffman, for instance, the first "art" dancer in American vaudeville, received a strict convent education in San Francisco; it included some social dancing, perhaps too much, for she ran away at fifteen to perform in the operetta chorus of the Castle Square Theater, became a rehearsal director, then moved up the theatrical ladder through sheer dogged intelligence. Ethel Gilmore, one of the few trained ballerinas of her time, was the daughter of a widowed Irish-Canadian ladies' tailor, Rachel Janet Gilmore, whose love of color had brought her to theatrical costuming and to New York. She put her three daughters into Elizabetta Menzeli's school—and all three of them made their débuts in the ballet chorus of a Florenz Ziegfeld show, *Miss Innocence* (1906). Ethel, the middle one, was picked in 1908 to replace the great Danish-English ballerina Adeline Genée in Ziegfeld's *The Soul Kiss*, and Ray, the youngest, became the top "picture girl" model in New York.

It was usually the mothers of these dancers who formed them, who stood as bulwarks guarding the light-heartedness, the freedom needed for young dancers, yet who taught them the disciplines of poverty. They held on to certain defiant beliefs about women's inner independence so they could teach their daughters things that weren't part of the American mission to save "immature, weak and ignorant creatures." Through personal catastrophe—their husband's death or desertion—these mothers had been left outside the pale already, on the fringe of the big cheerful family of the democracy.

Mary Dora Duncan, mother of Isadora and of three older children, was a fascinating and brave woman who taught her children as much of the civilized arts as she knew how to—music, dance, and aesthetic exercise, poetry and ideas borrowed from more sensual civilizations—arts of no use in an orderly American existence. It was almost a European education she gave her youngest daughter, almost a courtesan's training, but with an American crusading edge. The Duncan clan was aggressive; their heroes and heroines were past and present California Bohemians (such as Adah Menken), and they wanted to be a guerrilla band of serious artists inside what they saw as a misguided and thoroughly inartistic America. The story of Isadora's art consists of her discovering the seriousness of it after she had declared it loudly to be there. And she had the physical and theatrical skills to find this. Skills and training explain how Isadora grew up to become not only a desperate, chaotic, bold, and grandly tragic personality (as in a Henry James novel about a too proud American girl), but an artist who fashioned a new form of dancing.

In terms of pure dance invention, Isadora was the most significant figure in her generation. Her bold self-questioning was connected at the root to her physical training—that is, her mind and her body were inseparable, which is probably true of all great dance innovators. However, Isadora, while remaining an American "character," became a world artist who influenced the art-dance of Russia and Germany and England as much as or more than she did American dance.

It is not Isadora Duncan but another self-created dancer, Ruth St. Denis, who began the lineage of modern dance in America. Because Ruth St. Denis was a more specialized artist than Isadora, because she could have emerged only in America and she appealed mostly to American audiences, her story is to a great extent the story of this book. For a few years at the start of the century, Americans who saw her found in her dancing something that satisfied them deeply: a pantomimic shorthand of spectacle-extravaganza with religious overtones. The child Ruth Dennis was unlike those other early American dancers in several ways. She was a Protestant, whereas most of them were Catholics. Although her mother taught her some of the same aesthetic exercises Isadora's mother taught her, the intent behind Ruth's education was hygienic and spiritual not artistic. It was more in the American idiom. Ruth Emma Dennis was a highly religious and moral woman; her daughter's heroines were not the artistic ballerinas and actresses of Isadora's childhood but women reformers, aesthetics lecturers, Delsarte priestesses, and the pioneer women doctors of the nineteenth century, all of whom exhorted women to examine the conditions of their bodies as a manifestation of the conditions of their spirits. And besides her background of health reform, Ruth knew more than the other solo dancers about the popular theater and less about dance training, so that a significant part of her dance inventions derived from theater and the techniques of tragic actresses of her day.

Ironically, Ruth St. Denis became the mother of American art-dance because she never belonged completely to art, but believed equally in religion, hygiene, and the popular theater. She was a high-toned entertainer more than she was a schooled artist—and yet her imagination contained the freshness of an artist as well as the single-mindedness of a crusader. Ruth St. Denis' art was half-conscious. It came from the natural performer's unerring instincts for putting herself and her audience into another time and place—Egypt, the Orient—simply by acting out that time and place with costumes and movements. Lacking a dance education, she invented one, a kind of dance pre-history culled from her visions of antique and sensual civilizations and some scraps of information from public libraries. But she believed it. She never doubted she was giving her audience an ideology as well as a performance.

It is striking that Ruth St. Denis and the other American dancers, who all found dance metaphors in other civilizations, appeared just as the Russian Ballet made its blinding entry into Western culture and began the twentieth-century revival of ballet as an art form. The Russians, led by choreographer Michel Fokine, had also rediscovered ancient pagan civilizations. They introduced a pagan abandon into the traditional language of classic ballet and thus made new dance forms based on the old. The Americans had little experience with living theater-dance forms that made sense to them, yet blindly, almost co-incidentally, they found the right ones for their culture. It seems almost a sociological accident that the imaginations of some American women, on the periphery of American life, were so untamed and so fresh that they could divine something of what the Russians reached after decades of consummate tradition and education. It still appears sometimes as if American Modern Dance exists by accident. Ruth St. Denis, its accidental founder, set the tone of it by drawing ultimately on the stuff of her personality rather than on a system of theater discipline. How that personality emerged out of her unconventional early education, her entry into vaudeville, her years in the theater, her début as a cultural priestess, is an epic of her time. It is known today because her husband, Ted Shawn, built a learning institution, Deni-shawn, around her, and taught the students in it to re-enact—intently, systematically, at times grimly—the process by which the original Priestess had discovered her dance.

PART I

RUTH ST. DENIS

CHAPTER 1
Health and Beauty

It is ironic but not illogical that the mother of Ruth St. Denis had a body that constantly failed her. Ruth Emma Hull, born in 1845 or '46, was reared in the town of Canandaigua in western New York—a land known as the "burnt-over district" because of the intensity of its religious revivals. In the mid-nineteenth century when she was growing up, a tide of hopes and fears swept over America, and all kinds of spiritual kingdoms were prophesied. The Millerites, also of the burnt-over district, believed the Millennium was coming. People in other parts of the country decided to create it themselves: they built Utopias. Brook Farm in Massachusetts, Oneida in New York, New Harmony in Indiana, the North American Phalanx and the Raritan Bay Union in New Jersey, Mormon towns in the West, and new Shaker communities in the East and in the Middle West—all these sprang up within a short space of time and then most died away.

Ruth Emma Hull caught the habit of Utopias from the frontier and from her family's desperate situation. She was the thirteenth child of a heroic mother who raised the family alone after the father deserted them. The youngest daughter was nervous and intense and, because of her mother's struggle, concerned with the hardships of women. Despite her own fragile health she decided to be a doctor. When she was graduated from the University of Michigan Medical School in 1872, she was one of five women in her class. After that, she practiced a year in a Philadelphia clinic before her stamina gave out and she travelled back to Battle Creek, Michigan, to take the "water cure"—a regimen of sitz baths, douches, enemas, and cold abdominal compresses considered by some to be the most "natural" and the least fashionable treatment for women with nervous prostration.

There were many such women in those years. After the Civil War, it became apparent that an epidemic of ill health had settled on American women—or at least on those women who aspired to a life of the mind beyond their frontier mothers' life of toil. They themselves were the advertisers of their condition. Catharine Esther Beecher, self-appointed spokeswoman of silent American womanhood, wrote about the situation in her 1871 *Statistics of Female Health*:

> . . . the more I traveled, and the more I resided in health
> establishments, the more the conviction was pressed on my
> attention that there was a terrible decay of female health

all over the land, and that this evil was bringing with it
an incredible extent of individual, domestic and social suf-
fering, that was increasing in a most alarming rate.

The vigorous and widespread public discussion in the late nineteenth century of women's fitness camouflaged the deeper question of
what women were supposed to be fit for: wifehood and motherhood
alone, or some sort of personal happiness? In her survey of ill health,
Catharine Beecher and the women she interviewed equated their
nervous conditions ("delicate," "sickly," "bilious") with their actual
physical symptoms ("pelvic disorders," "sick-headaches," "dropsy").
There was a confusion between the symptoms women induced in
themselves and the ones that were caused by simple germs. It appeared
to women that a frail constitution, whether real or imagined, was inevitable among those who dared leave the old frontier life of service
for a new life with some culture, leisure, and even higher education
in it.

In short, they feared that nervous diseases were the punishments
for solitary pleasures. Abundant reading was supposed by some to bring
on ill health—women imitating romantic literary heroines whose pure
burning spirits always undermined their physiques. But some nervous
American women such as Ruth Emma Hull read only religious and
medical treatises, hardly any novels. Moreover, to all the women who
were plagued by very real pain, such as Catharine Beecher herself,
or Ruth Emma Hull, the causes of it were not so important as the need
to eradicate it. Catharine Beecher (and Ruth Emma Hull on a smaller
scale) devoted her life to the campaign for fresh air, sunlight, sensible
food, and plain clothing—to the principles of hygiene and the practice
of domestic science. These were all metaphoric remedies for an excess
of guilt, physical stimulation to reduce mental fearfulness. In one sense,
American modern dance emerged from these late-nineteenth-century
women's anxious idea of their physical selves: their supposed condition
of chronic disease was the background; the search for renewed health
was the impetus.

The only solution to the problem of women's health seemed to
lie with an older instinctive wisdom that had been lost to modern
civilization—through the fault of the male-dominated medical profession. Ruth Emma Hull had chosen to attend a medical school, but
she shared Catharine Beecher's distrust of such establishments. Beecher
pointed out that medical students and professors themselves were

unhealthy, working in stuffy rooms, ignoring Nature's laws, and studying artificial drugs like mercury and calomel. Conventional treatment
of women's diseases was especially wrong-headed—and even sadistic.
The best-known doctor of that time for women's nervous conditions
was Dr. S. Weir Mitchell in Philadelphia (he was a famous novelist
besides), whose famous rest cure for women consisted of forced inactivity in bed, no mental exercise whatsoever—no writing, no reading
—a constant diet of milk and bland, starchy foods, and complete sub-
mission to the physician administering the cure. The absolute passivity
implied by such a program was outrageous to think about: it produced
the wave of counterremedies such as the water cure and the pre-
scriptions of open air and exercise.

Ruth Emma Hull was a practicing young doctor in S. Weir
Mitchell's own city of Philadelphia when her breakdown occurred;
his treatment was an obvious choice for her. In discarding it for Dr.
Jackson's water cure, Ruth Emma was turning her back on her own
college education in favor of a wealth of folk medicine and miracle
cures nearer to the frontier customs she had known in her childhood,
and to the advice of the preachers, evangelists, quacks, temperance
lecturers, militant feminists, dress reformers, phrenologists, Grahamites,
mystical table-rappers, animal magnetists, and the like who had passed
through Canandaigua and were still crisscrossing the country in
the 1870s. However, educated women doctors also adopted these
home remedies and folk cures, which were actually a form of preven-
tive medicine. Dr. Harriott Hunt, a famous woman doctor whose
career was at its peak in the 1840s, often told her women patients to
forget their medicines, start a diary, and think of their mothers who
had somehow survived. It seemed obvious to these women doctors
in the face of such widespread feminine fragility that something in
women's daily habits must be wrong, that certain natural laws were
being flagrantly violated. Ruth Emma Hull, after her year-long water
cure, felt she had to preach to women about natural laws; instead of
returning to medical practice, she decided to go out on a lecture tour
on the subject of natural health and beauty. But that plan never
materialized. She was living by then in a former New Jersey Utopia,
the Raritan Bay Union, and there she met Thomas Dennis, an English
engineer and freethinker who had moved to America and was trying
to invent a flying machine. They married and settled in what was left
of the community.

In its day, the Raritan Bay Union had made important contri-
butions to the subject of health and beauty. A school had been

founded along with the community in 1853 (by Marcus Spring, a wealthy Quaker philanthropist), and that school, Eaglewood, became one of the most progressive in the country. It was still there when the Dennises were living at Raritan Bay, and it bore the mark of the heroic nineteenth-century feminists who had helped form it— Angelina Grimké, wife of director Theodore Weld, and her sister Sarah; both had insisted on absolute equality for the girl pupils. The school was the first in the country to offer its girls physical education —calisthenics indoors and boating and diving in the bay—at a time when exercise was supposed to destroy femininity even more quickly than book learning. The enlightened Grimkés had even worn bloomers in the 1850s when bloomers were first proposed—and in the 1870s Eaglewood girls still wore them for exercise. Ruth Emma Hull lived in a radical community of women and men abolitionists and freethinkers, a community that partly defined itself by its ideals about *women's* health, and these ideals, which belonged to a reformist viewpoint quite firmly consolidated by the late nineteenth century, she would pass on intact to her daughter.

Among all the possible plans to wrest women from an unnatural, passive, sickly, and distorted state, none seemed more basic than changing the kinds of clothes they wore in everyday life. The radical feminists of the fifties had thought the answer was the bloomer—that outfit of bodice and knee-length skirt over full, Turkish trousers (a free adaptation by Amelia Bloomer, upstate New York postmistress, of an Orientale operetta costume). Bloomers did not flatter every figure, though, and so never really caught on. Dress reformers of the 1870s were more cautious; they knew they must learn aesthetics if they were going to bring about the changes that were now even more crucial than twenty years back. American women were notorious for their mindless devotion to fashion—European fashion, since that was the only kind there was. Abroad, two traits distinguished American ladies: their ill health and their slavery to foreign ideas of style. By the 1870s this docility had got them committed to a complicated set of clothing which severely restricted the possibilities of physical motion available to them.

A woman's ordinary costume consisted of an outer dress whose waist was tightly buttoned over a corset with a tight-laced waist of its own; underneath the corset were other items, the "lower garments," one on top of another. The problem was inescapable:

Every one of the lower garments has a binding fastened
around the waist, and this binding is composed of a straight
piece of cloth folded double. Drawers, underskirt, balmoral,
dress-skirt, over-skirt, dress-waist, and belt, furnish accord-
ingly, sixteen layers of cloth girding the stomach and the
yielding muscles situated in that region.

This was a description of conventional dress put forth at a large
1874 dress-reform convention in Boston. According to other reports
drawn up on that occasion, not only were grown women subject to
fashion's tyranny but little girls in this country were threatened in their
very bones and internal organs by their clothing. Corsets were made for
girls starting at about the age of three; a child could pass through fifteen
or twenty graduated corset sizes before she became an adult. Of course,
not all mothers pressed corsets on their daughters, but even modified
versions of this shape slowed children down. A Dr. Mary J. Safferd-
Blake described a visit to a city grammar school where twenty-nine out
of the forty-two girls in the first class wore corsets, and none of the
forty-two could raise their arms over their heads (the corresponding
class of boys had no trouble doing this).

Of the five women invited to speak at the 1874 convention, four
were women doctors who had never been connected with the dress-
reform movement. But all of them testified to case after case among
their women patients of atrophied internal organs and stunted growth
—a condition they attributed mostly to clothes, to the clothes' "continuous pressure upon that life-endowing nervous center, the solar-
plexus, and upon the central glandular organs." Each woman doctor
advised different kinds of new, looser designs for inner and outer
garments—and also contraptions like suspenders, extra buttons, one-
piece underwear—anything to take the pressure off the waist and
lessen the intense heat forced on the solar plexus and the pelvis by so
many layers of cloth.

Hygiene was as drastic a concern as comfort. Skirts were not just
heavy but too long; they dragged on the ground and picked up mud
and germs on the underhems. Everything about a fashionable woman
seemed unnatural *and* unhygienic, and so the rhetoric of the dress
reformers was constantly invigorated by righteous physical outrage, and
by strong images of congestion and dead matter. The false hair, for
instance, worn under pompadours, was an unnecessary mass of stuff
". . . which continually calls to itself floating impurities and gives only
heat, weight and weariness to the head, while it destroys the beautiful

outline of the head and all symmetry of proportion between its size and that of the body."

Gradually, from under the accumulated artificial conventions of dress a "symmetry of proportion" was emerging as the new dominant value in women's clothes and bodies. The dress reformers refused to acknowledge the thousands of women who enjoyed the tight lacing of their corsets and the elaborate coquettish arrangements of their hair. They were blind, in short, to the charms of artifice. But history was on their side. The dress reformers' speeches and campaigns were shaping the new aesthetic which by the 1890s would allow most women in America to exercise and ride on bicycles, and eventually to participate in the fashion revolution of the teens. Already in the 1870s and 80s the force of the protest had given a few women a new sense of their bodies. Ruth Emma Hull as a doctor was one of the first of them; she wore plain, free-flowing garments and dressed her black hair in a loose bun at her neck—no puffs and no rats. Ruth Emma did not exactly have a personal aesthetic—it was her spiritual faculties that were cheered by her natural clothing. But some dress reform *was* concerned with style; in England for instance, hygienic clothes were nearly identical to the aesthetic ones invented on medieval and Greek models by the Pre-Raphaelite painters. In America the dress reformers were less responsive to aesthetics. They were content to protect God's Handiwork in women's bodies, hoping to reconstruct those bodies on what they vaguely referred to as "the true principles of physiology and art." However, their concentration on hygiene was beginning to open them up to other ideas about how women might be reclaimed from an artificial condition of life and from their various nervous afflictions. Some of these new ideas were directly connected to art and self-expression: one especially—a new pseudo-spiritual system of exercises called "Delsarte."

By the time the Delsarte system arrived in America, Ruth Emma and Thomas Dennis had moved away from their Utopia and settled on a farm called Pin Oaks in Somerville, New Jersey, where their· daughter Ruth was born in 1879. Ruth Emma, determined to raise a healthy child, hit on Delsarte through a shadowy figure named Mme. Aurilla Colcord Poté, teacher of reading, dramatic art, and vocal and physical culture à la Delsarte in her Carnegie Hall studio. Ruth Emma might also have felt Delsarte appropriate for her, because it implied revisions in dress and actually recommended a "Greek"

costume, and because its chief American prophet, actor-director Steele
Mackaye, was a former resident of the Dennises' own Raritan Bay
Union.

The Delsarte system had been fabricated in the mind of a
nineteenth-century French philosopher, François Delsarte; it was a
codification of human gesture, a spiritual labeling of every part of the
body according to certain zones—Head, Heart, and Lower Limbs,
which corresponded to Mind, Soul, and Life. Life was the dangerous
part—it was connected to the legs, those "beasts of burden" of the body.
Mind and Soul were more ideal, which made the upper body the
spiritually expressive part. Delsarte's science was mostly meant for the
stage—or so thought Delsarte himself, who coached some of the greatest
French actors of his time, including Sarah Bernhardt. Steele Mackaye
thought so too when he introduced Delsarte's ideas to America by a
monumental lecture-tour of Shakespearean monologues illustrated with
Delsarte gestures. But Delsarte in America soon passed beyond the
theatrical milieu into the domain of the growing numbers of women
obsessed with health and bodily freedom. The "aesthetic gymnastics"
invented by Steele Mackaye and perfected by his disciple, Mrs. Genevieve Stebbins, provided a more effective way of reviving women's
"natural" motions than simply changing the cut of their clothes. These
motions would open their lungs, and circulate the air around them.
And because spoken texts, colorful dancelike drills, and other ornamental games were included in Delsarte practice, by the 1890s it was
making numerous converts of those fashionable women eager to ex-
plore the frontiers of self-awareness.

In the 1880s, though, Delsarte still belonged to the reformers.
Its attraction for Mrs. Dennis was its unmistakable correspondences of
spirit and body. For all her scientific training, Ruth Emma remained
an intensely religious Methodist—religious to the point of superstition
—and Delsarte provided a bridge between her medical knowledge and
her faith. The exercises she taught her young daughter were all aimed
at spiritual self-betterment, according to certain "fundamental laws"
of the body the Delsarteans claimed to obey. And aside from questions
of religion, these exercises really did provide sound and logical training
for a growing body. Mrs. Stebbins, popular New York Delsartean and
author of manuals, began a course with "poise" exercises, went on to
"relaxation" (also called "decomposing"), continued with "energizing,"
and ended with vigorous "gymnastics."

The physical value of Delsarte was its clear concept of the body in space. Like ballet, Delsarte placed the body in an imaginary circle, and designated horizontal motions within it—forward, oblique, lateral—which intersected with certain vertical body "zones"—upper, middle, lower. You could move the head or foot or arm forward-front, forward-diagonal, up, down—you learned first to move one member in one plane before combining gestures in advanced figures like "Rocking Legs, Circling Arms," or "Fan Action with Opposition Head." In Mrs. Stebbins' manuals, all the exercises were symmetrical; the counter-weights and balances of a body's gravity were utilized, plus opposition of the left and right sides of the body and the body's natural spirals and twists. Advanced actions, like the serpentine of the torso and leg-swings from the hip, produced a clear sense of space-as-volume. And the ubiquitous spiritual meaning of the "zones," plus the gestures directly attached to certain poems and inspirational texts, guaranteed all Delsarte motions a higher significance. Any reader of Mrs. Stebbins' manuals was reassured that she was "training the body easily to express a beautiful soul—or vice versa."

Ruth Emma Dennis, whether consciously or unconsciously, planned to make her young daughter an embodiment of her theories about a better life on this earth. She dressed her in unfashionable clothes —the younger Ruth remembered peppermint stockings cast off by relatives—she fed her wholesome foods made of graham flour and the like; she taught her coordination, alertness, and health through exercise. Ruth was very tall for her age and growing fast; she had a small, freckled face, clear light eyes, close-cropped brown hair—and she spent most of her time running wild over the farm, climbing trees and swinging on swings. The family was isolated not only by its odd habits but by poverty and dissension inside. Thomas Dennis, still a dreamer, had taken to spending his evenings at the Somerville tavern. He was not a Christian like Ruth Emma; he clove to the "good old anti-Christians" Tom Paine and Robert Ingersoll. This drove his wife further toward religion. The family had grown; a boy was born when Ruth was eight, they were forced to take in boarders to meet the mortgage payments, and Mrs. Dennis developed a paranoic fear of losing Pin Oaks Farm—the one realm where she was able to apply her reformist ideals.

This nervous, deeply committed person, who had gradually reduced all public commitments to the health crusade, who had given up medical practice and lecture tours, now turned more and more to religion and to her young daughter for consolation. On the nights when her husband was out, she sat up with Ruth at the kitchen table, reading the Bible over and over to calm herself. Daughter of a strong and self-sufficient woman, heiress of the pioneer woman doctors of the nineteenth century, Ruth Emma Dennis had failed in her own life, but she passed on her mission to her daughter: to remake the world as a spiritual matriarchy, something her daughter found out how to accomplish years later on the stage. Ruth St. Denis inherited from her mother a near-fanatic self-reliance and a habit of secret spiritual meditation. Mother and daughter were the crux of the Dennis family. The small brother, gentle and droll, was barely noticed—no one even gave him a name until years after he was born, when they actually christened him "Brother." The father was gentle too, devoted to his family, yet utterly weak. Ruth St. Denis once remarked years later in an interview that she thought every female artist was the product of a mother whose strong will had been thwarted; the child would later prove, in a transposed idiom, everything her mother knew to be true.

The young Ruth spent as much time alone as she could, with her imagination and some books for company. She seized upon the two or three novels she found among the medical, religious, and philosophic tomes in the family library. One was Dumas' *La Dame aux Camélias*; she imagined herself the heroine, destined for a tragic fate. She read another book of her mother's that was more Theosophist tract than novel—Mabel Collins Cook's allegory *The Idyll of the White Lotus*—in which an Egyptian religious sect finds a young boy with "the gift of the unclosed eyes"; he alone can see the Lady of the White Lotus. At the end of the story the boy is martyred for his purity by the corrupt priests. What Mrs. Dennis dutifully understood by this legend was quite different from what her daughter read into it. The young Ruth saw glory and light—a vision—and desired it. Her imagination was so hungry that it seized on even the few crumbs of exotica to be found in such a religious tract. If her mother's imagination had embraced morbidity, diseases, spiritual self-chastisement, Ruth craved color and fantasy, for the sole reason of their innate power over her senses. Isolated as she was on a New Jersey farm, Ruth still belonged to her own generation of American girls who were rapacious for experience—the girls in the novels of Henry James, the girls in the cartoons of Charles Dana Gibson. These mythical American girls—

who became "famous" characters to Europeans—were pictured tall, taller than any other breed of women before them, with patrician features on their haughty faces; they walked briskly, they feared no one, they had opinions on every subject in the world; they were desperately eager to acquire for their families, themselves, their country, all the trappings of grace and worldliness. Ruth Dennis was subject to these longings too, although her senses were as starved as any Quaker child's; in fact her very isolation made her ripe for any vision of richness or fantasy she could find.

It was the theater of spectacle-extravaganza that provided it. She went only once in her entire childhood—when a friendly visitor to the Dennises' farm took her, age seven, with little Brother and the boarders' children to New York for P. T. Barnum's circus. She never forgot it. For this 1886 edition of the circus, Barnum had hired the Hungarian extravaganza specialists, the two Kiralfy brothers, to mount a dazzling production of *Nero and the Destruction of Rome*. Not only circus but formal stage productions were constantly written and staged by the Kiralfys, who had first come to America as actors, then shrewdly taken full charge of the lavish spectacles that popular taste demanded—panoramic downfalls of past empires, combined with re-splendent displays of current technology. The features of the Kiralfys' post-*Black Crook* spectacles—ballets corps, plots, settings, and some of the pantomime—were slung together in cheerful disregard for his-torical time or stylistic unity. In the final tableau of the Roman debacle for Barnum, the Kiralfys had set one hundred dancing girls in multi-colored ribbons floating above the ruins of the Imperial City. Ruth Dennis went home and cut up a sheet for her first dancing costume. Her fate was sealed. The stage would take her away from a plain and careworn world; her passport was her Delsarte-trained physical exuberance.

Ruth was thirteen before she saw her next spectacle, and already something of a dancer herself. It was *Egypt Through the Centuries* (1892) at the Palisades Amusement Park, directed by Augusto Fan-cioli, imitator of the Kiralfys. The subject was eleven thousand years of Egyptian history, which would have mystified the audience without the voluminous program notes—sober geographical facts mixed with fantastical lore about such ceremonies as the Sacrifice of the Virgins. The scale of production, for the sheer purpose of display, was un-imaginably splendid. Palisades Park boasted brand-new facilities with electric lights—both arcs and incandescents—gas illuminations and calcium spotlight effects, and a vast stage where immense tableaux, processions, and ballets could be mounted, such as this prelude to Cleopatra's appearance, a solemn parade

> . . . of EMIRS and CADIS with their insignia; REPRE-SENTATIVES of the KHEDIVE of Egypt, DERVISHES, guardians of the Mosques with their banners; the CAMEL of the MAHAMIL SLAVES, the MOBILLIGS of the mountain with their lances and oriflammes, Turkish KA-WASSES brandishing their cimiters, BEDOUIN CAV-ALIERS of the Plain, MUFTIS carrying the Koran; DELEES, soldiers and TUFICKEES, armed with spears and shields, SAADEES, eaters of serpents, and ELVAN-EES, eaters of fire, and ALMEES, GAVAZIES, GYPSIES AND JUGGLERS, etc. Guardians of the Night close the march in which also appear three gorgeous SYMBOLIC FLOATS.

In these two spectacles of wildly jumbled exotica, Ruth Dennis saw and recognized the kind of theatrical dancing available to her. It was spectacle-extravaganza ballet, closer to "art" than any other kind of dancing—but a mechanical art that Ruth would eventually need to reconcile with her beloved Delsarte self-expression. The "Grand Ballet of the Virgins" and the "Grand Oriental Ballet" at the Palisades Park were not atmospheric interludes but rather field exercises, with lines and phalanxes of girls in toeshoes advancing and retreating to the musical beat. These were formations modeled on that earlier, European idea of the corps de ballet; even the soloists were obeying conventions laid down by the Romantic ballerinas who starred in the parade of spectacles in the nineteenth century.

To Ruth Dennis, the toe-dancing of these Egyptian Virgins ignored the whole world of curves and spirals that existed in Delsarte. Ruth had already experienced these contradictions; her talent in Delsarte had sent mother and daughter on an investigation of conventional dance training. They had put on their best clothes for Miss Maude Davenport's School of Social Dancing in Somerville, where Miss Davenport, noticing that Ruth's exuberance hardly suited her dainty waltzes and quadrilles, had sent the girl and her mother to the Swiss dancing master Frank Carl Marwig in New York. Marwig offered the

most advanced instruction available: social dancing for couples, enriched by some classical steps and fancy dancing from the old French
and Italian schools of ballet and sometimes by some of the new arm
gestures from Delsarte. Most pupils of these dancing masters like
Marwig were society girls interested in deportment. Humbler "ballet
girls" in the theater couldn't always afford lessons or else they went
to the Italians Bonfanti or Menzeli. On this occasion, Marwig, in his
quaint black satin knee breeches, gave Ruth a trial lesson, found
the girl promising, and agreed to teach her free, but the weekly
train fare into New York was too expensive. The Dennises abandoned
the idea.

Even without proper lessons, Ruth could dance very well before an
audience. She could do stunts: splits and cartwheels and a spectacular
slow kick, lifting a leg in front to touch her forehead, lowering it,
then lifting the other leg in back to touch her head. The boarders at
Pin Oaks named her "Delsarte"; it was one of them who gave Ruth and
her mother tickets to a Delsarte performance of Mrs. Genevieve Stebbins. The event, probably a charity benefit, was significant for both
mother and daughter. Mrs. Stebbins wore a long Greek gown that
hung gracefully from the shoulders; her hair was simply dressed and
she stood onstage in a strong beam of light that made her look to Ruth
Dennis "like a pearl against a dark setting." Mrs. Dennis saw a woman
who was proud to appear in what was almost a dress-reform uniform,
who had a body that proved the virtue of both her clothing and her
theories of exercise; Ruth saw a woman who had made these principles
theatrical. The performance contained poses copied from Greek statues
and bas-reliefs in European museums—everything from the "tragedy
of Niobe to the Joyousness of Terpsichore," according to Ruth Dennis
years later, and also Mrs. Stebbins' *Dance of Day*, based on ritual
motions of Eastern religions which she had studied and come to ad-
mire. The impact on Ruth of these soft and sinuous motions labelled
Oriental must have been intense after the recent unacceptable Egyptian Virgins at Palisades Park. Mrs. Stebbins' very gestures were
familiar to Ruth; they were her own Delsarte exercises ornamented
for the stage and surrounded by spiritual allusions to appeal to the
imagination.

Mrs. Stebbins was not unique in the 1890s; she represented many
new concerns that were entering the English and American theater
by the back doors of Art and Reform. A solitary woman in a Greek
gown was becoming an obsessive image in those years, on both amateur

and professional stages. At the same time that Miss Ellen Terry was
being admired, painted, and photographed in neo-classic style as
Ophelia, a more notorious Delsarte figure than Mrs. Stebbins was
holding forth in the salons of London, Newport, and New York in a
"brain costume" of Greek robe with barbaric brooches: Henrietta
Knapp Russell. She was a dress reformer who had learned Delsarte
through her efforts to improve her oratory, and now served as an
inspiration to rich Edwardian ladies on two continents. In England
a novel about Mrs. Russell's kind of art appeared in the early nineties—and in 1894 in America. It caught up these art and reform
features of the age and disseminated them through a gigantic and
unexpected fad. This was George du Maurier's *Trilby*. The decade
was marked by Trilby soaps, Trilby songs, Trilby dresses, dolls, dances.
. . . The naïve artist's model Trilby, heroine of this tale of the Latin
Quarter of Paris, becomes a great singer when she is hypnotized by a
sinister musician, Svengali. The book may have created single-handedly
the magnetic legend of Paris' Bohemia, which would draw such
crowds of young American artists for the next forty years. Meanwhile,
the person of Trilby also generated a new feminine type—robust,
natural, unspoiled, and proportioned like a classical statue. In the
miraculous song recital that climaxes the story, Trilby appears in a
simple aesthetic Greek robe with her hair hanging loose, just like
her living counterparts Mrs. Stebbins, Mrs. Russell, or the young
Isadora Duncan, who by the 1890s was already gesturing to Homeric
hymns spoken by her brother Raymond and accompanied by her
mother at the piano.

Ruth Dennis was also tall, graceful, statuesque, and trained to
move harmoniously. And she wanted to dance. Yet she and her mother
had no actual contact with the fragile new forms of art-theater or
aesthetic lecturing. They had been living in a backwater, and Mrs. Dennis' information was a decade out of date. Consequently the Dennises
knew only about the kinds of theater that every other American knew
about—and it was this popular theater they encountered shortly after
this time. They had no skills for dealing with it—only Ruth's natural
energy and talent. They would go where chance sent them. In this
way they would make a kind of blind and bumpy progress through
the subterranean avenues of 1890s show business—which was just
then in a state of gigantic upheaval. From the dime museums to the
vaudeville stage, through musical comedies and serious melodrama,
Ruth would slowly rise. Each of these genres would leave its mark on

her unspoiled imagination, yet finally it was her own and her mother's dreams and ambitions that would be realized in a new American art of expressive dance.

CHAPTER 2
The Theater

*Ours is a profession of intense and sympathetic temperamentality,
less tangible than a dream, highly strung and emotional, graced
with the dearest and best and most Bohemian-like people in the world.*

—DAVID BELASCO ON THE THEATER
> (*spoken on the occasion of the first actors' strike
> of 1919, which he opposed*)

It was a whim of Mrs. Dennis' that put Ruth on the stage. Some time in the early 1890s she decided to produce a "theatrical" to raise money for a new flag for the Somerville Schoolhouse, and she chose Denman Thompson's beloved melodrama *The Old Homestead* —one of the war-horses of nineteenth-century theater circuits. Into the story Mrs. Dennis inserted a "skirt dance," in the latest popular style, for Ruth, and some little clog routines for the neighborhood children. (It was an Irish neighborhood, and clog routines were known by everyone.) The experience of putting on a play diminished the Dennises' isolation. They developed a passion for "theatricals" and at the same time they found a milieu to indulge it: an actors' boarding house on West 26th Street in New York, whose proprietress, Mrs. Nancy M. Miller, also held the mortgage on the Dennises' farm. Mother and daughter went to New York several times to visit, and at some point Mrs. Dennis resolved that Ruth might really try out for the stage. One day they made an expedition to Worth's Museum, on 30th Street and 6th Avenue, where Ruth, in her best clothes—a sailor jacket and wide-brimmed hat—did her slow-motion kicks for the manager. He hired her on the spot, to start the next day at a salary of twenty dollars a week.

The dime museums were in decline. Fifty years before they had been grand institutions, filled with embalmed "curiosities" and live specialty acts, the first respectable places of entertainment for the whole family. Now, they functioned as smaller, seedier versions of vaudeville houses: the actors—balladeers, clog dancers, comics, sopranos, impersonators, jugglers—performed eleven times a day on tiny lecture-room stages, in uncomfortable proximity to midgets and fat ladies on pedestals, octopi and two-headed calves in glass jars. Ruth's number was a skirt dance, like the one in the play. It was called "Gavotte d'Amour," and it contained many backbends and cartwheels with flourishes in between, and a slow split at the finish, set off by a coy toss of the head. Her timing was like that of a good circus trick act, with stops for applause. Her costume was a creation of Mrs. Dennis': a little cream-colored dress with three tiers of lace over a net foundation, ruffled panties underneath, and a great bow in her long loose curls.

After two weeks, Ruth got a place in a small vaudeville house— the usual step up for anybody with talent—and she continued on and off in vaudeville for some months, but had to drop out around 1893 when the Dennises finally lost the farm and moved to Brooklyn. Vaudeville did not pay enough. However, it was crucial to her career: vaudeville, the dime museums—these were the stages, the only stages, where solo dancers could practice their art, and dancing on them Ruth got her first sense of an audience. It was fully eight years after she started performing that she began to invent a style of her own. And although that later style—slow, atmospheric, Orientale—was partly a reaction to the flurry of vaudeville and to the kind of instant impact its performers must make on an audience, it also incorporated a few of her early skirt-dancing vaudeville tricks. She knew—and this was one of her strengths as an American dancer—that any and every audience she entertained had something of the vaudeville crowd in it.

When Ruth, in the last moment of the previous act's exit, ran out in front of the footlights, winked at the audience, and began her high kicks, she was obeying the conventions of a flourishing genre. Vaudeville, or variety, had grown out of nineteenth-century minstrel entertainment—white males in blackface who sang and danced and ribbed each other in quick-paced but ceremonious manner. Troupes of them toured all over the country in the 1860s, 70s, 80s. Tony Pastor, the portly czar of New York's 14th Street Theater, created variety shows out of minstrel shows when he added ethnic numbers— Irish, Scottish, German—and even a few women entertainers to the minstrel fare. With the exception of this new material, variety shows unfolded like minstrel shows, with a quick barrage of songs, gags, and dances for the opening, performed by all the actors arranged onstage in a semi-circle, the "olio" in the middle for specialty acts, and at the end, the "afterpiece," a short burlesque dramatic scene in which everybody took a role. Variety moved fast; each act was clocked to the second, and the whole show, acts and transitions, lasted the same number of minutes and seconds every night. Rhythm and timing were the prime skills of all variety troupers, not just dancers, though dancing was solely dependent on tricks of rhythm and sleight-of-hand. And this is what dancing meant to most American audiences; they had no use for higher allusions or sentimental auras in a short dance number. Most of the audience could perform some kind of folk or character dance themselves, and they came to see their betters. In some variety shows, dancing *contests* were part of the regular entertainment, with three judges sitting in: one for Style, one for Timing, one for Execution (the first two watched from out front; the last judge was positioned under the stage—he only listened).

The kind of dancing that was practiced in variety shows came out of folk techniques brought over by British immigrants—Highland flings, Irish jigs and reels, and especially clog dances, wherein the dancer's wooden shoes made complex percussive patterns on the floor (just as in the progeny of clog, which was American tap). On the circuits, clog dancing proliferated: Lancashire clog, American clog, hornpipe clog, trick clog, pedestal clog, and statue clog were popular. Meanwhile, in certain notorious and wicked nineteenth-century urban places—New York's Five Points District, New Orleans' Storyville, a little later San Francisco's Barbary Coast—clog dancing was minstrelized, syncopated, and jazzed up by a mixture of underworld immigrants and ex-slaves. Some of these dance-hall tricks returned to the variety stages in the guise of new, ingenious, syncopated specialties billed as Sand Dances, Egg Dances, Spade Dances, Candle Dances, Bottle Dances, and the Transformation Dance (called "Transformation" because the performer switched dance styles as layers of costumes were whisked off him one by one by a backstage helper with a string).

Men were still the specialty dancers in seventies and eighties variety shows (girls danced elsewhere, in lines and phalanxes in the faëries and extravaganzas of bigger stages). Since variety-show audiences were mostly male, it was hardly proper for a girl to do a solo dance—or any kind of solo act—except in wild and rough places like the California circuits, with their worldly audiences left over from the Gold Rush. In mainstream variety, girls danced only with brother, father, sister, or partner—until the 1890s, when a new solo genre emerged for women: skirt dancing, which is why when the Dennises came on the scene they decided on a skirt dance for Ruth as proper to the variety stages—they never even considered an aesthetic Delsarte vignette.

Skirt dancing was a mongrel style in which fancy steps learned from dancing masters were grafted onto humbler clogs or jigs—but popular because it brought some refinement into variety shows. A skirt dancer looked like a cross between a ballet girl and a clog dancer in her routine of fast footwork, acrobatic stunts, vigorous swishings of the skirt, twirls, and coy curtsies. Sometimes she even wore toeshoes, and hopped on pointe. No one knows who invented it, but skirt dancing soon surpassed all other possible styles for female dancers—probably because it was not a set form, not geared to hopping over bottles or candles or some other strenuous acrobatic feat: it gave the dancer a chance to display her own manner inside the dance. In the nineties, new middle-class audiences were suddenly more interested in behavior and charm than in tricks. Skirt dancing, hardly a form of its own, was a compromise style for a new time: it retained the old variety-show emphasis on speed and constant activity, but it costumed this in refined clothes—long tutus, or flouncy skirts. It introduced naïve and gullible Americans to the distant atmosphere of English music halls or French cabarets.

The dynamic changes inside variety shows in the 1890s were part of the impetus that would eventually make dance into an art. Art needed respectable audiences; variety at this time was going "clean" and classy—it was becoming vaudeville. Some managers thought a respectability campaign would attract a better class of people, including that whole half of the population who had never been to the music hall—the ladies. In Boston, the famous vaudeville manager Benjamin Franklin Keith lined the seats of his house with silk and banned all suggestive words ("son of a gun," "holy gee," etc.) and obscene gestures. From a nucleus of Boston houses, Keith built up his nationwide Orpheum Circuit, which became the deluxe itinerary, the Mecca, for aspiring vaudeville acts inside an ever more complex hierarchy. In the best houses, like Keith's, rowdy acts, off-color jokes, and some of the stoogelike action disappeared in honor of the new women patrons— the "huge-hatted ladies of America," as Henry James named them. And if they brought respectability, they also brought new appetites to vaudeville. They appreciated high style, they were curious about the exotic, and they loved sentiment.

The excitement of vaudeville in its heyday—the nineties and the turn of the century—lay in the personalities of the performers and the emotions they generated. Vaudeville *material* still consisted of the same classic songs and dances in march time or waltz time, but now the performers were obliged to transcend it. The new audiences, cooler, more polite, and actually seated farther away from the stage, demanded more than an actor's skill: they wanted his aura. The idea of a variety *troupe* whose members played together every night in the afterpiece burlesque disappeared, and the show became a collection of self-contained acts—it became all "olio." Now the different and separate acts competed for top billing. Foreign stars came in with new songs, new jokes, whole new kinds of charm—Harry Lauder the Scots comedian, Yvette Guilbert the French diseuse, Vesta Tilley the British ingenue—and American mass taste opened itself to a new range of insinuations. But the most popular new talent of the vaudeville stages was American, the performers with the widest range of moods, the softest and yet the brassiest touch, the ones who took outrageous liberties with the audience and with the old variety formulas—the solo females.

Ruth Dennis started out like any of the rest of them, entering the theater at a time when anything seemed possible, when a giddy aura of license reigned, especially for women's acts. It was a remarkable time, when performers and audience shared a newness of approach, and the young Ruth Dennis probably realized early what infinite variations were possible in a solo act—especially if the performer projected an unmistakable personal style. All the women headliners were idiosyncratic performers. The legendary ones at the turn of the century—Lillian Russell, Nora Bayes, Elsie Janis, Gertrude Hoffman, Eva Tanguay—all appeared as if from nowhere, like Ruth Dennis herself. None of them was from the dramatic theater; almost all came from families as humble and rootless as the Dennises. And they all displayed the desperate raw energy of their era—the kind of energy that devastated their personal lives but expanded and transformed the stages they played on.

Eva Tanguay, born a year earlier than Ruth Dennis, raised like her in poverty on a farm, became the highest-paid performer in vaudeville history. Tanguay cheerfully admitted her lack of real skill as a singer or dancer; she relied on her brassy clothes, her dazzling and raucous warmth, her instant intimacy with audiences: she flirted on a vast scale. She spurned the sweet woeful ballads of earlier sopranos and she shouted her songs to the upper balcony: "I Want Someone to Go Wild with Me," "It's All Been Done Before But Not the Way I Do It," and her signature number, "I Don't Care, I Don't Care." Her gestures, contrary to strictest vaudeville practices, were unpredictable: "She skipped a step here, ran a few paces there, danced in a slow dreamy tempo, and then suddenly rioted in a mad revelry, a whirlwind," said one review. The blast of Tanguay's personality created a new persona, the American hoyden.

Judging by her later extravagant behavior, the young Ruth Dennis, but for her spiritual anxieties, would have been somewhat like Eva Tanguay. Onstage she had Tanguay's irreverence, even in her first appearances—as witness the public's reaction: she was a favorite. A theatrical agent saw her perform and signed her up; Stanford White, architect and notorious cavalier of chorines, discovered her in a private performance at the Opera Club and became her informal protector (at a distance monitored by Mrs. Dennis). Even Thomas Edison spotted Ruth in his search for dancers to record on his new moving-picture machine—and in 1894 he made a two-minute kinetoscope of "Ruth Dennis, Skirt Dancer," with Ruth high-kicking in a patch of sunlight by the side of a building. It is strange how Ruth, whose mother's ideology had fitted her out for a Delsartean's career, or perhaps a dress reformer's, found herself such a successful coquette. It is even stranger that the solemn, bitter Mrs. Dennis encouraged this gift of her daughter's.

Women of the theater were thought to be frivolous "dolls of the world," consciously artificial and therefore the opposite of Mrs. Dennis' ideals. Of course the first reality for Mrs. Dennis was economic; the salary coming in might help get the farm back. But after Mrs. Dennis entered the world of theater, she seemed to throw all caution aside and temporarily abandon her convictions. So did many mothers like her. Theater in those years was a fast-growing business; child performers were in demand, and their mothers naturally came along. A striking number of these mothers were idealists like Ruth Emma Dennis, who had lived proudly independent lives until they gave up everything of their own for their daughters' careers. Lillian Russell had such a mother, Cynthia H. Leonard, a well-known and implacable feminist before her blond, sweet-natured daughter became the belle of New York. Mrs. Crabtree, mother of the famous soubrette Lotta; Ma Janis, mother of the spirited Elsie; Mrs. Pickford, mother of Mary; Mrs. Gish, mother of Lillian and Dorothy; Mrs. Sweet, grandmother of Blanche—all were upstanding women like Mrs. Dennis, possessed of strong moral convictions, but an even stronger desire to ensure their daughters' financial security. They married their girls to the theater and then settled down in the role of mother-in-law. The husbands of these women were shadowy figures like Thomas Dennis, in some way estranged from their wives and children. What the women had most in common was, of course, poverty. They had first come to the theater—some of them actually brought their babies to the stage door—because they knew the salaries of child performers exceeded anything they could earn themselves as plain, careworn, middle-aged women.

Yet the phenomenon is too striking and mysterious to be explained by economics or even biology. Onstage the daughters were the exact opposites of their mothers. Ruth Dennis was a cunning creature—like Elsie Janis or Mary Pickford—snub-nosed and freckled, with light hazel eyes, a rosebud mouth, and an infallible instinct to dramatize herself. Where did these youngsters get their theatricality? They had no worldly experience, no way of knowing what the adult audiences wanted. Yet they knew they had the power to cheer these audiences, and they were never afraid on stage. Most of them came of hardy, midwestern frontier stock, via their mothers. But the mothers' dour energy hadn't turned fanatic in the daughters; instead it turned into a splendid and audacious charm—and a striking commitment to the Pretend. In the protected and artificial realm of the stage, these young girls came alive. This era, from the turn of the century through the 1920s, would produce more young actresses and dancers with that precious theatrical quality of imaginative concentration than any other time in the American theater.

The common stage career of the Dennis mother and daughter, begun at this point, lasted the rest of their lives together. Mrs. Dennis, once unable to move from her sickbed, now found time to talk to managers, keep financial accounts, make costumes, take care of husband and son, and be there in the wings day after day, fixing her daughter's curls just before Ruth went out on the stage where, somehow, Mrs. Dennis was vindicated as a mother. The neighbors in Somerville had known Ruth as the tomboy child of the queer Dennis family, but in vaudeville, crowds were applauding her health, her charm, her high spirits.

Ruth's vaudeville career was interrupted just as it began. When the Dennises lost Pin Oaks Farm and moved to Brooklyn, she traded uncertain theater bookings for a steady job as a cloak model at the Abraham & Straus department store near their new home. Perhaps she was handicapped in vaudeville by her small voice; she could in fact sing and speak lines, and soon would do so onstage, but she never wanted to become a personality through speaking. Ruth was a natural dancer, if such a type can be said to exist. She had ideas, but at this point in her life, her body was quicker than her mind; she *did* something before she explained it.

Mrs. Dennis had raised her not merely healthy, but defiantly healthy; she had to find physical outlets even while working at Abraham & Straus, and she did: she performed a Greek Delsarte improvisation at a private concert; she entered an amateur women's bicycle race at Madison Square Garden and came in sixth. Both Delsarte and bicycles were emblematic of the New Woman of the nineties, whose physical ease was her trademark. Mrs. Dennis' beliefs had produced a very young New Woman with an incorrigibly athletic body, as yet unconnected to a wild and innocent imagination. The body had acquired some stage experience; the imagination was filled with vast and vague spectacle-extravaganza dreams—of Camille, of Egypt, of Virgins and White Lotus Ladies—much beyond ordinary skirt dancing. There was no genre in the theater then that matched what Ruth dreamed about.

Since she wasn't really equipped to do major solos in vaudeville, her agent turned to musical comedies, with their choruses and bit parts, as a prospective field of employment. In 1898 he found her a specialty spot in Edward Rice's *The Ballet Girl*, an English farce in questionable taste about a love triangle of an American heiress, a French count, and the ballet girl in a cabaret. It travelled with Ruth Dennis to Boston and Philadelphia and did better on tour than in New York. Ruth's part was a back-up number in the cabaret scene, called "The Blue Pierrot," which she danced "on pointe." A specialty dancer often inherited pointe numbers, even if she didn't know how to perform them, partly because ordinary actors and actresses at that time knew how to perform other kinds of dancing. In Ruth's case, her large body with its natural Delsartean swing was wrong for the quick toe-steps, but she managed. No kind of dance existed to show off her new kind of American body —tall, with naturally weighted movement. For that to appear, the performers themselves would have to slow dancing down and give it some room.

The Ballet Girl closed. Ruth played a short run in the chorus of Augustin Daly's *The Runaway Girl*, another "continental," slightly naughty show, but Daly died in the middle of it and the show disbanded. Ruth's next part brought her into contact with subtler and more powerful performing than she had known in vaudeville or in musicals—and an overall, operatic style of drama that was eventually to lead her to her own dance. David Belasco, the flamboyant and immensely successful impresario, hired her for his production of *Zaza* in 1899 and kept her in his company for the next six years. During that time she lived in a realm of vast stage sets, crowds of extras, extravagant costumes and props, fully orchestrated scores for the plays, and fêted star actors and actresses. From these elements, Ruth, in her unconscious search for a kind of theater to mirror her idea of a Utopia, took what she needed. In Belasco she found an intense preoccupation with the actress who played the heroine, and a passionate concern with theatrical techniques—the unity of music, scenery, lights, action— which she herself adopted. Under Belasco's influence Ruth also dis- covered she loved the theater like a religion. The only thing she missed on his stage was repose. She wasn't actually looking for that yet, but eventually she would need something like Delsarte harmonious repose on *her* stage. With Belasco the keynote was agitation: the crowd scenes surged back and forth; the intimate scenes were more desperately sen- timental than quiet. The plots of these plays turned on betrayals— murders, kidnappings, rescues—which generated the violent emotions in the characters and their extravagant histrionic acting techniques. For a young woman imbued with a deep spontaneous interest in how a stage looked and moved, the years spent with Belasco were a rich time.

The first thing Ruth noticed upon entering Belasco's company was the aura that surrounded its temperamental leading lady, the Titian-haired beauty Mrs. Leslie Carter. Mrs. Carter was playing the role of the French tramp singer Zaza, who becomes a music-hall star and takes revenge on her worthless married lover. It was a difficult part, calling for moods alternately coarse and tender, and much strenuous declaiming. Offstage Mrs. Carter received all kinds of special benefits from Belasco—a private railroad car, trunks of new clothes— to enable her to perform. Ruth was dazzled by Belasco's star—as was natural for a chorus girl who had read about Camille and dreamed about the un-American figure of the courtesan. She wrote her family all about Mrs. Carter, about her dressing room "with gorgeous long mirrors, rows of lights, hooks of chintz." Mrs. Carter, usually oblivious to the company, had complimented Ruth on her singing, and Ruth wrote coyly in a letter, "You know she's a star of the first magnitude and I'm a scintillating satellite." Ruth's letters acquired so many French expressions that an old Somerville friend wrote back begging her to "stick to plain United States."

Her ambitions had surpassed ballet and ballet girls, and she now wanted to be an actress. This momentary ambition was a strong in- fluence on her later dancing style. She copied the part of Zaza, studied it in secret, and practiced Mrs. Carter's fiery mannerisms. Belasco encouraged Ruth early on; he gave her a speaking part in Act V, outside the music hall where Zaza had triumphed, which set Mrs. Carter up for one of *her* key lines: as Zaza stepped from the stage door, Ruth, a flower girl, handed her a bunch of violets and asked "How did you become so famous, Mademoiselle Zaza?" to which the actress stirringly replied, "Through much misery, much work, much grief and a little luck!"

There was not a person in the audience or on the stage, including Ruth Dennis, who didn't hear that line as a motto for Mrs. Carter herself as well as for Zaza. Belasco had literally created this actress over several traumatic years of training in voice, gesture, deportment, repertory. Mrs. Leslie Carter was already known across America when Belasco took her on; she had stood trial in one of the most notorious divorce cases of the age, and emerged a beautiful, broken, and lonely woman, whose innocence was still in doubt. Belasco, a daring businessman as well as an artist, believed America needed an actress like the French Sarah Bernhardt, a grand tragic actress with a flamboyant personal reputation—and he staked nearly all he had on making Mrs. Carter into that. Those were the years when actresses dominated the stage, especially in Europe and England, when much of the energy of new playwrights from Bernard Shaw to Victorien Sardou to Henrik Ibsen was focused on making parts for them. On the Continent, Bernhardt and Eleonora Duse were revolutionizing the gestural language of the theater, and in England Ellen Terry, Olga Nethersole, and Mrs. Patrick Campbell were injecting their magical personalities into the craft of acting.

America of the nineteenth century had a tradition of fine stock actresses, Laura Keene, Ada Rehan, Nance O'Neil who had her own company—but these women were not the most outstanding stars of the new theatrical age. A star system connected to the long runs and longer tours of Broadway plays had replaced local stock companies across the country, and the public began to adore actresses who were identified with one kind of role, whether a tragic part or an ingenue. In the 1870s and 80s the ingenue and not the tragedienne was America's most beloved and truly native theatrical figure. Lotta Crabtree of California, who sang, danced, played the banjo, and dressed up rakishly like a boy, achieved her gigantic popularity through monumental irreverence. She even smoked a cigarette on stage! She pre-dated the girl vaudevillians of the turn of the century, showing off her effervescent skills in tailor-made plays like *Little Nell and the*

Marchioness, based on Dickens' *The Old Curiosity Shop.* In the nineties Lotta retired to London with her mother and a fortune to be a lady.

David Belasco, who began as a California actor too, surveyed the scene as the ingenue Lotta was ending her reign and the tragedienne Sarah Bernhardt was beginning hers, with the first of her indefatigable tours of America in the late 1880s. Bernhardt brought a new serious extravagance to the legitimate stage, to the person of the actress, and to the repertory of American theater. Her kind of play was the *pièce bien-faite,* a construction of many violent twists of plot (Eugène Scribe and Victorien Sardou were the masters of the genre), usually with a strong woman figure at center stage, a queen or courtesan who seemed to call the vast action up out of herself. Bernhardt's plays were customarily named for their heroines, who were "bad" women: *Adrienne Lecouvreur, La Tosca, Magda, Théodora, Fédora, Gismonda, Frou-Frou,* and of course *La Dame aux Camélias.* And if Bernhardt, by the time she toured America, seemed to be playing variations on a single formula, she still elicited from it an astonishing force that she projected through the special techniques she had developed for herself. Bernhardt was a theatrical original. She had merged the classic gestural code of old French academic acting from Corneille and Racine's time with newer skills of Boulevarde melodrama and some of Delsarte's pseudo-spiritual expression. The mature Bernhardt chanted her lines like a torch singer and gestured boldly with her whole body. She created her characteristic moments of anguish or high lament by lifting her chest, throwing back her head, and stretching her arms to the skies. Americans went to Bernhardt's plays as though to an opera—for the awesome alien rituals; hardly any of them could understand what she was saying, since she declaimed in French. But gradually Bernhardt's appearances exposed American audiences to a richer display of French acting and of stylized feminine corruption than they had ever seen. In the course of the 1880s and 90s, as Bernhardt crisscrossed the country, her name became a household word, the way Anna Pavlova's would two decades later—and the stage demeanor of her savage and vengeful courtesans passed into the national consciousness.

It was this high-tragic style that Belasco wanted to bring into *his* productions via Mrs. Carter; that was why he bought the French play *Zaza* for her and why he chose as her next vehicle *Du Barry*—the dramatized life of that queen of all French courtesans, the consort of Louis XV. The play was a gorgeous and massive piece of entertainment. However, Mrs. Carter at its center proved not quite what he had hoped for the heroine. She was so completely Belasco's creature that she never became her own, and so had no recourse to the natural dignity needed to balance this strident part. Everyone agreed that Mrs. Carter displayed, in her heyday (the years when Ruth Dennis was fresh to the company), a professional competence and a raw, if sometimes vulgar, panache. But she verged on caricature. Broadway's senior critic William Winter described her in near-comic fashion, even though he generally supported both her and Belasco: "Mrs. Carter [as Du Barry] would work herself into a state of great excitement. She would weep, vociferate, shriek, rant, become hoarse with passion, flop and beat upon the floor." Another critic, Norman Hapgood, thought she was "hard as an arc light"—and in fact, when Mrs. Carter left Belasco in 1908 and tried to star on her own, she faded somewhat. She hadn't ever discovered exactly what she was doing in the dramatic theater.

In watching Mrs. Carter through the initial staging, the seasons, and then the tours of both *Zaza* and *Du Barry*, Ruth Dennis was constantly presented with the figure of the grand actress and her language of expression. She absorbed immeasurable amounts of the techniques Mrs. Carter depended on and the air of high intrigue that surrounded her on the stage. Ultimately Ruth rejected the cyclonic rhythms of Mrs. Carter's kind of heroine, but she took the extravagant, French, Bernhardt-imitation gestures as her own. However, as she grew up in Belasco's plays, Ruth began to show marked talent not as a tragic actress but as an ingenue. The skirt-dancer part of her was irrepressible. She regaled her fellow actors in the wings with jokes and songs in brogue and minstrel drawl, and Belasco saw.

Ruth's quicksilver quality gave Belasco the idea of making her a comic star on the order of Lotta Crabtree, the way he had made Mrs. Carter a tragedienne (Belasco had a long subsequent sub-career as a creator of actresses). He had liked Ruth from the first, when she showed up in *Zaza*, and now he continued to groom her. He gave her a special giggling scene of her own in *The Auctioneer*, the urban comedy he produced after *Zaza*, and then a name part in *Du Barry*— Mlle. Le Grand, danseuse of the Paris Opera. Ruth danced a solo minuet in Act III and sang a song, "Amaryllis," in a small but true soprano voice. As an afterthought Belasco also put her into the final scene, at the head of the screaming, jeering Jacobites who accompany Mme. Du Barry to the guillotine. Belasco knew that she could command the most raw energy and the most mischievousness in the company, and he came to her with a proposal to "re-create" her. When Ruth finally rejected Belasco's plan for her future, she wasn't rejecting his perceptions of her, she was choosing a wider range for herself than he could imagine. Her temperament and talent marked her as a soubrette, but her imagination was edging her toward the grand actress, the figure closer to the White Lotus Lady of that early religious novel, and to the Delsartean Genevieve Stebbins with her mystic authority. Ruth wasn't prepared to give up a cherished and secret vision of herself as a goddess, a theatrical matriarch. But her precise kind of goddess didn't appear in Belasco's repertory.

What Ruth took unquestioningly from Belasco was his stagecraft, wherein lay his genius. Belasco was by birth a creature of the theater. His father, a Portuguese-Jewish Harlequin of the London stage, had brought his family to California in the Gold Rush, and David had grown up in California frontier theater (like Lotta Crabtree and many of the outstanding theater figures of this time). Even after he became the top impresario-director in New York, he relied on the sense of timing bred into him by his experience in every conceivable character part in local stock repertory. Belasco has been called a master of theatrical "realism," but he was as fabulous as he was realistic; what he had really mastered was the inner rhythms of the genre of melodrama, which was a blending of music ("melo") and drama. A constant awareness of rhythmic motion on the stage was what Belasco contributed, through Ruth Dennis, to American dance. The legend of Belasco points to a truly physical grasp of dramatic action. He constructed his massive plays alone on the stage, improvising every part himself, working out the action stroke by stroke—and it was always strenuous. One of his memorable moments was Mrs. Carter's leap from a high ladder to a swinging bell-rope (to stop the bell tolling for her lover's execution) in *The Heart of Maryland* (1896); all his plays had such highlights of action. He also had an uncanny sense of the way actors worked with *things*: furniture and props. Most of the "realistic" details he introduced into his productions—real water for rivers, real food for dining scenes, real diamonds and pearls to adorn the actresses—were there to help the cast feel the atmosphere. So were the new range of electric light effects with which he replaced gaslights in every theater he worked in, and the musical scores he commissioned for every play.

By the time Belasco produced *Du Barry* for Mrs. Carter (1901) he was orchestrating a huge production staff, a cast of ninety-odd players, most of them in full-dress satins and laces; elaborate sets ranging from the twisted streets of Paris to the façade of Versailles, to the sumptuous bedchamber of Mme. Du Barry herself (furnished with some of the original Du Barry's baroque antiques). The glory of this vast enterprise was how it moved. The verbal texts were the least important feature of his theater—most of them were pirated anyway—rather, it was the timing, the precise control of the light, music, and histrionics; the sense of how intimate scenes should alternate with epic crowd displays; how the hordes of players spilled from one side of the stage to the other; how vast sets succeeded one another as the play unfolded. Belasco directing was like a naval officer commanding a battle; his stage was a sea of color, sound, and motion, and he, on a larger than human scale, was a choreographer. David Belasco was Ruth Dennis' real dancing master, as well as being her dramatic coach.

Belasco was also a theatrical imperialist; any new idiom he encountered he had to try out in his theater and give to his public. In the Paris Exposition of 1900, which Belasco and the cast of *Zaza*, including Ruth Dennis, visited after performing in London, Belasco saw the brilliant Japanese actress Mme. Sadi Yacco, the first of her country to bring Japanese theater to the West. Belasco came home and mounted his own Japanese play, *Madame Butterfly*, in 1900—one of his usual seduced-and-abandoned stories, but told in this new surprising Japanese mode—and he followed it up with a sequel, *The Darling of the Gods*, in 1902. Ruth Dennis was Belasco's protégée; he let her watch rehearsals and talk to him about things Japanesque. This new look of the scenery with twisted gardens and distant volcanoes; this weird and delicate music, and the long pantomime scenes Belasco wrote into these two plays, much quieter than the maelstroms of *Du Barry* he was directing at the same time, stirred Ruth profoundly. In them she glimpsed the qualities she was longing for.

Ruth, too, had seen Sadi Yacco, and taken away an excitement so intense it inspired her first experiment in dance-drama. It was in 1900, after only a year with Belasco, that she made a solo dance sketch in the Japanese mode—or at least in Japanese costume. She named the dance "Madame Butterfly," in honor of Belasco's new play, and she performed it with his permission in small vaudeville houses—even though she never mentioned this in later narrations of her career. Nevertheless, with this solo she began to think of dancing as something other than a vaudeville act to show off a personality. What she had made was a genuinely new thing: a dance that was the distillation of a story, a play with the drama taken out, a modest composition, but one saturated with the modern quality of "atmosphere."

Mme. Yacco's attraction for Ruth was her "aura of stillness—so different from our Western acrobatics." Ruth had sensed that Sadi Yacco's
art came from an older and more honorable source than Belasco's commercial formulas—although she had no quarrel with these. But in
Sadi Yacco she saw the dignity this tradition gave to the Japanese
actress's motions. Perhaps it was Japanese society, perhaps it was
Japanese theater, that had created this courtesan-figure she played—
the woman who has many lovers and who lives by artifice—but in
either case Mme. Yacco's stage characters were distinctly different from
Belasco's. They were absolved of guilt and anguish. They were not
caught up in desperate struggles of retribution. In short, Mme. Yacco
showed Ruth the possibility of a grand actress-heroine who wasn't a
"bad woman," one who used ritualistic and rhythmic gestures as her
natural mode of expression.

If Sadi Yacco was Ruth's external catalyst, inside she was impelled toward rebellion by an intense confusion about who she was at
home and who she was in her profession. All through her years with
Belasco, Ruth continued to live with her family while in New York,
and she wrote constantly to her mother while on tour. She wrote about
the things they had always talked about together: nerves and religion.
"I'm so sorry you've been having such bad nights," she said in a typical
note. "If I was home we would have a nice talk, probably on faith,
and by and by after much reasoning and arguing you would feel a
little better, n'est-ce pas?" Since Ruth's habitual function at home was
to comfort and soothe, no wonder she was drawn in theater to a
Japanese actress's serenity. She herself now wished to do on stage what
she had done all her life: calm down her mother—and everybody else
—offer a quieter, richer world as compensation for distraught nerves.
A book she picked up during her last year with Belasco, Mary Baker
Eddy's *Science and Health*, revealed that her own mind might get
her to this quieter, healthier, mystical place. The author had written
(in 1875) that worrying about ill health might be an activity à la
mode, like buying clothes in Paris: if one stopped thinking about it,
one stopped wanting to do it. In its use of her mother's religious
rhetoric, the book suggested to Ruth the ultimate remedy for Mrs.
Dennis' chronic nervous pains, and a release from anxious sympathy
for herself. Ruth thought she *felt* spiritual ecstasy.

But this was the same Ruth who in the theater was a backstage
favorite and a jokester, mischievous companion of Belasco and Hamil-
ton Revell, the male lead in *Du Barry*. Her threadbare childhood had
bred a deep thirst for luxury and magic. All her life Ruth would feel

the classic longing of the American Protestant, the abstainer, for the rituals of "the other," the sensual religion—be it the Roman Catholic Church or be it theater. A passage she wrote years later for her autobiography provides a clue to these complicated exchanges inside her mind between abstinence and indulgence:

> With the mixing of the grease paint and the making up of eyes and mouth, the powdering of face and neck, there is enacted something like a mass for beauty—I have felt this since my earliest days in the theater. We come to this strange little sordid temple. There is a discipline to be endured. There is a ritual to be enacted—at the other side of which we emerge as a new being. The smell of greasepaint is to an actor what the smell of incense is to the devotee.

Ruth belonged in the theater; she just had to bend it a little toward the sacred, and create the roles that would satisfy both her body and her soul. Meanwhile she had been playing in one or another production of *Du Barry* for nearly four years. It was in the final thirty-eight-week cross-country tour of that play when Ruth, dancing the same minuet, singing the same song, above all watching Mrs. Carter rant and rave every night, found the strength to rebel. A sign came to her in Buffalo of what she must do. She and a friend, drinking a soda in a drugstore, looked up to see a poster advertising Egyptian Deity Cigarettes. Under the brand name was a splendid picture of a bare-chested goddess, Isis, seated between two stone columns under a twilight sky, her head lifted, her hands resting serenely on her thighs. This was a vision, stronger even than the Japanese, of the things Ruth wished for in her theater—control, serenity, Sphinx-like reserve, absolute feminine authority. For the rest of the tour she devoured books on Egypt in every available library. In San Francisco, she had herself photographed as Isis, in a square black wig with a paper lotus flower in it, a band of silk across her chest, a draped skirt, and bracelets on her arms and ankles—the first of many costumes improvised by Ruth Dennis out of nearly nothing. This photograph was the most direct way to audition herself as the Egyptian Deity—a figure as powerful and as seductive as Mrs. Carter's and Sarah Bernhardt's heroines, yet calmer and more mystic. There was something about the angular Egyptian design, the severe and the sensual combined, that exactly matched the spiritual hedonism inside this rather fanatic American girl.

.   .   .

At the end of the *Du Barry* tour Ruth left Belasco. She was twenty-six, and she was throwing away a theatrical future practically guaranteed. But the Dennis family had dreaming in their blood, and the Dennis women a streak of stubborn independence. Ruth's vision of her *Egypta* was not so different from Mrs. Dennis' plan for health and beauty lectures—it was simply on a grander scale, requiring scenery, costumes, and crowds of extras as befitted a Belasco disciple. When she got home to New York, Ruth found that the family, on the strength of her excited letters, had moved to a bigger flat to give her more space to work. Guided by her Belascoesque nose for exotica she discovered something useful in Coney Island: a whole village of Hindus, entertaining with their native dances. This was as close as she could get to Egypt—and nautch girls, snake charmers, and Hindus were finally just as compelling as Egyptians. Ruth shifted her focus temporarily to India. Most Americans lumped Egypt and India together anyway—in the questionable context of the kootch, of belly dancing. The hootchy-kootchy, probably named for the Indian province of Cooch Behar, had been popularized in America not by Indians but by an Egyptian dancer called "Little Egypt" at the 1893 Chicago Exposition. By 1905 when Ruth left Belasco for exotic dancing, everybody knew the song about the hootch at the 1904 World's Fair: "Meet me in St. Louis, Louis. . . . We will dance the Hootchy Kootchy."

But Ruth was not learning that hootchy-kootchy; instead she was re-discovering the Oriental in a serious way significant to her own female American sensibility. In her reading she found the Indian legend of the mortal maid Radha loved by the God Krishna. She looked at pictures of Radha and Krishna on their lotus leaf, of Radha wandering the night alone. To Ruth these legends answered the need for an idiom somewhere between the spiritual and the theatrical. To become Radha she garbed herself in a gauze skirt with a gilt rim; she covered her midriff bodice with dimestore brooches and "decapitated hatpins," she put two jeweled circles in her hair at the nape of her neck, and she stained all the skin of her body brown. For a while she even tried a version of a nose ring. Inspired by her transformation, she proceeded to create the dance, to the lush and mysterious divertissements of the French opera *Lakmé*, by Léo Delibes. It was the fullness of the music that enabled her to combine mime and tableau poses from drama with some sections of count-by-count dancing.

In Ruth Dennis' *Radha*, the figure of Radha dances for her devotees (impersonated by several down-and-out East Indian sailors and clerks) with the symbols of the five senses—bells for hearing, flowers for smell, a bowl of wine for taste, handfuls of jewels for sight, and kisses on her own palms for touch. (Her poses with these objects resembled Mrs. Carter's exaggerated pantomime gestures with props.) For the next part of the dance, a symbolic rendition of despair, she borrowed the writhing motions of Sarah Bernhardt, whom she saw in person in Sardou's play *La Sorcière* at the same time she was working out *Radha*. For her finale when the music speeded up, Ruth's old skirt-dancing instincts came back to her in a series of high kicks, backbends, and tour-de-force twirls with gauze skirt rippling up and down. The dance ended in a symbolic faint—a signal of the transcendence of the senses. However, the real significance of *Radha* was not its symbology but its rhythms; this was the first time in commercial theater that the body of a dancer had realized its own natural pace and begun to occupy all the space and time on stage that it craved. Ruth Dennis was a big-boned, healthy, even voluptuous American girl; this dance expressed some of the glory of that.

When Ruth made the rounds of theater managers with *Radha* she added two shorter dance sketches—an exotic ingenue vignette, *The Cobras*, in which she played a snake-charmer waif in a marketplace, and the more abstract and mystical *Incense*, her Delsarte number. At first, agents and managers thought the act was too close to Midway dancing of the lowest sort—hootch and peep-show styles. Finally, though, Proctor's Vaudeville House on 23rd Street slotted her into a show between a pugilist and a group of trained monkeys. Although she scored a mild personal success there, it took the daring, restless eye of a New York socialite, Mrs. Orlando Rouland, to recognize the purity of her intentions in *Radha*, and also the prophetic note of high chic she had struck. Mrs. Rouland arranged for Ruth to give a private matinée at the Hudson Theater. This was a time when reckless young society girls were reading Omar Khayyám's *The Rubáiyát* (a rose-colored and musk-scented edition had appeared in 1897), and those in the vanguard of taste were beginning to cultivate atmospheric décor—about two decades in arrears of the English aesthetes.

Within this small social set, Ruth Dennis' Oriental act fell on fertile ground. The billing on the Proctor's program was *Radha*: "wonderful, mysterious, exquisite *Radha*—a spectacular foreign act said to be almost Belascoesque in its construction." Ruth's own name was on the verge of disappearing until Mrs. Dennis, remembering a time when David Belasco had exploded at Ruth's girlishness and called her "Saint Dennis," wrote it down—*St. Denis*—on a trunk bound for the Hudson Theater matinée. It stuck. It satisfied Mrs. Dennis' religious conscience. After thirteen or so years of theatrical experience, mother and daughter began their second career in nearly the same state of charmed innocence in which they had begun the first.

CHAPTER 3
Europe and Isadora

The small group of society women gathered uneasily at the Hudson Theater on Thursday afternoon, March 22, 1906. They had come to see a young "Temple Dancer" called Ruth St. Denis, in a private matinée—on the recommendation of their adventurous friend Mrs. Rouland (wife of the painter), who had rescued this original and mystic act from vaudeville. The theater lobby was darkened for the occasion; real Hindus were gliding about inside it and incense was in the air. The curtain rose; a girl in veils appeared, set down her sacrificial tray, and rippled her arms like smoke. In the second number the girl, now arrayed in dirty turban and ragged dress, impersonated a waiflike snake charmer in an Indian street bazaar, filled with gesticulating Hindus. But the third piece, *Radha*, was the prize. The stage was transformed into a gold-encrusted shrine, whose doors opened to reveal the goddess sitting on a pedestal, covered in jewels, with a bare midriff, brown stain on her skin, and bells on her ankles. She bowed to her crouching devotees, she twirled, she made extravagant gestures with significant objects—a small bowl from which she drank, a garland of flowers she pressed to her breast. The dance mounted to a frenzy as the goddess whirled ecstatically and finally fell, spent, in a symbolic faint. At the end of the performance the ladies went to their waiting hansom cabs, still in awe, according to next day's newspapers, of what they had seen.

Ruth St. Denis' *Radha* became a cult item in restricted aesthetic circles of New York. The *Evening Sun* mentioned her in a gossip column, called "Matinee Girls," in which one of the girls resolves:

> We shall mold our hands until they are wedge-shaped, dye our fingertips with henna, and hire a Nautch girl to teach us Delsarte.

The other girl answers:

> From what I've heard about Loie Fuller, Radha must be the most original of all.

Original was a new word of praise; it applied to unknown matters like Eastern decoration, and self-expression. When Ruth Dennis emerged from David Belasco's stage in her own spectacle—as Ruth St. Denis— she found herself a part of a new thing just barely discernible, a fad of expressive dance.

The most famous new dancer, and the one who had first gone

to Europe, was Loie Fuller. Europe was where Ruth St. Denis knew she must go as the next step in her career—and she did, in the summer of 1906, to London, to Paris, and to Berlin, where her Oriental dances were much acclaimed. And she was not unique. Before she arrived, not only Loie Fuller but Isadora Duncan and Maud Allan, both Americans, had made names for themselves. (Maud Allan, born in Canada, had moved to San Francisco at an early age.) Over the two and a half years Ruth St. Denis stayed in Europe, solo dancing grew even more popular, and by the fall of 1908 she, Maud Allan, and Isadora were playing in three London theaters at the same time—with enough audience to go around.

There are ways in which these several American girls with their original dances constitute a movement, since all of them were products of America's naïve dreams about art, and of American dance training, however haphazard. Europe produced nothing like them until the next generation. On the other hand, Europe recognized what they were doing; without the excitement in Europe about new forms in all the arts, Fuller, Allan, Duncan, and St. Denis would never have lasted. In Europe each was taken up and patronized by artists and poets and intellectuals on a scale undreamed of in America. They were thought to be not just new kinds of artists but new kinds of personalities. Each of the four had brought her mother with her, yet American-style they, the girls, seemed to be in command. Their brashness, their cheerfulness, attracted fatherly Europeans who "adopted" them.

It was a strange and marvelous meeting: they found in Europe the approval of an old, refined, and self-aware culture; Europe found in them a pre-civilized freshness. Moreover, each of them embodied some features of Art Nouveau, then at its height. Curling lines, organic spirals and curves so beloved of artists then, appeared in their dances, and so did glimpses of the current imagery of fauns and nymphs side by side with Salomés, Cleopatras, Belles Dames Sans Merci. Because these American girls came from a country which all but ignored the lure of the femme, they could play at being erotic with no deadliness attached. They were child-women with a pagan innocence and power—and they puzzled and fascinated Europeans. Images in all the arts anticipated them and then reflected them: the poems of Yeats and Mallarmé, the paintings of the Fauves, the statues of Rodin. They stepped into the scene, and as if by a trick of ancestry their heritage was suddenly revealed.

Loie Fuller was the first, and she came to Paris from America in 1892, as if from another planet. By sheer doggedness she got herself onto the stage of the Folies Bergères, where she became a sensation with her Fire Dance, her Lily Dance, her Butterfly Dance, and her famous Serpentine—skirt dances glorified by her own lighting inventions and silk manipulations. Miss Fuller was a native of small-town Illinois who had made her way through the whole spectrum of nineteenth-century American theater. She was basically an all-purpose soubrette like the famous Little Lotta Crabtree, although she had begun as a child temperance lecturer exhibiting colored charts of the liver. She had played the boy hero in *Little Jack Sheppard* opposite the great comedian Nat Goodwin, she had toured with Buffalo Bill's Wild West Show, appeared in *Aladdin's Lamp* (a faërie extravaganza like *The Black Crook*), and written and mounted her own play, *Larks*. It was while rehearsing in a comedy, *Quack, M.D.*, that she accidentally discovered her dance—or so says the legend. Offstage one day a beam of sunlight caught a piece of silk she was draping on herself and in the mirror she was transformed. Being of a scientific turn of mind, she began to experiment with ways to move the silk around in the sunlight, and she perfected a number of motions—twirls, waltz steps, little skips —that made the silk swirl.

Loie recognized she had found something resembling the new aesthetic costumes on European stages (Ellen Terry's Greek gowns, Sarah Bernhardt's Oriental) as well as the dress-reform ideals in this country. Loie was a genius at picking up things in the air. She decided her new trick was "artistic" and belonged in Europe—near Sarah Bernhardt, whom she admired extravagantly. It was with this flimsy conviction that she went to Paris. She didn't know anything about culture; she hadn't been to a museum, she didn't know statues were single items made by sculptors—she thought they were made en masse in factories. But the quickness and shrewdness bred in her by America's rough and ready theater became her guide—she sensed what her audience of that moment wanted to see, and she sensed correctly. Europe proclaimed her a wizard of light, color, motion, and impressionism. The millionaire collector Camille Groult (of the flour and meat-paste fortune) showed her his Watteau pastels, his Turner canvases, his preserved butterfly wings—and told her that she was also part of his collection. Everyone from Dumas-fils and Anatole France to Rodin and Mallarmé became her admirer; their serious opinion of her art inspired her to keep on perfecting it. It was she who first lit herself from beneath the stage, through frosted glass panels; she and her electricians made the secret chemical dyes that gave her lights their shimmering, mother-of-pearl, rainbow hues. Special sticks that she wielded under the fabric became the instruments of awesome motions: in the Lily Dance she spun the white silk into a moving spiral; in the Fire Dance she whipped the yards of translucent stuff, lit rose and vermilion, around her shadowy form. Everyone said she had captured Nature by technical means—its plantlike and flamelike curls and spirals, its tendrily lines that united everything and wrapped around everything and linked everything in endless growth and decay. Almost by chance Loie became a potent symbol of the age, an age when electricity was new and glorious, and colors were resplendent—and both were used by artists in their creation of a grand artificial version of organic nature.

What Loie had done theatrically was to abstract the idea of the 1880s and 90s spectacle-extravaganza, with their trompe-l'oeil marvels, their ballerinas, and their cloud machines, into a solo dance spectacle. A decade later Ruth St. Denis would abstract romantic-historical drama in similar fashion. However, underneath the silk, Loie was using dance motions of an earlier tradition—music-hall skirt-dance motions. Her music was nothing like Debussy's or Richard Strauss's modern tone-washes; rather it was straightforward Delibes pizzicati, or Johann Strauss waltzes. In two film fragments of Fuller performing, it is apparent that she constructed her dances in short sections: she would undulate the arms, for instance; still undulating them she would start to twirl, then she would supplement the twirls with a low dip backward and serpentine arm movements. Through all this, the moving silk gave an illusion of daring musicality. But the dance made no attempt to mirror the melodic rise and fall of a particular piece of music; it proceeded by accumulated gestures, and it could fit almost any music. There is no denying that Loie possessed dance instincts, and that she was sincerely attached to her new kind of spectacle. What she had found, though, was actually more an idea than a new method. It was ordinary dancing concealed and surrounded by veils, and since Art Nouveau audiences loved things like veils and women's hair—flowing textured matter associated with skin—they didn't miss choreography. Loie's audience was all the more intrigued with her moving body for intuiting it through the silk. They never tired of watching her demonstrate over and over the mysterious, self-renewing, glorious, and terrible *motion* so essential to their modern aesthetic.

In 1896, four years after she made her début as an unknown at the Folies Bergères, Loie returned in triumph to New York's Koster and Bial's Music Hall, the house that imported the best foreign acts—at twice the salary of American headliners. The newspapers were impressed by her French aura and her dances retitled in French *La Nuit,*

Le Feu, Le Firmament, Le Lys de Nile. Also impressed were two young ballet girls, Ruth Dennis and Isadora Duncan, who could not help hearing of La Loie Fuller on her first homecoming tour. Perhaps they saw her at that time. Four years later both of them encountered her at the great Paris Exposition of 1900, that supreme manifestation of Art Nouveau, where Loie had her own theater—a low, cavelike structure graced by a giant statue of herself and swirling drapes. Ruth Dennis was in Paris with the Belasco company of *Zaza*; Isadora by then had cut herself adrift from American theater and joined the Bohemian artists of London and Paris. Loie Fuller was not the sole reason that either St. Denis or Duncan went to Europe, but her career had bloomed at a time when they were only obscure chorines with inchoate theatrical ambitions. Loie made everyone aware that dancing was more than trick steps and jollity, that it could call forth the deeper sentiments that usually belonged to modern painting, music, and drama.

It is clear that Ruth St. Denis and Isadora Duncan both stemmed from Loie Fuller, though each took off in a separate direction. Ruth St. Denis explored the mood part of dancing—she made dance *scenes*, with literal costumes and stage sets where Loie's had been abstract. Meanwhile Isadora identified what Loie had implied about the body itself as a means of expression, with or without veils. Loie's dancing had come out of the theater she knew—and that was all she knew.

Both Isadora and Ruth St. Denis were something else before they were theater dancers; both of them carried compulsions from their lives into their theater careers—similar compulsions, but worked out in different environments. Isadora and Ruth were approximately the same age, born around 1878. Both grew up in poor families, on the fringes of society, and both were indoctrinated into dress reform and Delsarte and defiant feminism. However, Ruth Dennis was essentially a Protestant child and Isadora, through her mother, a lapsed Roman Catholic; Ruth grew up on the East Coast; Isadora in California, in the lively, wicked, hedonistic, and above all theatrical city of San Francisco. The key to their samenesses and their differences may have been the grief they each inherited for a world their mothers had lost before they were born. However, whereas Mrs. Dennis' rightful milieu consisted of women doctors and health reform, Mrs. Duncan's was one of culture and elegance.

Mary Dora Grey Duncan came from a wealthy Irish-Catholic

family of St. Louis, a city that boasted old enough cosmopolitan blood—French, German, Irish—to educate its Catholic young boldly and liberally. Even the girls were allowed to read French novels and learn not just pretty pieces on the piano but the literature of the instrument. Mary Grey married a San Franciscan, a banker-gambler-poet, Joseph Duncan. When this husband abandoned her and her four children, Mrs. Duncan became a piano teacher and also, like Mrs. Dennis, something of a classic non-conformist. But instead of clutching her religion to her, she rejected it and turned instead to the theories of the Irish agnostic Robert Ingersoll. He justified her worship of art and culture.

Ingersoll was a splendid and lugubrious orator who travelled around America preaching his Gospel of Humanity and providing an umbrella for all kinds of quarrels with conventional God-fearing beliefs. Ingersoll did not believe in God, but he did believe in human kindness and in a sweetened sensuality. He worshipped women and the feminine aura; he thought life should be lived fully on this earth, not in heaven, and that some pagan religions hadn't been all wrong. Even though his main arguments weren't aesthetic, Ingersoll's theology supported Americans' very new curiosity about art and the artistic part of a person.

The four Duncan children mouthed Ingersoll; they could also recite the Romantic poets: Keats and Shelley and Robert Burns, who conjured up lost pagan sensations, and Walt Whitman, who connected these to the American landscape. Whitman was beloved of the youngest Duncan, Isadora; her favorite poem all her life was his "Song of the Open Road," about the joys of travelling light and the desire to embrace everyone else travelling too. Whitman taught the importance of those surges of feeling inside a person, the rhythmic rise and fall of nearly inexpressible emotion: "You air that serves me with breath to speak! / You objects that call from diffusion my meanings and give them shape!" These rhythms of the romantic soul were heard by the Duncans not just in poetry but in the piano music their mother played for them—Beethoven, Brahms, Chopin, Schubert; rubatos, crescendos, gusts of melody.

The miracle of Isadora's childhood is that this rich mixture of oratory and melody was experienced by her physically, because it mingled in her childhood with certain physical attitudes she was being taught—among them dress reform, Delsarte, and a California worship of the outdoors. Californians were proud of their giant landscape, their Pacific Ocean, their redwoods. In the years of Isadora's childhood,

California artists and writers like Jack London, Bret Harte, and Frank Norris were finding that they could transfer the pagan ethos of ancient Greece to their own wilderness. Isadora's father was a poet of their set. He may have belonged to the Bohemian Club, a group of gentlemen who put the landscape literally to use every year in a theatrical revel on a natural woodland stage called The Grove. The most memorable of these was a masque, in 1892, called *The Hamadryads*, wherein the actors played spirits coming out of the trees. The Grove plays may have impressed Isadora early on with the thought that theater could invoke powerful ancient spirits. She knew about these plays through her special friend, the poetess Ina Coolbrith, who was also the Oakland librarian and guided Isadora's reading.

It could have been Ina Coolbrith, or Mrs. Duncan, or Isadora's sister Elizabeth who also taught Isadora about uncorseted, free-flowing clothes—dress reform. Aesthetic dress was almost a uniform of San Francisco artists— and Greek and Pre-Raphaelite costumes certainly fit the Duncans' view of themselves as an artistic family and as artistic Californians. Ruth Dennis' dress reform was an ideology; Isadora's was an aesthetic of the "natural." Mrs. Duncan made sure that a historic example of Nature-worship, Botticelli's *Primavera*, hung in a prominent place in whatever boardinghouse the family was just then occupying. It was also a model for Isadora's clothes and later her costumes. Dress-reform rhetoric shows up constantly in Isadora's later articles and speeches, but it was always connected to the unique California way of seeing Nature. Unhampered bodies and "natural" rhythms were synonymous to Isadora—and somewhere within the combination was "true dance." "What is 'true dance' in opposition to what might be named 'false dance'?" Isadora asked in an article she wrote around 1905:

> The true dance is appropriate to the most beautiful human form; the false dance is the opposite of this definition —that is, that movement which conforms to a deformed human body. First, draw me the form of a woman as it is in Nature, and now draw me the form of a woman in a modern corset and the satin slippers used by our modern dancers. To the first all the rhythmic movements that run through Nature would be possible. . . . To the second figure these movements would be impossible on account of the rhythm being broken and stopped at the extremities.

The "corset" of "our modern dancers" and the corsets of conventional dress were both odious to Isadora. Yet no matter how fervently she claimed that her own body remained "as in Nature," as a child she did study dancing systematically. First of all she had learned the Irish jigs and reels of her grandparents when she was a baby. Then, when she was about five or six, her sister Elizabeth came home to Isadora's family from the grandparents who had raised her. Elizabeth had become a professional dancing teacher, with a school where well-bred children of the city learned the dances they were expected to know in the 1880s and 90s, character dances like mazurkas, czardases, schottisches, varsoviennes, an occasional daring waltz. These were rhythmically complex and expressive in their own way. Such dancing schools as Elizabeth's did not count as academies because they had no overall logic in the teaching. However, training for advanced students was challenging; random ballet steps were taught along with the character figures; "pas de bourrée," "sissonnes," "assemblés," and the like might be worked into advanced routines at amateur exhibitions. By the 1890s some of those dancing schools had already incorporated Delsarte exercises—which Isadora clearly learned at an early age. She had rapidly become her sister's best pupil and helper. If her mother and the whole California milieu had given her the image of an ideal pagan person, it was her dancing lessons that would enable her to *be* that, or anything else she fancied, on a stage.

What actually got her on the stage was San Francisco's own rich theatrical environment. The young Isadora was not an isolated girl on a farm like Ruth Dennis, but a precocious urban child with three older siblings, Elizabeth, Augustin, Raymond, who adored theater. In the seventies and eighties the city was at its most theatrically alive; great actors of the day all played there: Joseph Jefferson, Edwin Booth, Helena Modjeska, Nance O'Neil, Sarah Bernhardt on her first American tour. Besides these stars the city boasted a rich array of variety shows, of 5—10—15¢ melodramas (the eternal *Uncle Tom's Cabin*), of 25¢ operas (favorites were *Faust* and *Lohengrin*), and frequent visiting concert musicians—singers, violinists, and solo pianists. The Duncans breathed in all these theatrical strains through the city's very air, and through the enthusiasms of a sister of their mother, beautiful tragic Aunt Augusta, who was stage-struck. The Duncans' back yard became the scene of amateur theatricals—imitations of melodramas and comedies on the real stage; these were so popular that the Duncan children took off on tour up and down the California coast. It was an obvious thing to do in the open-ended theater world of the Far West; on such mule-back and stagecoach expeditions David Belasco, Lotta Crabtree, David Warfield, and Blanche Bates too learned their trade. In the Duncan troupe Isadora, then twelve years old, danced; Augustin and Raymond recited, and all took part in a short comedy.

This format appears to have been a tiny variety show with a "forward," an "olio" for specialties (the dances), and an "afterpiece" burlesque. In 1889, when the dancing soubrette Lotta Crabtree was still at the height of her career, Isadora might have imitated her. Minstrel-like routines pleased country audiences more than Delsarte posing, and Isadora possessed the prerequisites for skirt dancing—a repertoire of jigs, reels, and character steps and an appetite for showing off. It is logical to think her first performing included some kind of fast musical dancing, if only because her later dances show such ease with old dance forms and their rhythms. She had heard these rhythms constantly in her mother's piano pieces, mazurkas, polonaises, *tanz-stücke*; she had danced them in Elizabeth's lessons, if not actually on these small California tours—and so fixed them forever in her body. Unlike Ruth Dennis, whose youthful knowledge of dancing came from the one or two stage spectacles she had seen and the exercises in Del-sarte manuals, Isadora lived among people who were doing theater, no matter how amateurish, and dance too, no matter how conventional. Her early dancing gave her the means to work with movement itself: where it was going, its starts, its crescendos, its natural closings. Ruth Dennis would learn from Belasco to objectify a scene, with herself in it gesturing expressively. Isadora could objectify the very movements. From her earlier, less conscious experience she knew more clearly than Ruth St. Denis what her gestures were and what they implied. Isadora didn't see herself inside a tableau, but it inside her; in her mature dances she was the equivalent of the scenery, the object of the lights, the sole source of shifting rhythms and paths across the space. Isadora's awareness of gestures-plus-steps developed so much beyond either Loie Fuller's or Ruth St. Denis' that she can be called a choreographer at a time when that word wasn't in use.

However, before she emerged as herself, Isadora, like Ruth St. Denis, served some time in New York's commercial theaters and New York's aesthetic salons. In 1896, when Isadora was nineteen, she and her mother headed East, to find audiences, or just to find a job. This was the time when Broadway was consolidating its sway over all of American theater through the touring circuits, and local theater life, as in San Francisco, was slowly dying out. In Chicago, Isadora intercepted producer Augustin Daly (the same who was to hire Ruth Dennis two years later for *The Runaway Girl*). He gave her a chorus role in *The Geisha*, New York, 1896, then a gypsy dance in *Meg Merrilees*, 1897, and the fairy dance in his *Midsummer Night's Dream*, 1897. But Isadora never felt as easy as Ruth Dennis in the commercial theater; she says in *My Life* that she wandered alone backstage and read Marcus Aurelius.

In 1897, years sooner than Ruth Dennis, Isadora retired from Broadway "to compose her own dances in her little Greek tunic." Between her 1897 decision and the Duncans' 1889 California tour, a mere eight years, Isadora had embraced the artistic and buried all trace of the music hall. She now became a salon soloist on the order of Mrs. Genevieve Stebbins in New York and Henrietta Knapp Russell in Newport and London. Her new repertory combined gestural illustrations of poetic texts spoken by her brother—a selection from *The Rubáiyát*—with some short dances to artistic music like Ethelbert Nevin's "Song of Narcissus," and additional numbers called "Spirit of Spring" and "A Dance of Mirth."

No one knows what she really did in those early concerts, but her programming closely resembled that suggested in Delsarte manuals. Scores of these were available in the 1890s, guides for visualizing poems or poetic ideas. One typical manual, *Delsartean Pantomimes*, by Mrs. J. W. Shoemaker, 1891, supplied musical accompaniments in addition to the texts and the gestures—the whole was designed for "home, school and church entertainments." The book's opening page proclaimed: "Association's mystic power combines / Internal passion with external signs"; inside was a text for every kind of "passion"—a faërie, "Paradise and the Peri"; a comedy, "The Bachelor Brides"; an adventure, "Paul Revere's Ride"; an idyll, "The Voice of Spring"; a dark selection, Poe's "The Raven"; and an Eastern romance, "Queen Vashti's Lament." Gestures for the texts were diagrammed line by line; these gestures were quite sophisticated both rhythmically and metaphorically, and they were entertaining too. Home, school, and church audiences were no doubt charmed by any young girl in a Greek gown as she described wide flowing circles in the air and addressed Spring:

> I come, I come, ye have called me long
> I come o'er the mountains with light and song!

Delsarte, though, meant more to its practitioners than charm: these gestures implied their own dynamic flow which complemented the

rise and fall of the words. Delsarte expertise represented experience in
the connections between "heard" rhythms and pantomimic gestures—
a sensory cross-over that Isadora already understood well, partly
through her Delsarte work. Young Miss Duncan, interviewed in New
York by the *Herald Tribune*, called Delsarte "the master of principles
of flexibility of muscles and lightness of the body."

In America in the late nineties Isadora was no more than a skilled
Delsartean—at least on the surface. Inside she had the makings of a
dancer, but it would take Europe to bring it out of her. The
Duncans moved to London in 1900. There, confronted as Loie Fuller
had been by new experiences both visual and musical, Isadora devised
the kind of art she is remembered for. She and her brother Raymond
haunted museums and met as many artists and art specialists as they
could find. The experience of seeing the real Elgin Marbles and real
Renaissance canvases, plus the idea of her various English protectors
that she use this art, and better music, to initiate her dances, transformed her repertory. In London's New Gallery in 1900 she appeared
in dances to Mendelssohn's "Spring Song" (costumed in pastel gauze
after her beloved *Primavera*), three Chopin Preludes, and a minuet
from Gluck's *Orfeo*. In another New Gallery concert she mimed or
danced several paintings, another Botticelli (*La Belle Simonetta*), a
De Predis (*Ange Jouant de la Viol*), a Titian (*Bacchus and Ariadne*),
and a contemporary neo-classical *Orpheus Returning from the Shades*,
by Sir William Richmond.

What is interesting is not just that she accepted the source material suggested by her English patrons, but that she solved the artistic
tests they had put to her—in ways significant to *her* future work.
Working with these paintings, she found motifs and actual movements
she would use throughout her career. Certain themes appeared again
and again in her dances: the legend of Orpheus and the Furies was
one; the Primavera tableau with its pregnant Flora (goddess-mother
of Spring) and the Three Graces was another. And not only did she
repeat themes, she wove the same motions again and again into different dances. London programs show that as early as 1900 she was
finding those essential motions which formed her language, which
she would fit together differently in each dance, and which she
would also use as the basis of her teaching.

Isadora's dance language had originated in Delsarte gestures. But
in Europe, after days and days of all but living in museums with
Raymond and coming to feel at home with classical statues—the Elgin
Marbles, the Tanagra Figurines, the Venuses and Amazons and

Winged Victories—she had learned the physical truths the Greeks had known: the way a body finds its own effortless, asymmetrical balance; the way a marble Venus, for example, stands into one hip with the opposite shoulder sloping down. Their gestures of repose Isadora had already made her own in performance. Now in Renaissance art she experienced a new dimension and she began to show the movements of several figures within a space. She added to her language those gestures of surprise or suspended motion one sees in Renaissance canvases—the effects of figures on each other. One of the clearest signals she took is the stylization of "I am being pursued"—a nymph pursued by a satyr, a Diana chased by Acteon, Ariadne surprised by Bacchus. . . . The gesture of this appears again and again in Duncan dances: the dancer in a sideways lunge, her hands fending off the pursuer as she looks back over her shoulder. The pursuer is seen in the same dances (mimed also by the solo dancer): he lunges forward and reaches out toward the imaginary pursued. Gestures like these existed in Delsarte too; but Duncan's versions were broader—they were no longer gestures but motions because they led to other motions. Their purpose was not to transmit a mimed message but to show an action. It is extraordinary that a young dancer decided that by herself she could offer an audience not just the pantomimic intentions of one figure but the flow of question-response among several figures inside the formal space of a painting-frame or a stage.

One is reminded of Walt Whitman, and his constant desire through poetry to take other identities into his own body. One also thinks of Rodin and his great works, with two or three figures sculpted in a single gesture, or with thousands of them merging together in the massive bronze door called *Gates of Hell*—which apparently influenced Isadora very much. Isadora watched Rodin at work. Her contact with him and other modern French artists, Matisse, Maurice Denis, and Émile Bourdelle, who revered classical proportions but transformed them for the present, was probably as important to her as her own study of the antique originals. Rodin took the serene classical poses and twisted them, arced them, forced them to anguish or ecstasy, broke them with his bare hands—almost set them in motion. It is likely that Isadora, watching him, boldly decided that she could go beyond him or any other visual artist, because she could make statues travel, cover ground, move in a dance. There is no doubt that the young Isadora harbored a monstrous boldness inside her person, and that she knew it. An invitation she sent out to a private concert in those early years in France, 1902 or 1903, is almost self-mocking:

Miss Duncan will dance to the sound of harp and flute
in her studio next Thursday evening, and if you feel that
seeing this small person dancing against the waves of an
overpowering destiny is of some benefit to you, why—come
along!

Some of this boldness is essential to choreography—especially the kind
worked out by these American women, from the inside out, starting
with their own bodies. A vision of one's body as the center of the
universe—or the stage—generates absolute clarity in the position of that
body and the intent of its gesture. In those early years of Isadora's
dancing, she trusted that her body would tell her what she needed
to know. Those were the years when she stood "quite still for hours,
her two hands folded between her breasts, covering the solar plexus,
that 'central spring of all movement. . . .' "

It must not be forgotten that the solar plexus was the area most
maligned by corsets and most championed by dress reformers. Whether
or not Isadora remembered her childhood pride in her own uncon-
strained waist and ribs, she certainly *felt* this and continued to feel it.
The solar plexus became the starting point of motion for a Duncan
dancer. In the Duncan exercises and dances that have survived, it is
the solar plexus—the lower ribs right above the stomach—that animates
the dancer's body. In the light expansive leaps onto one leg it is the
lifted ribs that buoy the dancer; it is the ribs also that contract and
coil in to send her forward again into a leap, a skip, a run. In short,
the solar plexus responds to the music in Duncan work. This was
Isadora's great discovery: the expressive upper body—from Delsarte,
from Greek sculpture, from Renaissance painting, from modern art—
combined with the ebb and flow of musical melody in the feet. No one
else had articulated that connection; no one had "travelled" those so
familiar gestures. In Isadora's dances the feet describe the rhythmical
patterns of the music, waltz, march, mazurka; the ribs give expansive-
ness to the musical phrase, more depth, more impact, more space—and
the head and arms gently acquiesce. Isadora incorporated a new upper-
body space, and along with it the air above the stage, into dance.

Isadora's art also grew through the music she was more and more
emboldened to use. No dancer before her had ever interpreted music
written not for dance but for concerts. In her early years Isadora had
followed Delsartean and Loie Fuller models, using Strauss waltzes
and idyllic airs as a generalized background to the gestures. Her dances

in 1900 to Chopin Preludes in London meant a new departure, but probably not a firm decision about music.

It is possible that she was pushed toward using classical music by the example of another American girl dancer, Maud Allan, who made her début in a solo concert in Vienna in 1903. Allan, essentially a San Franciscan like Isadora, had come to Europe not as a dancer but as a young prodigy at the piano. Friends, though, convinced Miss Allan that her beauty, her classic jaw line, clear light eyes, and masses of brown hair, would be wasted if she simply played the music—she must dance it. She did. In her first program, wearing a Greek tunic like Isadora's, she "visualized" selections from Bach, Beethoven, Schubert, Schumann, and Mendelssohn. Isadora, dancing in Budapest, very near Vienna, may well have heard about the content of this performance. It was only then in 1903 that she herself began to use all the music in Gluck's operas instead of just the dance divertissements; and only in 1904 did Isadora dance her first Beethoven in public. By now she was famous all over Europe, and in the summer of 1904 she interpreted the dances in Wagner's operas at the Bayreuth Festival, by special invitation of the master's widow, Cosima Wagner.

By this time Isadora had found the elements of her art: its musical patterns, its gestures, its three-dimensional melody. Her dances were rhythmic statements that complemented the music: questions and answers and repeats and surprise thoughts paced according to the musical forms. They existed in formal space. Loie Fuller's earlier dances were two-dimensional—a literal translation onto the stage of Art Nouveau's moving ornamental line. But Isadora's dances had become not mere pictures but structures of motion.

The earliest Duncan dance that survives is a short Chopin Prelude she made in 1904, which builds phrase by phrase on the gentle crescendo of the music. The dancer comes forward toward the audience; she runs to one side of the stage, then to the other; at a note of anguish in the music, she turns away, first to one back corner of the stage, then to the other. As she runs, she allows her upper body to bend and her arms to trail, but she never loses her clear path on the stage. At the music's final swell she turns to the audience, opens up her arms in a wide circle, and as her hands reach her sides, she lifts her face to the sky almost lazily. This was her complete acquiescence to the dynamics of the dance and music. In order that the dancing be seen for itself, Isadora was now performing in a light silk tunic, abstracted from the costumes Botticelli and Titian had put on their nymphs and goddesses; it was gathered underneath the breasts and at the hips, and slit at the front of the thighs to give free play to the legs. For scenery she used long neutral blue-gray curtains that hung behind the grand piano. She paid close attention to the lights (according to the recollection of Ruth St. Denis and others), dancing among simulations of shadows on the stage, and subtle color-changes, sometimes amber, sometimes rose. However, the lighting was never a character in the dance as it was for Loie Fuller. For Isadora, the single dancer was the spectacle; she alone was the music, the scenery, the other imaginary people onstage. Not until the next generation of American dancers, not until Martha Graham began fiercely to pursue formal choreography, would such a range of expression be discovered by a solo dancer.

When Ruth St. Denis arrived in Europe in 1906, both Isadora's art and her own had moved so far beyond their common Delsarte origins that they were barely comparable. Ruth did have scenery on-stage, and other characters (her Hindus), and elaborate costumes. Her dances, though, were actually miniature dramas made out of dance motions—with ritual replacing dramatic suspense. Unlike Isadora, Ruth hadn't come to Europe to find new sources for her art; she had enough sources in her new-found Eastern legends and her inherited American stage techniques. She came to Europe to find new audiences for her *Incense, The Cobras* and the splendid *Radha*, and to win Europe's artistic seal of approval—and she did. Germany, with its appetite for artistic massiveness, best appreciated her extravagant décor and the fully orchestrated *Lakmé* music she danced to. Richard Strauss had already constructed a whole opera, *Salomé*, around one Oriental dancer, and he was in the midst of creating *Elektra*. On the surface, *Radha* looked like an addition to this gallery of goddess-queens.

However, Ruth St. Denis herself, the last of these four American art-dancers to arrive in Europe, was untouched by the ferment of modern culture there. Of course she was moved to be thought an artist in a community of artistic colleagues. But her own cultural identity left her no room for aesthetic discoveries. In picture galleries she saw only "Spotted things, rosy-fleshed and stippled ladies, or hospital scenes —painted with alarming realism—very obstetrical." Her experience was utterly unlike Isadora's, and she found nothing that reminded her of her own art. The music of Strauss, she conceded, was grand and visionary but full of "curious dissonances," and a Wagner opera did not inspire her. She marveled at how the audience could sit still for such long musical expositions; as a commercial artist she felt Wagner's timing was off. Ruth's own sense of timing, nurtured on Belasco's stage, remained the same throughout her nearly three years in Europe. She didn't change anything in her dances, except costumes, which she was eternally tinkering with anyway. In London, 1908, she added two new dances to her repertory, a *Nautch* and a *Yogi*. Both of these, though, had been in her mind since before she came to Europe. The earthy nautch and the ascetic yogi were two facets of Ruth's private dichotomy between the spirit and the flesh. The costumes as usual reflected the estates of the characters: the one figure all aglow with emerald skirt and gold sari, the other humble in rough girdle and one string of prayer beads. These two new dance "scenes" combined with her other vignettes made a full and varied *East Indian Suite*, which Ruth presented in her 1908 London season.

In London in the fall of 1908, while Ruth was playing the small select La Scala Theater, Maud Allan was filling the Palace Theater with her notorious new *Salomé* and Isadora was dancing *Orpheus*, accompanied by some of her tiny German girl pupils, at the Duke of York Theater. By this time, each of the three had learned whatever she could from Europe and from the others. In Europe dancing was becoming the respected equal of music, of art, of literature. The Russian Ballet was poised on the horizon, ready to burst on Paris the following spring, and these American girls who preceded it had grown famous. After London, Isadora left for her first season in America performing as a serious artist. Ruth and her family went back to Germany for one more round of tours, climaxed by an offer from the citizens of Weimar to build her a theater, if she would stay in Germany for five more years. She could not. She and her mother missed home; Ruth missed the jokes of American theater people and the moral scruples of American artists. She missed being in a theatrical company. Loie Fuller, Maud Allan, and Isadora Duncan now belonged more to Europe's art than to America's. But Ruth St. Denis belonged to the theater that had produced her. She was the only one of the four who could go home and play vaudeville; she was the only one who *wanted* to go home. So, after one last turn around the British Isles in the summer of 1909, the Dennises sailed gratefully for New York. And so it was Ruth St. Denis' love of the grand gesture, her consummate, humorous ease on the professional stage, that became the starting point for a modern dance art in America.

PART II

DANCE SCATTERS AND MOVES WEST

CHAPTER 4
Salomé

While Ruth St. Denis was abroad (1906–1909) her conviction that dance could be artistic finally caught on in America, and a new kind of theatrical dancing was born. It was nothing like vaudeville with jolly soubrettes in clogs, nor was it ballet, with naughty girls in tights and flounces. Those modes were too flippant in the light of serious modern theater, where the heroines of Sardou, Sudermann, Ibsen, and even Belasco moved about the stage as though in their own rooms, and revealed their states of mind by extremely naturalistic actions. Boldness in the plays' subject matter had produced this frankness in the acting, and actresses' bodies were understood to have a new license on the stage. Audiences that had seen Mrs. Fiske's *Tess of the D'Urbervilles* shiver and retch, or Eleonora Duse's *Magda* lie down and scream, were ready to watch dancing which also approximated "private" behavior, which was bold and relatively lifelike. But dancing, after stern quarantine by generations of Puritan descendants, was flammable stuff: it was fated to arrive in the form of a scandal.

On January 22, 1907, the Metropolitan Opera mounted its *Salomé* by Richard Strauss, just once, before the Met's outraged backers —J. P. Morgan, W. K. Vanderbilt, and August Belmont—withdrew it from the stage. This grave insult to an artistic institution caused the press to enter the fray, pro and con. "Salomé in her transports of rage or gross sensuality is no less respectable a person than the Saphos, Zazas, Mrs. Warrens and other red-light heroines of the contemporary stage," said *Theatre Magazine*. But her dancing—the shedding of the seven veils and the fondling of that "decapitated head"—these "sickened the public stomach." Nonetheless, Salomé's appearance in 1907 was one sign of a social and cultural upheaval that anticipated the reckless twenties. No sooner was she banished from opera than she surfaced in vaudeville, via the Met's prima ballerina, Mlle. Bianca Froelich, who had been the dancing Salomé to Olive Fremstad's soprano in the solitary performance. Plump, saucy, and Viennese, Miss Froelich simply repeated her Salomé movements in the small Lincoln Square Variety Theater, and in that context was branded a kootch dancer. A few months later, the wily Florenz Ziegfeld served up another Salomé to an elegant public in the first of his high-class vaudeville shows—the Follies of 1907. He had transformed the rooftop of the New York Theater into the Jardin de Paris. Under the city sky, amid bright new awnings and potted palms, after fifty "Anna Held Girls" had paraded in red drummer outfits, Grace LaRue had sung "Miss Ginger of

Jamaica," and Annabelle Whitford had posed as a Gibson bathing beauty, the dancer Mlle. Dazié emerged as Salomé. She wore a low-slung gauzy skirt, a circle of pearls over each breast, an aigrette on her forehead, and she had four peacock-costumed girls in attendance. For Ziegfeld she perfectly embodied his theatrical strategy, which was to transform popular, even off-color, material into a new and high-class chic.

Ziegfeld had picked Mlle. Dazié because she had a certain mystery about her; before emerging as Salomé she was "La Rouge Domino," who had baffled the public for two years, cropping up in world capitals gowned and masked in red—a costume dreamed up by her publicist. In real life Dazié was Daisy Peterkin from Detroit; although she had studied ballet in Europe and could really dance on her pointes, she would have gone unnoticed without such a stunt. But now that the Follies and her Salomé were a hit, Dazié and her publicist (now her husband) seized the occasion to open a school for Salomés, two hours every morning on the theater roof garden. By the summer of 1908 she was sending approximately 150 Salomés every month into the nation's vaudeville circuits, each armed with the same routine—an incoherent mix of gestures and undulations addressed to a papier-mâché head.

A hue and cry arose on main streets, in churches, and in the press. "It grovels, it rolls in horrible sensuality . . . can we endure this indecent physical display?" No one spoke about the actual dance motions of the Salomés. Probably no one noticed them, since the shock of the Salomé costume and the Head was enough for even seasoned vaudeville audiences. Besides, they had had no experience with dance as a dramatic language; they knew only about lively steps on the beat. If any of these first Salomés was gifted, her audience wouldn't have known.

It took a clever and top-level vaudeville player to reveal Salomé's dancing potential, and she did it by showmanship. Gertrude Hoffman was born in San Francisco, and after a childhood in which she absorbed equal parts of worldliness from that city, and purity from her convent education, by the age of fifteen she was already leading the line in the Castle Square Theater operetta troupe. But she faced the same dilemma as Duncan and St. Denis: how to combine dancing with ambition. No dancers commanded much respect in the theater world. Hoffman's solution was to widen her sphere: still in her teens, she went to New York as a rehearsal director—an unheard-of thing for a woman. Soon she was coaching sixty-member shows (Oscar Hammerstein's *Punch, Judy & Co.*, 1903) and staging vaudeville routines like Elsie Janis' and La Rouge Domino's—until one night in Philadelphia in 1906 she stepped in for a sick dancer in Flo Ziegfeld's *The Parisian Model* and stole the show imitating French star Anna Held in her song "I Just Can't Make My Eyes Behave." (Held herself imitated Enrico Caruso in another scene.) As a regular thereafter, Hoffman also imitated Eddie Foy in his ballerina act and Georgie Cohan singing, until the show closed. Then she played Hammerstein's Victoria, New York's top vaudeville house, with her own "imitatrice" act, which prompted Hammerstein to send her to London to copy the biggest-drawing Salomé yet—Maud Allan's. Hammerstein hadn't thought about Hoffman's dancing skills, he hadn't picked her because she started in a dancing chorus; he simply assumed, like everybody in vaudeville, that if you were a mimic and could make your body look like somebody else's, you could also make it dance.

Gertrude Hoffman outdid herself with her first serious act in the fall of 1908, at the Victoria. In a bluish light, from the depths of a painted Eastern garden, to the sounds of a full orchestra conducted by Max Hoffman, her husband, she emerged—"garbed in the draperies and gew-gaws of a bloody age." Her legs, reviewers noticed, were daringly bare under her thin tulle skirt. A good many reviewers also noticed this time what she was doing: how she undulated around the stage, espied the head of John the Baptist, danced wildly with it, and then fell, spent—all in the space of six minutes. The Hoffman whose heavy-lidded eyes, long thin face, and lanky body had always made an audience laugh now made it sit up and marvel. And her Salomé, begun as an imitation, became the first coherent dance creation since Isadora Duncan had left the country in 1900 and Ruth St. Denis in 1906. The new Gertrude Hoffman, aesthetic dancer, did not, however, follow her predecessors to Europe; instead she went on a national tour—and so did her imitators. This second wave of Salomés brought sophistication to even the smallest towns; it indicated to the whole country that the forces of Art and Sin had conquered Broadway and were claiming the future.

"Now [these days] we mustn't be reminded of the old-fashioned hard-working New York that we sprang from," mourned the old comic Ned Harrigan, of Harrigan & Hart, in 1908. "That's too vulgar for us. Now we must have our Salomés and our dance poems and our what I call four-cornered plays—you know, a husband and a wife and a mistress and a lover."

. . .

The Salomé furor took place in the short space of two years. By the time Ruth St. Denis came home from Europe in 1909, the public had "weathered a cataclysm of Salomés" and then calmly applauded a second production of Strauss's opera, starring Mary Garden at Oscar Hammerstein's Manhattan Opera House. They were now enlightened. A dancer, they dimly understood, was not just a pretty face and a tease, she was a magical being with the power to call forth in her audience the sensations of a faraway age (an age not stuffy in matters of dress). The public was ready for Ruth St. Denis. Her London and Berlin triumphs had been recognized in the press, and her name had been featured at Hammerstein's Victoria in Gertrude Hoffman's sequel to her *Salomé*—a full-scale imitation of St. Denis' *Radha* with Hoffman as the goddess surrounded by thirty "Cingalese" natives. There was no better publicity than a Hoffman imitation. As soon as the Dennis family was safely settled on a Staten Island farm, Ruth moved back into her old matinée spot at the Hudson Theater, in November 1909. "Out-Saloméing all the Salomés, Miss St. Denis burst upon dazzled audiences . . . ," ran the reviews. Ruth, whose commercial instinct never failed, had in fact replaced Radha's skirt and bodice with Salomé's jeweled harness. However, her *East Indian Suite* featured other exotic costumes besides, from the gaudy silks of the nautch dance to the humble tunic-wrap of the yogi. The full-length show was striking enough for manager Henry B. Harris to risk some evening dates—which meant an audience of husbands and fathers as well as the faithful matinée ladies. In 1909 Ruth St. Denis was at the height of her solo career: her dancing was fashionable because it sparked imaginations already sensitized to a whole range of exotic phenomena.

"Where do you think I've been—in the dressing room of the great dancer," wrote Betty Biddle in her New York *Sun* column (November 1909).

> This afternoon we sat in the box and watched the wonderful Eastern pictures unfold themselves just like natives unfold those wonderful pieces of woven cloth. Little snatches of Omar Khayyam kept running through my brain and the weird music and that fascinating incense.
>
> The Yogi dance was perfect. Oh girls, wouldn't it be lovely if our religion meant so much to us?

After the show Miss St. Denis was sitting at her dressing table drinking malted milk and eating crackers, for the last one is so fatiguing. Her figure suggests a closed lotus bud, it had that peculiar Eastern curve, not often seen in Western women.

Wonderful cashmere shawls and bits of Persian embroidery were strewn around the tiny room in artistic disorder. It made me feel I was living in one of Kipling's short stories—*Kim*, I think, especially in the temple scene with the old priest with his bare brown body, white beard and immense turban. It enthralled my senses; I saw nothing and heard nothing but *Radha* and the call of the East.

I was sure Miss St. Denis had been in India but she said no, she is a native of Somerville, New Jersey, the land of the mosquito, she calls it. . . .

Ruth's admirers thought she so perfectly embodied the "East of Suez" that they hardly heard when she lapsed into New Jersey tones. Orientalism had appeared as 1890s chic in the interiors of the new Waldorf Hotel, 33rd and Fifth, which were Turkish. It took ten or fifteen years for the style to filter down to middle-class wives and daughters, who then designed "Turkish corners" in their living rooms, with tasseled cushions, potted palms, and ostrich plumes in big vases or majolica jars. Ruth's East Indian skits were perceived as the very spirit of the Turkish corner, expressions of a refined sensuality new to the American palate. The newness was entertainment enough for her audiences. Whether the style was authentic or not didn't concern them. It was to Ruth's advantage that she wasn't Indian or trained by Indians; the audience preferred her to be American, like their home brand of Orientalia. Neither the décors on the stage nor the furnishings in private homes were meant to be faithful copies, but rather visual signals of a realm somewhere on the brink of taste. Moreover, no exotic strain ever showed up alone; the "East Indian," for instance, was always mingled with some of the "Moorish" or "Turkish" or "Hellenic" or "Byzantine" or even "Renaissance."

Stanford White, partner in the architectural firm of McKim, Mead, and White, was probably the firmest arbiter of New York's taste at this time. He was a big, red-haired, and mustached man who designed everything in all styles: jewelry, picture frames, yachts, posters, city fêtes, a group of châteaux on upper Fifth Avenue, and the massive, carnival-like Madison Square Garden. He saw nothing wrong with mixing styles and eras: any object was possible, "if it was good." His taste was theatrical, and the theater was within his connoisseuring domain. Actresses to him were as beautiful as buildings or pictures: Ruth Dennis in her earliest chorus days was one of his "finds," and so was Evelyn Nesbit, whose husband Harry K. Thaw shot White in 1906 on the Madison Square Garden roof. He had lived long enough, though, to see Ruth Dennis become St. Denis the exotic dancer, and to be justly proud. *Radha*'s color and animation were in tune with his deepest beliefs.

This was the end of an era when New York had been transformed, largely through the efforts of White and his colleagues, from a city of small dark brownstones to one of elegant and spacious hotels, banks, clubs, churches, and railroad stations made of light stone, yellow brick, terra cotta. Gentlemen artists like White and his friends mounted a life-long campaign against tightmindedness in the American spirit. His aim was to bring beauty to the people of his city; he costumed New York and undressed her too, and as more and more art objects appeared before the public eye, the spirit of censorship receded—somewhat. When White first put Augustus St. Gaudens' nude Diana on top of Madison Square Tower, women and children were kept away from the "Garden goddess gloated over by clubmen and Johnnies." Gradually the city adopted her.

White's bold and eclectic taste, however, was often misunderstood. To ordinary people, Art meant anything exotic, fussy, or risqué —Turkish seraglios or nudes out-of-doors—anything, in fact, that was unnatural. In the realm of Art, Americans mistrusted their own instincts. That is why the urban nouveaux riches preferred to collect painters who, if not dead and pedigreed, were academic and static like the French William Bouguereau—instead of the experimental Impressionists. Bouguereau's subjects were posed mythology. His nudes had a Renaissance aroma without much life, and they suited American propriety, whereas Renoir's or Degas' sensual women with their skins painted as part of the moving surface of the world, did not. Sometimes paintings of Spanish gypsies or Moorish harems could hang in American houses, because geographical distance obscured their sensuality. But extreme caution was required for official murals in public places. When one of these pictured a sacred principle such as Wisdom, Progress, or Manifest Destiny in the form of a

woman, she usually wore a white drapery—that piece of clothing somewhere between dress and undress, which both concealed her body
and associated it with classical antiquity. Mural painters like John La
Farge and sculptors like St. Gaudens could thus invoke woman's body
as ideal form without confronting her corporeality.

The public's feelings about the dancers who came after the
Salomés paralleled what it felt about painting and sculpture: here
was a necessary risk. A good deal of the time, bare bodies were implied
if not displayed. However, since dance was now almost a high art,
it was assumed like painting to contain ideals that were edifying—
even if these sometimes resembled the basest desires. In 1909–1910,
when many people saw Ruth St. Denis dance, they also flocked to see
Isadora Duncan, Maud Allan, and Loie Fuller—all of whom visited
America in that season. The New York concerts were usually elaborate
matinées at Carnegie Hall or the Metropolitan Opera: Isadora Duncan
in her tunic dancing to music of the entire New York Symphony
Orchestra; Maud Allan, also with an orchestra, for her Salomé (now
passé) and her Greek and Botticelli sketches; Loie Fuller with her
thirty girls and her range of styles—from the original light and silk
numbers called "dances of the future" to the "waltzes of all the modern
composers from Chopin to Strauss" to the "purely classic Greek."
(Fuller's "Greek" interpreter was an American girl called Orchidée
who wore draperies and held a live wolf in photographs.) The term
"classic" dancing was widely in use; it had nothing to do with classical
ballet but referred to anything vaguely antique—even Ruth St. Denis
was called a "classic" dancer for her "purity of line." All these solo
artists, with or without companies, represented America's emergence
from its Victorian cocoon into a confused realm of beauty and moral
uncertainty. "Dancers Shed Clothing and Put on Ideals," "Line Drawn
Between the Nudity of Woman and the Undraping of the Artist,"
ran the headlines. There was no mistaking that they were art—they
looked like figurines, the odalisques, the triumphant muses in the
murals, all come alive and proclaiming what one poet called the "joy-
ance" of the senses.

The bodies of the dancers in their light draperies or strings of
jewels had a special appeal for women—because of their very unre-
straint. They were not painted or sculpted images; they were real and
they projected an astonishing physicality. Fashionable women in the
audience, notwithstanding the popularity of bicycles and the advent
of physical culture in women's schools, were securely laced into corsets

that amplified their fronts, swelled their hips, and diminished them drastically in the middle. They were supposed to stand in an S-curve, their faces peering down over high-boned collars or pearl "chokers," their fronts as well as their behinds extended, their arms pulled back at the elbow, their long skirts trailing the ground. This final caricature of Victoriana, however reassuring to the wearers and the viewers, had outlasted its time. It was unfit for a new century that stressed speed and thrust in mechanical matters, fluidity and undress in artistic ones. No wonder women filled the matinées to see the "classic" dancers: the mere spectacle of graceful, musical, and uncorseted motion was an impelling sight, a prophecy.

Florenz Ziegfeld seized on the same spirit of bodily liberation when he dressed his Follies girls as symbols of the new century. Instead of the customary flounces and tiered skirts handed down from French and English music halls, he put them in strange abstract costumes—the satin shorts suits of the 1908 taxicab girls with the "For Hire" signs in their caps; the briefer suits and striped capes of the 1909 girls, and the illuminated ships on their heads. It was the first time the chorines were not simply a titillating bloc of scenery. Julian Mitchell, Ziegfeld's eccentric, half-deaf, but brilliant stage director, dissolved the eternal chorus *line*. He grouped the girls in graceful plastique poses, modeling them with stage lights, and he kept them reacting onstage, listening to the tenor, smiling at the comic. Since Ziegfeld's shows were not part of serious concertizing, he was free to stress glamour instead of art, and in this area his instinct was uncanny. He had seen, as early as 1906 (*The Little Duchess*) when he framed the small, buxom, and French Anna Held with six tall Broadway chorines, that American girls were the opposite of French ballet girls. They were not "delicious"; they were graceful and coolly dazzling. So he put fifty tall and haughty "Anna Held Girls" into the first Follies, along with Dazié and her peacock crew. Thus, inside this fairly modest 1907 event—in all other respects a regular corny and tuneful vaudeville show—Ziegfeld introduced the American chorus girl, a natural princess.

Ruth St. Denis' beliefs placed her among the "classic" dancers, but her strategies put her with Ziegfeld and the showmen. There was no more queenly person on the stage in matters of dress. When she was thinking of a dance, she usually imagined the cloth and colors first—and had done this ever since the first moment of her dancing career, when in 1905 she had dressed herself like the

Egyptian goddess on the cigarette poster. By 1910, exotic solo dancers were so popular that her manager H. B. Harris, who held the purse strings, gave Ruth permission to do *Egypta*. On December 10, she premiered it in five immense, Belasco-like scenes: the Invocation to the Nile, the Palace Dance, the Veil of Isis, the Dance of Day, and the Dance of Night or Hall of Judgment—each filled with the appropriate courtiers, soldiers, peasants, slave girls, or demigods whom Ruth had recruited and trained. She played a different character at the center of each scene. Her eyes were lined Egypt-style out to the sides of her face and her head covered with a square wig braided with shells and beads, and held on by a forehead bandeau. Her face, a full oval with clear, light eyes, small nose, and rosebud lips, was close to ideal for its time. It was a baby face, and its contrast with the decadent, geometric costumes—the tunic skirt and collar necklace, the long, clinging, half-transparent shift—pleased the audience. They loved to see their American girls dressed in pagan magnificence. Ruth's Hindu and then Egyptian versions of contemporary chic sustained audiences through this essentially one-woman show in static tableaux. When she closed *Egypta* in New York, she took some of its scenes, plus her *East Indian Suite*, on a successful cross-country tour; in late summer, 1911, she came back to New York to play a week in Hammerstein's Victoria; then she went out again to tour the best vaudeville palaces in Chicago and Boston.

Ruth St. Denis wasn't misplaced in vaudeville, nor was she ashamed to play it in its glorious years, as she later protested she was. It is doubtful whether the other solo dancers could have held a headliner spot. Art outweighed spectacle in their dancing, and they attracted large audiences only because of the bursts of publicity surrounding their visits to America. St. Denis, constantly in view for two years, continued to cast spells in popular houses with her hocus-pocus gestures, her dazzling costumes, her natives, and her incense—her cloak of the Mystic. Her staging was always impressive, but Ruth's real secret lay in something her contemporaries took for granted—her personality. This, not Radha or Egypta, was the heart of her performance.

Whether consciously or not, she had constructed her dances on a tried-and-true vaudeville formula, just like the grand woman entertainers of the day: Lillian Russell, Blanche Ring, Eva Tanguay. A singer's custom was to open her act with the rhymed verse of a song, usually nonsensical, so the audience could examine her, and then to launch into a rousing spirited chorus ("Waltz Me Around Again,

Willie!"') and take the audience along. Ruth's act was a danced version of this. She began slowly, with downcast eyes and languid gestures, she worked up to fuller decorative gestures and let go in a fast "chorus," a series of spinning turns with ankle bells and flaring skirt, before she dropped into a final defiant pose. In the course of the dance she took her audience into her confidence with a smirk, a wink, a signal of infectious self-delight that put them at ease with the "artistic" side of the dance. Unexpectedly, unconsciously, they understood her; they could enjoy the dance and still call it spiritual. Ruth was in earnest about both aspects of her performance. She was a "classic" dancer with a philosophy. She was also an entertainer whose personality flowered on stage and she knew that audiences had a claim on that side of her. As a choreographer her resources, her range, and her use of space may have been limited, but they served her purposes exactly.

Dancing as a virtuoso art arrived in America with the Russians. First Anna Pavlova and Mikhail Mordkin gave two short evenings at the Metropolitan Opera (February 1910). Even though the Russians had evolved a modern art of dance out of classical training, most of the American public assumed that they came from no tradition, like American girl dancers, and that Pavlova was one of the "classic" dancers—one of the best—since she wore the familiar "Greek" draperies, danced to Chopin like Maud Allan and Isadora Duncan, and ended the evening with a wildly popular Bacchanale ("Autumn," from Glazunov's *The Seasons*). She returned to tour the country the next fall (1910) with Mordkin. Not even an astute critic like Carl Van Vechten realized the two were sustained by a formidable school of technique— ballet—a level of technique heretofore seen by Americans only in *The Black Crook* ballerinas. Van Vechten had to invent a way to describe her dancing, since he, or his readers, lacked even a basic term like "arabesque." "Pavlova twirled on her toes," he reported. "Then with her left toe pointed behind her, maintaining her body poised to form a straight line with it, she leapt backwards step by step on her right foot."

When Diaghilev's Ballets Russes triumphed in Paris in 1909, efforts were made to bring them to New York. However, the Italian director of the Metropolitan Opera, Giulio Gatti-Casazza, opposed the idea—probably out of loyalty to Italian ballet. Two years later, it was a beloved vaudeville personage, Gertrude Hoffman, who brought the first elaborate but pirated edition of the Ballets Russes to America. Hoffman had been in Paris that summer; her years as a mimic had taught her to see dancing clearly, and she realized at once the Russian Ballet's importance to Western culture. She began to study Russian technique herself on the spot, first with a Diaghilev company dancer and then with a teacher whom she brought from St. Petersburg to America. By 1911 she had also assembled about one hundred Russian and French dancers in New York, including Theodore Kosloff, her ballet master, Lydia Lopokova, and Alexander Volinine, a seventy-five-piece orchestra conducted by her husband, Max Hoffman, and bold Fauvish scenery painted by Golow of the Moscow Imperial Opera. On July 11 at the Winter Garden Theater, she premiered her "Saisons des Ballets Russes"—three of Michel Fokine's ballets, *Schéhérazade*, *Cléopâtra*, and *Les Sylphides*, reconstructed by Kosloff—without Fokine's permission. Permission, however, had not been needed before for Gertrude Hoffman's or anybody's imitations, and this was actually another imitation on a grander scale. "Les Saisons" was a success. The company, after playing New York all summer, then set off on a cross-country tour to Los Angeles.

A pure dance spectacle on this scale was new to Americans, yet according to newspapers they sat through it for nearly three hours, even though they were accustomed to spoken lines or comic relief on the stage. Thanks to Ruth St. Denis, they could recognize the Persian and the Egyptian and even distinguish crudely between the two: "*Schéhérazade* is as redundantly voluptuous in its Persian curves as *Cléopâtra* is severe in its Egyptian angles," said one newspaper. As for the dancing, official critics did their best to understand. They dutifully quoted Theodore Kosloff when he explained that the new Russian techniques were a blend of old French and Italian ballet with modern pantomine—"Mimodrama," he called it. "We have tried to do what modern Russian painters and poets have done—invest our art with realism and life," he said. Reporters noted in bewilderment that Russian dancers studied daily from the age of eight—and at the expense of the Imperial Government. Their regime of exercise and diet was so healthy, reported one paper, that old "Patipas," the "father of Russian Ballet," had lived to be a hundred and three. Beyond these observations the critics were at a loss, for they still had no terms, no understanding of the ground rules of the art. All they had seen of dance-as-art was their own barefoot girls who made up steps to suit girlish moods instead of revolutionizing a dance technique already in existence.

To Europeans the Diaghilev Ballets Russes was the apotheosis of an artistic movement all over Europe which combined new ideas with a free borrowing from antiquity—in Matisse's words, "an awakening of the old sensual foundation of man." The same spirit was obviously at work in some quarters in America, among photographers, architects, painters and poets, and a few dancers. However, no one in a responsible critical post recognized that the new Russian Ballet had implications for all the arts. No one in America in 1911 thought to follow the trail of Gertrude Hoffman's Ballets Russes to Paris and back to Russia. That this new dancing stemmed from historical sources in the theater was an idea alien to most Americans. They assumed that Gertrude Hoffman was simply offering a novelty on a grand scale, a larger version of the barefoot dancers' free-form inventions. The most important American visual arts magazine, Alfred Stieglitz' *Camera Work*, published from 1903 to 1917, discussed not just photographers but playwrights, sculptors, painters, even a few "classic" dancers, but it never mentioned Diaghilev or Nijinsky or Fokine.

The problem was more basic than the lack of exposure to the real Ballets Russes, which didn't perform in America until 1916. American critics weren't even curious about the mechanisms of their own solo dancers' art. It was the Europeans and especially the Russians who analyzed and built upon the dance inventions of Loie Fuller and Isadora Duncan.

In America people failed to grasp that a dance was a construct in space and time, involving principles of composition as palpable as those in painting or sculpture. No one ever asked Isadora Duncan how she arranged the movements she danced with such apparent artlessness on the stage, or even where she got them. The mere fact that she and other dancers were moving through space and light, setting in motion poses resembling those of figures in classical paintings and sculptures, made the public too giddy to examine the art. Those figures were distant and mythological, and appropriately half-dressed. The dancers who imitated them were disturbingly alive in the here and now.

One of the most intelligent and open-minded writers on *Camera Work*, Charles Caffin, was aware of critical blindness to dancing and diagnosed the cause in a 1909 article on the Post-Impressionists, in which he compared Isadora to Henri Matisse. Arbiters of aesthetics thought Matisse a madman to paint Nature with two or three quick brushstrokes; Isadora Duncan was scorned by the same official minds for her "simple" dances to orchestral symphonies. But Caffin believed

Isadora Duncan was truly modern like Matisse because she was as consciously primitive as he: her dancing distilled what Caffin called "the corporeality of things" ("the perfume of the flowers, the ripple of brooks, the sway of pine trees . . ."—he went on through a catalogue of natural rhythms). Where were the American critics who could understand this? The music critics knew how to hear motion but not to see it; the old-time art critics couldn't see it either, because Isadora Duncan wouldn't stay still to be analyzed. As a result, her dancing, all dancing, remained in people's minds a dilettante's art, a vague swirl of artistic qualities and personal expression. This same offhand tone even appeared in the dancers' own descriptions of their art, Isadora's flowery rhetoric and Ruth St. Denis' pseudo-sophisticated remarks. Miss Ruth could always be counted on to say something glamorous, irrespective of what she was actually doing. "My new dances," she announced to *Vanity Fair* in 1913, "will be fantastic little things with tone and color and intimacy in which rhythm and the poetry of motion will dominate."

After 1911, most of the "classic" dancers went back to Europe, all except Ruth St. Denis, who remained in America as her career disintegrated. She could barely find a place to perform. It wasn't her fault: the demand for soloists had abruptly ceased. Ruth could have settled into one of the smaller vaudeville circuits and toured forever with *Radha*, but she never had seen herself as a conventional entertainer. Instead she subsisted for the next year on private performances at the balls of the very wealthy—like the one Mr. and Mrs. Philip Lydig gave in January 1913. Mrs. Lydig, an exotic beauty, had caused a theater to be built in her home for one performance of the apocryphal drama *Judith*, starring the fashionable actors M. Édouard de Max and Mme. Yourska as Holofernes and Judith, and Ruth St. Denis as the Persian dancer. All three professionals, however, were incidental: the real actors were the three hundred prominent guests who disported in costume amid Moorish lamps and tables piled high with Eastern fruits. In instances like this, St. Denis was reduced to a minor role in a show starring her patronesses. Their husbands simply applauded and paid the bills.

Society women were now the "classic" dancers of the country, and they were indulged in this pursuit by their husbands, by the press, by the artists whose services they bought. The costume balls that had featured them since 1900 as amateur Aïdas, Brünnhildes, Thaïses, Radhas, Schéhérazades, and Salomés had begun to merge with everyday life. Gertrude Vanderbilt Whitney was one of the most prominent to devote her life to art. She was Ruth St. Denis' age, tall, talented, and eccentric-looking enough to earn the French epithet *belle-laide*. She had grown up in one Fifth Avenue palace, moved across the street to another when she married, and later built a third with her husband farther up the Avenue. Stanford White was the Vanderbilts' and Whitneys' designer. Mrs. Whitney was one of the first American women to wear a Poiret gown, to take up sculpture, to patronize native painters, and to dance, à la Orientale. She even took some lessons from Ruth St. Denis, whom she adored, and she went on to win contests in New York and Newport—where she was crowned "one of the seven best amateur society dancers in the world." Even her daughter, little Flora Whitney, according to the select society magazine *Clubfellow*, liked to "drape curtains and portières about her body and trail them alongside the ground (in the privacy of her room)."

The impulse toward theatrical gestures, dances, and costumes was extravagantly present in fashion, which was just then in a turmoil. In Paris, 1906, Paul Poiret had made his first gown to be worn with a new kind of corset that was slimmer, subtler, rubberized. Poiret's designs were the culmination of several decades of artistic (and hygienic) dress-reform experiments tending toward the "Greek," plus his own enthusiasm for modern neo-classic forms and his vision of women's bodies in motion. Poiret profoundly understood Isadora Duncan's dancing in her early years in Paris; like her, he had decided from the Greek statues in the Louvre that the natural point of support in a woman's body was not the waist but the shoulders. In the next few years his simple gowns released "that gracious line that begins under the arm and drops to the ankle" and grew to be the rage. These gowns weren't just shapes; they were also costumes, allusions to antiquity; they were variations on Hellenic or Turkish or Japanese, and they had names like "Pénélope," "Lola Montez," "La Perse," "Isadora." It was a revolution based on period forms, but forms which Poiret had streamlined for the present. Poiret's showmanship was the catalyst that finally changed the way women all over the world walked, held themselves, gestured, ate, spoke. Within several years he had caused all dressmakers to raise waists, narrow skirts, and add flowing tunic effects to gowns. It was as if some gigantic hook had let go of women at the base of their backs, releasing them into sinuous plastic poses. The new dresses almost inversed the old; they were gathered under the breast and draped down the back, so their wearers no longer sailed upright into a high wind; they glided easily on an impulse from within their bodies, or they stood in repose in public—exactly what the "classic" dancers had always urged women to do.

In America, all levels of society were aware of these changes. The *Vogue* Paris correspondent in 1908 was one of the first to see Poiret's implications: "We are at present enjoying not only the most salutary but the most artistic style since the Greek era, in which we are neither sloping nor square but just natural graceful beings," she wrote. Even the humbler arbiter of *Ladies' Home Journal* fashion journeyed to Paris to advise her readers how to sew the new designs at home. American women unquestioningly imitated Parisian styles— there were no others. But Poiret's revolution not only gave all women a chance to design their own silhouettes—it gave Americans the edge. The new fluidity of shape emphasized the health and physical ease the country had lately boasted of in its girls. American women found they were very good at sculpting themselves in motion; perhaps their own daring lessened that first wonderment at seeing free-form barefoot dancers on the stage. Because of the new undulating fashions, they themselves were the potential "classic" dancers; if not they, their daughters were.

It seemed that the pioneering of Duncan and St. Denis had pro-duced a crop of amateurs, not only among the wealthy but all through society. The cross-country tours of all the barefoot dancers had spread inspiration, and new performers sprang up in small communities— wherever young girls displayed artistic tendencies. They boasted they were "sky-taught, sea-taught, Nature-inspired." Sometimes they were forced by local women's clubs to wear coverings on the limbs down to the knees. Even miniature Isadoras appeared on the stage, like eight-year-old Virginia Myers in New York. "To the music of Chopin's Funeral March the tiny girl trod a strangely stately measure . . . her technique has not been hampered by conventional training." News-papers announced that the American girl's dream had shifted from operatic singing to artistic dancing, and that girls were dancing—"even though the rather dubious moral standpoint of the art might make the Puritans turn in their graves."

Times were dark for the Dennis family in 1912: once more Mrs. Dennis took boarders into their New York apartment, this time on West 89th Street. But Ruth didn't stop working out her theatrical visions. She was preparing a Japanese dance-drama she had had in mind ever since Mme. Sadi Yacco's performance in the 1900 Paris Exposition. In the spring of 1910 Ruth had sought out a former geisha in Los Angeles for lessons in Japanese dance—the first sustained work in a formal technique since her childhood Delsarte. However, in the midst of final preparations for the Japanese epic, Henry B. Harris went down with the *Titanic*, in April 1912, leaving the Dennises bereft of funds. Only after a long delay did Ruth manage to raise money and rent the Fulton Theater, where on March 12, 1913, she premiered *O-Mika*. It was in two scenes, the Courtesan's Dance and the Warrior's Dance, and it was the most daring thing she had yet done. The newness was not in the story—another tale of a courtesan turned goddess—nor in the costumes—which contained the usual stunning colors and fabrics: "five kimonos worn one over the other, salmon, violet, amber, rose and green," according to the *Evening Journal*. The innovation lay in the authenticity of the piece as a whole. Ruth's personality, which had shone so easily out of her *Radha* and *Egypta*, was partly submerged in *O-Mika*'s slow, precise Japanese motions. Her face, framed by an elaborate black wig, was "tiny, cold, mystical"—unrecognizable. And she did not break the mood with crescendos of backbends or spinning turns.

O-Mika was not a success, even though St. Denis was invited to perform it at the 1913 opening of the splendid new Palace Theater. It was inaccessible to the general public, and in performing it she was giving up all claims to her earlier mass popularity. The dance was consistent with itself in mood and style, but too delicate and abstract to grip an audience. The spare gestures with a fan or sprig of flowers were artistic rather than vaudevillian. They produced an effect like the artistic photographs of Clarence White, Arnold Genthe, and the Baron de Meyer, who placed their models amid light and fabric, in just such delicate poses as these. *O-Mika*, like those photographs, looked far too ethereal to most people. They thought St. Denis had veered off in the direction of distorted, and therefore useless, abstract art. "I fear the Futurists, who have laid violent hands on painting, have extended their paws to the dance," said one critic after seeing *O-Mika*.

To the average viewer in 1913, dancing was a pale art, a jumble of sketchy styles. Even the brave "classic" dancing was no longer a strong instrument for a strong solo artist, but fair game for ridicule. Serious and comic modes were now one and the same. In the 1913 Ziegfeld Follies a "drunk" comedian did a "Classiceccentrique" number, and in Marie Dressler's 1913 All Star Gambol a dancing couple did a skit called "The Evolution of Dancing," a quick historic run-through of styles from the "Ancient Greek," to the "Old-Fashioned Step," "Original Spanish," "Classic Toe," "Lightning Turkey Trot," "Soft-Shoe Dancing," "Wooden Shoe," "Russian Dancing," and one final "Classic Dance." By 1913, seriousness had come and gone from American dance, which now belonged to society ladies, little girls, and vaudeville funnymen.

CHAPTER 5
Ragtime

A deadly blow to "classic" dancing was struck by ragtime music and dance when they arrived in the teens. Some rag music had been in the air since the minstrel shows of the 1890s, some cakewalking had been tried out by the general public, but then rag dancing had returned to the dance halls and brothels of the red-light, "tenderloin" districts of Chicago, St. Louis, Sedalia, Kansas City, Memphis.

In San Francisco it emerged again. After the 1906 earthquake had destroyed much of that city, in the rubble grew up a shantytown which was so violent, so chaotic, and so unabashedly sinful that it drew tourists in droves. It was called the Barbary Coast. Here in vast palaces of gilt and tinsel the dregs of humanity danced "to the savage beat of tom-tom, cymbal, horn and banjo"—inspiring the onlookers, especially entertainers in the West on tour. In 1910 Anna Pavlova went anonymously to a Coast dance palace, coaxed her partner Mikhail Mordkin onto the floor, and began to dance to a ragtime beat, whereon the tawdry crowd grew silent and retreated to give them room. Pavlova on her own stage had shown the public a wild and abandoned kind of dancing, and so had Isadora Duncan, but in them it was called Dionysian; now the same impulse reached the masses via the syncopated music and the raunchy ambiance. New York producers grabbed onto the whole idea of ragtime: in 1910 the Ziegfeld Follies featured a "Barbary Coast Bear Café"; Lew Fields's 1911 show *The Henpecks* imported a Barbary Coast "coon shouter," Blossom Seeley, who ragged across the stage, singing "Toddlin' the Todolo"; at the Beaux Arts club, Barbary Coast dancers taught the customers a jaunty walk in close embrace and the craze was on for turkey trots, grizzly bears, bunny hugs, humpback rags. Shock was expressed, and some private amusement. A few young people who "trotted" or ragged at unseemly moments were tried in court; but then the defense lawyer sang "The Grizzly Bear" and the whole courtroom joined in on the chorus, "Everybody's Doin' It."

However, by 1912 these wild dances had vanished, "victims of gracelessness," said *Vanity Fair*. Instead appeared the smoother one-steps, hesitation waltzes, South American tangos, and maxixes—called the "glides." In them, a ragtime exuberance was contained, smoothed out, and subtly dramatized. The couple's positions were formalized—in fact, because of their formality, these dances were closer in spirit to Carnegie Hall "classic" concerts than to Barbary Coast ragging. They involved a conscious acting-out of the musical mood—the one-steps and "walks" were quick, light, and sunny, the Latinate "glides" dark and smoldering. To do any of them took a dramatic imagination and a loss of embarrassment, connected with a lithe body and a daredevil sense of timing.

It was the character of the music that invited this dancing wit. Written ragtime was the creation of several virtuoso musicians—Scott Joplin, Louis Chauvin, Ben Harney—who synthesized romantic piano music and Afro-American folk sounds. They put the chromatic ardors of Chopin and Liszt inside robust rhythmic phrases, and so changed that European melancholy into something more playful, elusive, and devil-may-care, but still lyrical. Ragtime was constantly shifting moods over its springy beat—from bombastic to sweet, from pompous to tender. And just as quintessential ragtime was a humorous comment on romantic music, so the ragtime couple dances also quoted from romantic "classic" dancing—they took over not only graceful poses but whole steps: skips and kicks and skittering runs. Ragtime dancing used the same tug and pull at the music's momentum that Isadora Duncan had incorporated into her style. However, the serious origins of ragtime music and dancing were soon obscured by their rapid popularization. Around 1912, urban culture began to manufacture something like a ragtime universe.

With the dancing fad, all the dinner orchestras in restaurants and clubs demanded new and novel tunes—so Tin Pan Alley came to the rescue. Composers like the young Irving Berlin made pseudo-rags with self-advertising lyrics, "Alexander's Ragtime Band," "The International Rag," "Everything in America Is Ragtime." Berlin had an ear for slang; he matched it with his tunes, and soon most rags had catchy semi-nonsense lyrics—"He Had to Get Under, Get Out and Get Under," "Hello Frisco, Hello," "Who Paid the Rent for Mrs. Rip Van Winkle Rag," "Très Moutarde," "De la Fumée (Some Smoke)." Songs made mockeries of sacred concepts—inventions, legends, affectations, and anything that claimed to be Art. The poor devitalized "classic" dance came under attack when Irving Berlin ragged the "Greek" Spring Song ("That Mesmerizin' Mendelssohn Tune") and Yiddish-ized vaudeville Oriental ("Sadie Salome"). In fact, ragtime's mischief put a temporary stop to America's complaining about its own artistic inferiority. "Some people rave about Wagnerian airs / Some think the Spring Song is divine / Talk like that is out of season / What I like is something pleasin'," declared Joe Snyder's lyrics to Scott Joplin's "Pineapple Rag." The songs and their dances presented American irreverence in such clever fashion that Paris, London, Berlin, and the whole Continent caught the fever. Ragtime became a major cultural export, one of our first.

Meanwhile, in American cities, a kind of high life emerged. It was lavishly modern, featuring electricity, loud music, fancy décor, but was so unfamiliar it seemed fantastical. Critic James Huneker called the night-time New York of the teens a new Babylon, a lost Atlantis raised from the sea, with all its hotels, theaters, clubs "rising tier upon tier, starry with illumination." Most of them contained spots for dancing. The Beaux Arts was the first to remove its dinner tables from the floor, Bustanoby's followed, then Reisenweber's, the Café de Ninévé, Rector's, Sherry's, and then the tea parlors, theater rooftops, hotels—the Astor, the Vanderbilt, the top of the Strand, the Biltmore, the McAlpin, the New Amsterdam, the Ritz, Claridge's, Healey's, Madison Square Tower—these hosted daily and nightly crowds of people who came for the brassy music, the dancing, and a few drinks or bites of food in between. Electric lights and mirrors illuminated the vast salles, and painted flowers, winged bulls, slaves, nymphs, satyrs, and mermaids adorned the walls—a hallucination of the exotic taste Stanford White and the gentlemen connoisseurs had wished on New York.

An orchestra, or sometimes two—one for ragtime and one for tangos—dominated the room in raised palmy enclaves, and so did an array of statuary; at the Biltmore it was the plaster Neptune and his surround that gave the name to the operation, "Les Cascades." On the floor thousands of little wicker or grille chairs and tables were strewn outside the low railings that marked the dancing space. And here people of all ages and classes—society ladies with feather aigrettes, businessmen in black dinnerwear, lounge lizards, chorines, and in the more democratic spots, shopgirls and clerks—rubbed elbows while tangoing and one-stepping and polkaing. Dancing was praised and decried as the great equalizer. Indeed, it seemed that coordination and stamina were the only useful attributes in this dancing society—the older virtues, a good name or an education, were momentarily super-fluous. The suddenness with which new fortunes were made at this time, the overwhelming mix-up of the social order, created something like chaos in the ballroom. Ragtimers themselves were bewildered at why they, ordinary upstanding citizens, would submit themselves night after night to an atmosphere of haste, jostling, and barbarism worse than that of a political convention.

Discussion of the dancing went beyond simple good and evil. Of course there were still ministers who believed dance halls were the Gates of Hell, temperance orators who said dance halls helped the liquor interest, social workers who declared they corrupted young working girls. But ragtime had risen in the world, as high as select clubs and ballrooms in private homes, and that put the dancing in another light. It stood for the social chaos that characterized the American teens. There was a helplessness about the anti-dance rhetoric in those years. How could dancing be evil when the sons and daughters and wives of leading citizens were dancing along with everyone else? Who was left to set an example to the uncultured classes? Those were the fears of all Americans who were comfortable with the old order. But the old order was vanishing with America's great "success" in world commerce. This ragtime melee established the conditions necessary for change; in it the "best people" were indistinguishable from everyone else. Cities were growing, and city life had dispensed with small-town values. Social configurations had to become blurred, especially in New York, since waves of newly rich from the Midwest—Edith Wharton called them "the invaders"—were arriving to live in the great over-stuffed hotels and dance in the tea parlors and on the theater roof-tops.

The old urban elite and the few serious art, theater, and music critics who had embraced modern European art were ironically forced into a conservative position. They feared that the already fragile American culture would disintegrate in the mad whirl of ragtime. James Huneker, critic for the New York *Sun* (1902–1917), ruefully remembered all the abuse heaped on the vaudeville Salomés of several years back; now when all women were Salomés there was nothing left to say. It wasn't the carnality of the dancing that bothered him, the "knee to knee" positions of the couples, it was the exhibitionism—young people flaunting themselves as on a stage. The social drift toward this tendency had shown itself even before the dancing appeared: first there had been late supper orgies after a play, then cafés with some sensational singer or dancer in the aisles; now that respectable café patrons themselves were "performing," where could it end but with those same patrons "mounting the vaudeville stage and doing flip-flops and splits and such things before a hired audience of reformed ballet girls"? This is what the high-society youths in Rupert Hughes's 1914 novel *What Will People Say?* fantasized for themselves—and they were sincerely alarmed at their own recklessness. Everyone was alarmed somewhat.

Those who defended the modern ragtime dances nervously reminded the public of their sportive nature—at least dancing got the men out of their stuffy offices and the women away from their interminable bridge games. Inactivity, they claimed, was the ultimate American sin —worse than exhibitionism. Even some hygiene, dress-reform, and open-air fanatics conceded that ragtime, while low-down and "in-artistic," had physically awakened a number of people. But this was no real comfort for the astonishing transgressions implied in ragtime dances.

The country's real ambivalence about social dances might have kept people from seeing what was in them—just as it had with "classic" dancing—except that a number of chic young couples ap-peared: they danced on Broadway, presided in the late-night cafés and palaces, and conveniently embodied the whole dancing mania. The ragtime industry created them partly to be imitated—they posed on song covers, modeled clothes, wrote dance instruction manuals. But their main function was to demonstrate, which the best ones did with a daring and inventiveness that finally no one was ashamed to copy. The most prominent of these couples paired an American girl with an exotic, Latin-looking young man: Florence Walton and Maurice Mouvet, Joan Sawyer and Carlo Sebastian, Bonnie Glass and Rudolfo di Valentino, Mae Murray and Clifton Webb. The men had a reticent physical ease with women that their American counterparts couldn't quite attain. On the dance floor they not only partnered the girls but furnished a sort of environment to show them off: they blended in with the décor and lent a mystery to the routines. And of all the couples, the most beloved was an Englishman, Vernon Castle, and his American wife, Irene.

The Castles, because of their origins, were considered the most scrubbed and wholesome of dancers: Vernon was an engineering stu-dent who had stumbled onto theater as a hobby and then wooed Irene, a New Rochelle debutante, away from genteel life and onto the stage. Vernon was thin, his blond hair was receding, but his perfect manners elicited an air of mischief in his dark, slender, gaminlike wife. They had the distinction of "arriving" in New York with some Parisian re-nown; while stranded in that city they had invented a dancing act for the Café de Paris—and what they had invented, out of Vernon's in-complete recall of "coon-shouter" Blossom Seeley's "Grizzly Bear" from *The Henpecks,* 1911 (Vernon had played a bit part in that Broadway show), became the international dancing style of the next few years. In Paris the young and winsome Castles were the first entertainers to sit down with the guests and then rise from their center table to start the entertainment; back in New York they continued to attract both friends and patrons among the wealthy. In 1912 they played on Broadway in *The Sunshine Girl* and soon, with the backing of shrewd theatrical agent Elisabeth Marbury, they opened a select dancing club, Castle House, on West 46th Street, then a late-night café, Sans Souci, right off Times Square, and then an ultra-tasteful dance palace on Long Island, Castles by the Sea. Every few months they left their country estate and went out on the road in a series of exhibition-contests with themselves as soloists and judges. These events gave them a means to tour the country outside of the vaudeville circuits, and, unsullied by vaudeville, Vernon and Irene were a living advertisement for the handsomeness, the sunniness, and the slight piquancy of the "modern" dances.

The Castles' real contribution to dancing came not from their reputation but from their performing aplomb. Their every routine was choreographed and rehearsed minutely until they moved together in continuous and surprising harmony. They skimmed down the long polished floors, decorating their path with little kicksteps, hesitations, and lightning zig-zags that never interrupted the natural sweep of motion. At crescendos and stoptimes they had showier tricks: he flipped her up and around his body; he lifted her forward in the air as she showed a dainty foot; he held her at the waist as she bent back, rolled around his arm and then up—but always they continued to move, their little steps propelling them in one clear direction at a time. He was immaculately turned out in black tails; she wore white or diaphanous pastel with one or two tunic layers that belled out as he spun her. Their very coolness and lightness increased the excitement of the show; they seemed to be riding the wave of ragtime through no effort of their own.

What Vernon had done was to take a simple social amusement, couple dancing, and make it a highly expressive genre. First of all he gave a dance a shape on the floor. From the high, light, tandem stepping of the one-step he made the Castle walk, in which the gentleman propelled the lady backward to the other end of the room, then kept steering her in ever smaller circles until they had to stop, unwind, and start back in the opposite direction. The step was addicting and pleasing to think about, since its end was its new beginning. For their exhibition routines Vernon not only set floor patterns, he made steps

that fused several earlier dancing styles—minuets, polkas, and drawing room waltzes, the little tap and soft-shoe steps from the music hall,
discreet high kicks from the cakewalk, and the spirit of partnering from
the modern Russian ballet. In that kind of ballet the man's task was
to show off the woman's line, and in the Castles' dancing, no matter
how complicated the steps, their purpose was Vernon's presentation
of Irene. Her "line" was what people saw when the Castles danced,
and it was the line of Isadora's and Pavlova's "classic" dancing observed by Vernon. Irene's fluid back, her gracious bends forward over
pointed foot, her decorative over-the-shoulder glances, her pointed foot
raised in a little arabesque in back—all those were positions adopted
from the "classic" stage. Irene was one of the truer professional heirs
of Isadora Duncan. She was coolly and proudly "Greek," though
not with any of Isadora's grand heroic resonances. She was an
Amazonette, a Duncan reduced, streamlined, made portable by a
partner.

In the realm of popular fads, of which "modern" dancing was a
part, Irene Castle not only mirrored a new age, she improvised some of
its features—calf-length dresses, low-heeled dancing pumps, little
Dutch caps—and she was probably the first American woman whose
ideas had such an impact on fashion. When she had her hair cut short
(before an appendectomy), a host of women copied her; she put a
seed-pearl band around her brow to hold her short hair back, and so
did thousands: these were more faint allusions to the antique, or to an
aesthetic-hygienic style now diluted into high fashion. A newspaper
said the Castle hair looked like "a cross between an ancient Greek
runner and a child's bob." The country forgot, in its preoccupation
with Castlemania, that these clothing and dancing experiments had
begun with the "classic" dancers, Duncan and St. Denis: they were
the ones who had stood the ridicule of their own time, only to see
their queer dress and unhampered bodies become a fashionable
conceit.

Every smart dress was now a dancing dress. Simply to talk about
the cut of clothes, said fashion experts, was to describe dancing. Even
women who never braved the dance floor sought the effect invented
by Loie Fuller, Isadora Duncan, and Ruth St. Denis and fixed by Paul
Poiret—light stuffs wrapped around the body, with additional trailers
that moved and caught the light. The dresses dramatized the con-

nection between a moving body and the space around it. After the long nineteenth-century debate on women's natural forms versus corsetting, the now triumphant looseness in the torsos of gowns, the draped softness at the necks, prompted a whole new range of twisting motions. Women were encouraged by their clothes to spiral up from the waist, to look over their shoulders, to look up, to open their necks to the air. Asymmetrical curves and faintly Dionysian poses were crucial to sitting, walking, and dancing. The tangos and one-steps travelled fast but still required full expressive use of women's upper bodies, and full use of the arms with a partner, to give the bodies room to shift direction. All these ways of moving were reminiscent of the "artistic" poses taught in Delsarte recitation classes in girls' schools, with their stress on opposition motions and oblique lines. And the gowns indicated even more theatricality—they were costumes. They made reference to the artistic but jumbled realm of the Antique, of harems and woodland glades, nymphs and satyrs, and Paris and Oriental slave girls.

Vanity Fair, February 1914, picked out two gowns from among the crowd at the opening of the Castles' Sans Souci to epitomize the flights of fancy women permitted themselves when dressing up. One was "Oriental,"

> a concoction of white satin, seemingly with Turkish trousers. No one would have believed six months ago that any dressmaker would dare put so much material into a skirt as this one had. The plaits at the waist were allowed to flare into extraordinary fullness over the knee and were turned under and gathered to the shorter lining of chiffon cloth. It was slashed in front almost to the knees and filled in with ruffles of white tulle which fell over flesh pink stockings. The slippers were of black velvet with small buckles of brilliants.

The other, worn by a slim blonde, was "Greek,"

> . . . a gown of tulle, a tunic with an irregular edge, bodice a Greek surplice affair, caught with a sprig of apple blossoms on each shoulder. The colors are lavender, pink, faint blue and white, one shade overlapped the other, producing a lovely opalescent effect. The origin of the gown was evi-

dently the gown Mlle Pavlova wears when she dances to the strains of Mendelssohn's "Spring Song."

The ragtime craze mixed a vague artificial idea of Art (Pavlova never danced the "Spring Song") with the restless vitality of American life, and the figure of the American girl exemplified the mixture; she was a half-fanciful creation, more a cultural myth than a real person; but she dominated the era—in magazines, in books, in a string of Broadway plays that celebrated her escapades and her costumes: *Poor Little Rich Girl, Oh! Oh! Delphine!, The Lady of the Slipper, The Sunshine Girl, The Girl from Utah.* She was not the patrician and humorless 1890s Gibson Girl but a much more impish creature with delightful, if untrustworthy, whims—and she was useful for defining the contradictions of the age.

She was not independent, for husbands and fathers still chivalrously supported her, yet she was modern because she was a dancing addict and the sign of a future when no one would bother with social conventions and ceremonies. Self-expression, a suspicious concept, was born with her. Then, it didn't mean cultivating the personality; it meant crudely ignoring the proprieties and acting instantly on one's desires. Again and again, writers connected this girl to the aborted pace of modern life. *Vanity Fair* called her "the princess of an age that has turned the home into the hotel, the painting into the photograph, the book into the review, the letter into the telegram"—and, they might have said, the human encounter into a dash on the dance floor. But dancing, like this fond image of a girl, also kept hold of something old-fashioned. There was repose in it, the repose of the mesmerizing, broad-swinging tempi of ragtime. There were fanciful costumes and surroundings and a set of gestures that made clear to anyone who watched just how to move, to pose, to arrange oneself in relation to others in a fast-moving world. These rag dances were a teacher. For aspiring women who hadn't been to finishing school or for girls who were waiting to grow up, they gave an instant comprehension of just what airs and graces to put on. For all its reputedly obsessive pace, ragtime dancing maintained in the end that there was still gracefulness in human society.

As long as it served this urgent social purpose, dancing was more important as a communal sport than as a theatrical art, and it was crucial as a cultural myth. But the small band of "classic" dance enthusiasts now rose up to protest, claiming that ragtime occupied a very low order on the scale of dance evolution. Anyone on the side of pure art could easily discredit the ragtime myth: when *they* went to observe at the dancing establishments they found no passion, no abandon, no physical beauty, but only discomfort: bedraggled ladies trussed up in ridiculous garb, dodging the bellies of their suffocating, dinner-jacketed escorts. *They* encountered stale air, mournful brass bands, empty slang exchanged by helpless couples. The minor "classic" dancers, so rudely thrust out of favor, were the most vituperative on the subject of ragtime dancing—and reporters loved to bait them. Even the once-great Ruth St. Denis, now touring the small cities of the South with her new partner Ted Shawn, was constantly asked to comment on the "modern" dances. She usually replied in a huff that she knew only about dancing that was one thousand years old. In one interview (Bristol, Tennessee, April 1914) she lashed out at those pitiful young people who were

> solemnly gyrating in couples about waxed and polished floors of overheated ballrooms. Betimes they sit in pairs in open windows and exchange high-brow remarks such as "You certainly are one swell dancer, Miss Fewclothes" to which she replies "Oh, you are such a flatterer, Mr. Fudge," or, "Isn't the music simply swell tonight."

However, popular demand had obliged even Miss St. Denis to include modern ballroom numbers on her own program, danced not by herself but by Ted Shawn and a Miss Hilda Beyer in between her regular East Indian, Egyptian, and Japanese vignettes. As a solo dancer St. Denis could no longer hold an audience for an evening; alone on stage with all those Oriental trappings she looked almost dowdy. She was forced to give up her plans for a full-length *Veil of Maya* and concentrate on a smaller variety act—if she was to survive. It was her new partner, Shawn, at twenty-three almost a generation younger than she, who took on the task of translating St. Denis' original spiritual fervor into modern commercial terms. Shortly after joining her as a partner he married her. Together they would bring aesthetic dancing back into the country's entertainment circuits.

CHAPTER 6
Ted Shawn

Ted Shawn was a mixture, like Ruth St. Denis, of the commercial and the spiritual. But because he was male, fourteen years younger, and solidly middle class, Shawn had a different understanding of dance from hers. He did rescue St. Denis' "classic" dance from obscurity and extended its life over another generation, but he never equalled her spiritual fervor. Ruth St. Denis' art was not made to be "artistic"; it had sprung almost involuntarily from her deep private mysticism submerged in certain rituals of popular theater. But Ted Shawn's was "artistic" and nothing else from the start. He was born in 1891 and he grew up after a sweetened "Art" had become a part of middle-class America. A girl in those years had only to wear a "Greek" gown, a boy to carry a sunflower, and the neighbors understood: here was not an ordinary child.

Shawn, the son of a Kansas City newspaperman, passed his childhood among books and amateur theatricals. His bookishness got him to the University of Denver to study for the Methodist ministry, where he was called "the sweetest collegian" because of his looks: he had adopted the flaring black tie, low collar, and "abstracted mien" of Oscar Wilde and the English aesthetes of two generations back. Shawn was eager for religion, but he was also drawn to forbidden Bohemian worlds outside of it: a close friend was an older girl who spent her summers in an art commune near Buffalo, called Roycroft. She told him about Roycroft, the domain of Elbert Hubbard, who was a preacher of the arts and a propagator of all past eras of cultural history. It was Hubbard's folk philosophy, explained in books published by himself, that brought young Shawn to a state of mind where he was ready to accept dancing as a possible occupation.

Elbert Hubbard was a former soap salesman who had modeled himself simultaneously on Walt Whitman, Robert Ingersoll, Oscar Wilde, and William Morris. In 1895 he founded a small magazine, *The Philistine* ("The Smug & Snugly Ensconced denizens of Union Square called me a Philistine, and I said, 'Yes, I am one if a Philistine is something different from you'"), and set up his crafts colony in East Aurora, New York, for the manufacture of decorative homey items and small books. Hubbard, although he baited the literary establishment with his own vigorous and slightly lurid prose, did not propose any radical revisions of society. He was a culture popularizer, preparing people for aesthetic enjoyment. In a series of books called *Little Journeys to the Homes of Good and Great Men*, he meditated on the legendary figures of the past; in describing them he scaled them down, domesticated them, and introduced them jovially to the

American folk. The guest rooms at the Roycroft Inn were named after his favorites: Socrates, George Eliot, Beethoven, Edison, William Morris—and finally Susan B. Anthony, whose name commemorated Hubbard's one moment of true, though questionable, rebellion. He had allied himself out of wedlock with an intellectual suffragette named Alice Moore, whom he later married after divorcing his meek first wife. Roycroft thus became a refuge of the New Woman, and Roycroft's New Woman theme fascinated Ted Shawn. Allene Seacroft, his college friend, was the first New Woman to play guide and muse to Shawn's sensibilities. After she was graduated from the University of Denver, leaving Shawn to finish college alone, he paid teasing tribute to her in a short play about a woman-dominated Utopia.

Shawn's exposure to Roycroft would prove useful later, when he began his own culture-farm, Denishawn. More important to him now was Hubbard's definition of a recognizable façade for artistic men—or rather a combination of façades. Hubbard had reconciled two prominent ones, the European aesthete and the American Rough Rider, simply by combining them in his daily dress—lyrical flowing hair and flowing cravat mixed with burly homespun tweeds, heavy shoes, and Stetson hat. Hubbard, by his example, showed it was possible for young men to be both aesthetic *and* robust. This proved necessary during Shawn's college years. The Spanish-American War had been fought, Theodore Roosevelt was President, and physical preparedness was a crucial topic. Ted Shawn himself went to work summers in a logging camp above Denver and began to toughen up. The President was exhorting all boys to seek "the strenuous life" and become "good boys," the kind who "had it in them to thrash the objectionable boy when the need arose." Roosevelt, speaking to his own class of Americans, was advertising his well-known obsession with racial purity. Like many of his time, he feared that American "old stock" was dwindling in numbers and losing its vitality, just at the moment when Southern European immigrants were pouring into American cities with their hordes of dark-complexioned children.

Ted Shawn, who came of German and old American stock, subscribed to these eugenic sentiments and would later write about dance in markedly eugenic terms. Eugenics was the popular science of racial purity that enjoyed a tremendous vogue in the first years of the twentieth century, creating health and exercise obsessions along with new institutions—national parks, forest rangers, summer camps and resorts, and hygienic-reform clubs. One of these, the Ralston Club, operated by pledge; members promised to eat wheat cereal for breakfast, take long walks, perform daily exercises, and wear wool next to the skin. If enough of the right people took the pledge, the club thought, America would become the Utopia it was meant to be, its "old stock" reinvigorated and purified.

Having survived the logging camps, Ted Shawn was on his way out of a "goody-goody boyhood" when diphtheria struck in his junior year and changed his life. To regain his coordination he enrolled in a dance course taught by Hazel Wallack, a dancer home on leave from the Metropolitan Opera Ballet—and undoubtedly the best first teacher Shawn could have hit upon. *Her* teacher, the ballet mistress Lina Calvazzi, of the old Italian school—straight backs and low, correct leg extensions—was nevertheless the first European to notice publicly that American girls, with their beauty and brains, could make fine ballet dancers. Hazel Wallack taught with a thoroughness that revitalized Shawn's body, and a freshness that brought back all his boyhood theatrical fancies. He was plunged through her teaching into all the current controversies over the new, aesthetic dance. It was 1910, the peak time of the vaudeville Salomés. Shawn made his debut in that year in a small Denver club with his teacher. According to the newspapers, they danced an amalgam of ballet, ballroom, *and* Salomé styles:

> Miss Hazel Wallack and Ted Shawn will swirl to the mystic images of the wild and exotic dance of love . . . it is said to be the last note in aesthetics and the first in the expression of the elemental, the primitive, and the Orientalism of the East.

A short time later, Shawn saw on stage the true priestess of the mystic dance, Ruth St. Denis, who was touring the West with her *East Indian Suite* and excerpts from *Egypta*. She inspired him to leave the narrow confines of Denver, and he set off, not for New York, but for the nearer town of Los Angeles. Dance was to be his profession, but he would take at least two years to square it with Roosevelt's virility cult *and* with the aesthetic posturings of his earlier heroes, Oscar Wilde and Elbert Hubbard.

It is not clear why Shawn went to Los Angeles, unless he thought movie shorts on vaudeville shows could be an outlet for his dancing. If so, he was ahead of his time. The real movie centers were New York and Chicago. Southern California had been discovered as a landscape to use in films only a year or so before, and in 1911, Los Angeles as a city was still dwarfed by cosmopolitan San Francisco. It was a flat little town, hot and dusty. A few ornate hotels stood in the middle of empty desert and farmland; a dozen small film studios were shooting improvised Westerns in old farm buildings.

At first Shawn had nothing to do with the movies; he worked days as a stenographer, nights as a dancing teacher in the studio of another teacher, Norma Gould. But as the movies grew, Los Angeles acquired city features, such as dance palaces and ragtime bands. Shawn and Gould became taxi dancers, hosting Tango Teas in the small, select Hotel Angelus. Some evenings they also gave exhibitions at the baroque Alexandria Hotel, where the young movie world gathered. The Los Angeles *Examiner* said that Shawn and Gould had made up a new dance combining the waltz and the tango, adding that Ted Shawn was "a grotesque young man, chubby and glassy-eyed."

Undaunted, Shawn took some ballet lessons from Pershikoff, a Russian dancer in Gertrude Hoffman's Ballets Russes who had settled in Los Angeles at the end of the company's national tour. Presumably Ted Shawn saw Hoffman's company in 1911 (D. W. Griffith did) and took heart from the vigorous and exotic male dancing it offered audiences. To Shawn, this approximation of the Russian Ballet projected the artistic rigor he must have needed to choose Art over ragtime. Around 1912 Shawn and Gould themselves began to give "interpretive and classic" dance concerts in between their ragtime appearances: "classic" items mentioned in the press were *Dances of Henry VIII* and *Diana and Endymion*. In 1913 Shawn finally managed to make a short movie—*Dance of the Ages*—with the Edison Studios in Long Beach. The setting was a table surrounded by wisemen and savants; Shawn and his company, superimposed in miniature, repeatedly emerged at one end of it, each time in the garb of a different era—leopard skins, then Greek draperies, then Roman togas, then peasant ribbons and flounces, and finally modern ball dress and ragtime gowns. The dances were all composed of sketchy leaps, hops, and skips. Nevertheless, Shawn and Gould now had a reputation. When San Diego's new Majestic Vaudeville House invited them to open its floor show, the papers announced that they had created a repertory of over forty "classic" dances, all with scenery and costumes.

But Shawn's ambitions had grown too big for Los Angeles, and he craved talk and philosophy about dance. He found a book, *The Making of a Personality*, which justified the "classic" dance in the highest artistic and philosophic terms, and he resolved to go East to find its authors, poet Bliss Carman and health and beauty expert Mary Perry King. What drew Shawn was the book's flowery language, its emphasis on eugenics, and its equation of physical beauty with moral purity. Moreover, Bliss Carman had a considerable reputation as a poet with a supposed pure-minded approach to hedonism.

Carman was the author, with his friend Richard Hovey, of those beloved volumes *Songs from Vagabondia* (1894), *More Songs from Vagabondia* (1896), and *Last Songs from Vagabondia* (1901)—which had uplifted a whole generation of sensitive young men of the Midwest. Carman, Canadian and Harvard-educated, and Hovey, a product of Dartmouth, had once sported monocles and sunflowers themselves, and spent time at Elbert Hubbard's Roycroft. Like Hubbard they saw themselves as aesthetic missionaries to an America that was shutting them out, a society based, in Hovey's words, "on money-getting and not on the eternal harmonies." In the midst of *fin-de-siècle* Big Business, poets Carman and Hovey had to muster up all the eternal harmonies they could find for their side, so they filled their verse with woodlands and dryads and naiads—also with high seas, taverns, buccaneers, kings and pampered courts, and with Whitman-esque and Kiplingesque exhortations. Again and again they evoked those sensual rewards that don't cost anything: "Song that is the flower of love / And joy that is its fruit / Here's the love of women, lad, / And here's our love to boot!" Curiously, in wishing themselves out of the marketplace, they almost wished themselves off the map. Nearly every poem describes another land—Arcadia, or ancient Greece, or Lethe: "Just to live like lilies / In the lake! / Where no thought nor will is / To mistake!" These futile longings seemed to be the correct note in any poetry that aspired to be popular. The Washington *Star* praised the second *Vagabondia* volume because "the poems have just enough mystery to delight and stimulate the imagination without overtaxing it."

As time went on, both poets felt the need to bolster their poetry with some solid doctrine. This they found through an alliance with an extraordinary woman, Henrietta Knapp Russell, and with her "religion": she was a high priestess of Delsarte in the salons of London, New York, and Newport. Mrs. Russell was about forty when Carman and Hovey met her; they were thirty. She had a dramatic, worldly appearance: her hair was brushed "Egyptian fashion," her dress was "Greek" and studded with barbaric brooches—she called it her "brain costume." In her, Hovey and Carman found their New Woman, who could teach them about physical life, as distinct from spiritual posturing. Gratefully they dedicated the first *Vagabondia* book "To H.K.R. for debts of love unpaid / *Her boys* inscribe this book which they have made." Mrs. Russell married Richard Hovey and gave him a child; to both poets she gave her rhetoric and her theories.

Up to this time, Mrs. Russell's constituency had been women. In her own book, *Yawning* (1891), she described the body's instinctive powers to relax even in a civilization which, she said, had released a whole social class (the top one) from physical work and yet left it weary. Her province of dress reform and Delsarte exercise was that same branch of the health movement so familiar to the young Isadora and Ruth St. Denis. Mrs. Russell's books found their way into libraries of poor families like the Duncans and the Dennises, *and* the homes of rich and restless society hostesses—as did those of her disciple, Mary Perry King, who wrote *The Basis of Beauty* (1900) and *Comfort and Exercise* (1901). Both authors addressed themselves to the very real clothing problems still presented to women by convention—the constraint of corsets, the threat of germs carried in the long, trailing unhygienic skirts. Mrs. Russell and Mrs. King, like all dress-reform apologists, proposed to free women's bodies, thereby releasing the beneficent impulses of their souls. Wrote Mrs. King: "We permit ourselves to be hampered, limited, handicapped, galled and jaded by clothes. Is it any wonder that our spirits are distempered, our minds befogged and our sense of fair play radically perverted?"

The difference between Mrs. Russell and most health reformers was that she, perhaps through her extensive travels, had developed a lively taste for aesthetics. She wasn't afraid to tell her readers or listeners how to be beautiful, and she invoked all the pseudo-scientific Delsarte theories about the body as mirror of the soul, to artistic, rather than simply moral or religious, ends. Both Mrs. Russell and Mrs. King proposed specific beautifying measures, exercises and diets, to improve the person—and it was this emphasis Bliss Carman and Richard Hovey seized upon. Their own self-images, the clothes they wore, their male beauty, were prominent features of their poetry in *Songs from Vagabondia*—even as it was in Whitman's poem *Leaves of Grass*, which was Hovey's and Carman's inspiration. Men, of course, had trouble enunciating a male aesthetic doctrine for fear of straying into narcissism or homosexuality. However, it was just such a doctrine, discovered by Bliss Carman in women's books and restated by him in his own, that freed young Ted Shawn for a serious dancing career.

Disguised and unnamed Delsarte and dress-reform ideas allowed

Bliss Carman in *The Making of a Personality* (1906) to argue on a grand scale for an aesthetic of the body. Traditionally, he said, physical beauty (especially in men) has been treated as a pagan ideal, irrelevant to Christian societies, but now history has proved it essential. No "puny perverted race" ever accomplished anything noble. Conversely, the Greeks, those architects of nobility, were "enamoured of physical beauty" and devoted to the fine arts. There was a moral lesson in all classical art—the famous statue of the Winged Victory, for instance, was the best argument Carman knew for good posture, and good posture by Delsartean logic meant an upright soul. Carman's devotion to Greece was shared by most health reformers of the time. The Greeks in their excavated form—sculpted bodies of white marble—were racially pure and aesthetically pleasing to everyone, not only to Delsarteans but to dress reformers, to hygienists, to eugenicists, to artists, poets, philosophers, politicians, educators, "classic" dance enthusiasts.

The activity of dancing followed close upon the emulation of Greek statues, and some kind of dancing figured in the proposed Arcadias of almost all reform groups and minor artists. The Ralston Club believed in future settlements, where "Greek-like groves and academic aisles should be set forth in woodland orchards—for play, celebration and communal *dancing*." Charles Wesley Emerson, founder of Emerson College of Oratory, which offered a high level of physical culture, proposed exercises in curves, designed to teach true beauty. "I scarcely need refer to the ancient Greeks," he parenthesized to his audience. But Bliss Carman extended this thinking in *The Making of a Personality* so he could welcome aesthetic dance even in theaters, and praise the art of Isadora Duncan and Ruth St. Denis—although Carman frankly still preferred dancing out-of-doors, away from the stale air. This particular connection in Carman's writing was what inspired Shawn. Carman's blessing on these "classic" dancers and his desire to link race purity with some theatrical aesthetic finally convinced Shawn to abandon his unworthy ragtime activities and devote himself to pure dance.

However, the dance that Bliss Carman had in mind was only in its fetal stages; Shawn found this out when he reached Mary Perry King's Triunian School of Personal Harmonizing in New Canaan, Connecticut (where Bliss Carman was in residence). Shawn was by then a veteran performer: he had already danced in Los Angeles for three years; he had come East with Norma Gould as an entertainer on the Santa Fe Railroad, playing to tiny rural audiences up and down the South and Midwest. In Connecticut, Mrs. King and Bliss Carman disregarded audiences. Their ideal was "free gymnastics," based on so-called natural body movements—such as deep breathing, swaying, balancing, yawning—Mrs. King's translation of Delsarte doctrine, which she still did not mention by name. Slow motion, said Mrs. King, revealed to an individual his own true rhythms. Marching about, flinging the body, and jerking the limbs did not—these were "inartistic." Mrs. King's "artistic" resembled a warm bath, wherein Self-Expression lazed about in the stress-free state she (and other reformers) imagined for a democracy-Utopia. Her gymnasium was supposed to be a life-laboratory. Her pupils, by slow, repeated imitations of Greek sculpture, were supposed to ennoble their bodies and elevate their souls.

Ted Shawn, for all his devotion to Bliss Carman, was rapidly drawn away from the Triunian School, back to New York and its theaters. In 1914 he arrived in a city still in the grip of ragtime debaucheries, and not overly ready to welcome a male "classic" dancer.

The state of home-grown "classic" dance was revealed by the début of another male dancer in that year. New York of course had seen Mordkin, Pavlova's virile partner, and the Russian men in Gertrude Hoffman's company—but they couldn't countenance the same behavior in American men, even such a one as the well-known Paul Swan, another artistic mutation of the Midwest and Ted Shawn's only American competitor. Paul Swan was a painter mildly famous for his resemblance to the Praxiteles statue of Hermes, and his role as the "Figure of Perfect Manhood" in his 1911 Suffragettes' Parade. But Paul Swan encountered much skepticism when he decided to take to the stage as a dancer. *Variety* described his début at Hammerstein's Victoria, in a Sphinx Dance, a Chinese Dance, and an inevitable Narcissus:

> [While dancing] Swan floated about the stage, his arms moving snake-wise, his body twisting, almost squirming. However, there were snickers from the audience and the second and third dances seemed to be over the heads of most. Mr. Swan died in the final dance, and it's tough to die at Hammerstein's.

If the godlike Swan evoked ridicule, what about Ted Shawn, who was nowhere near so beautiful and couldn't even paint? But

Shawn's conception of dance had passed beyond attitudinizing. Shawn was over six feet tall and he made a wholesome impression whether he spoke or danced; now he was armed with Bliss Carman's view of dance as a moral good *and* he had a mission—to do for dance what Carman, Hovey, and Elbert Hubbard had done for literature. He wanted it to be loved by the American people.

Moreover, he had met Ruth St. Denis, his old idol, still a fascinating concoction of Irish slang and mystic meditation. She became his New Woman. When they began to talk to each other, they discovered a whole vein of Delsarte-inspired rhetoric in common. Shawn joined her just before her tour of the South in the fall of 1914. His function was to placate popular taste with the ragtime numbers and light pas de deux which he danced with one of St. Denis' back-up girls, Hilda Beyer, while St. Denis continued to offer her mystic solos. Soon, Shawn began to take over the direction of the tour. He set up pre-performance Tango Teas, and to the shows he added duet after duet for himself and Beyer—duets that could have stepped from the pages of *Songs of Vagabondia* (or any volume of *fin-de-siècle* American lyric poetry): "The Joy of Youth," "The Pipes of Pan," "Pierrot and the Butterfly," "Pan and Syrinx," "The Southwind and the Rose."

"Classic" dance, the company found, had not died out altogether in the provinces as it had in the cities, because the second-rate "classic" dance that reached the provinces was sweet and not overtaxing to imaginations, whereas ragtime was horribly insistent and seductive. Nor was it necessarily the small-town audiences who kept the "classic" dance alive but rather the local arts reviewers who nourished themselves on Bliss Carman's poems and Ted Shawn's rarified language, which was the opposite of vulgar ragtime slang. A Lynchburg, Virginia, paper welcomed the little St. Denis troupe:

> With all the world a-tangoing and doing other hesitating steps, it will be a pleasing change to skip away to the Far East. . . .

In Nashville, Shawn's offerings were understood as

> dances in which gods and mortals alike of ancient days found joy and beauty in the bare, unfettered rosy limbs, the graceful figures of youths and maidens, and joyous songs of multitudes . . .

The company followed its southern tour with a full cross-country trip, in which Shawn, by adroit management of the books, paid off all of St. Denis' debts and managed to save money as well. Shawn, now the manager, husband, and partner of St. Denis, was twenty-three years old. He had his art, he had his New Woman, all he needed to be a prominent eccentric like Elbert Hubbard was a domain like Roycroft, an Arcadia of his own. And he would have it, for he was entrepreneur as well as dreamer. Renewed response to the "classic" dance all across the country had convinced him a "classic" school could be a going concern. When the company reached Los Angeles, he and Ruth St. Denis bought an idyllic estate on the hill at 6th and St. Paul, in the heart of the city. Denishawn, their school, opened in the summer of 1915—a living example of a poem, a painting, or a photograph, in the latest aesthetic mode.

CHAPTER 7
Denishawn

Denishawn was secluded from the world by a wall of eucalyptus trees; inside on one and a half green acres were a large, Spanish-style house, a swimming pool, and a tennis court—which, with platform, barre, canopy, and mirror, became the dancing pavilion. The thought of open-air dancing proved slightly overwhelming to some of the local reporters at the school's opening:

Society Matrons, Blushing Maidens,
Queenly Clubbites Take Ruth St. Denis Route
to Health and Beauty

said the headline on a page of cartoons about Denishawn in the Los Angeles *Record*. Under a drawing of Ted Shawn was printed: "This is not a waiter but an urn-bearer." But Denishawn, no matter how eccentric a place, was also a true realization of one kind of American idyll, a chaperoned Utopia. The school flourished, and attracted film actresses. Ruth St. Denis provided the glamour, and Shawn was the genial host; meanwhile he also concentrated on training several young dancers—some from other Los Angeles dance schools, one or two from the pick-up company of the last tour—nine of whom were declared professionals by the end of the summer of 1915. Shawn then closed the school, rented the house to sometime dance students Lillian and Dorothy Gish and their mother, and took Miss Ruth and the new company across the country on a concert tour of forty-nine one-night stands. They ended in New York with a matinée series at St. Denis' old haunt, the Hudson Theater.

The standard Denishawn concert evening began with a benediction: Ted Shawn in long white robes dancing "The Lord Is My Shepherd"; it wended its way through a variety of Duncan-and-Pavlova-esque "Nature Rhythms," some St. Denis–style Orientale vignettes, and finished up on a modern note: a mix of ballroom duos and Ballets Russes–type solos—in all, thirty-three dances. This catch-all was a success, even in New York, where the matinées led to more matinées and then to vaudeville offers. Denishawn signed with the "two-a-day" Orpheum Circuit and opened at Keith's Palace Theater, New York, January 16, 1916, in a headline spot.

Ruth St. Denis was welcomed back heartily by the New York press. "I have never ceased plugging, that is the word, plugging," she told reporters, and she gave full credit to her mentor in the theater, David Belasco, who, she said, had taught her the beauty of unity. However, the new Denishawn Company owed its sudden transformation from small-time concert to big-time vaudeville not so much to the "plugging" as to the caprices of culture. Experimental theater from Europe, with its multi-sensory experiments, its new unity of the arts, had finally found a wary acceptance among American theater-goers. In fact, as Denishawn opened in vaudeville, the group that was the apogee of modern theater, Diaghilev's Ballets Russes, made its début in New York at the Century Theater.

Dance then was not separate from theater; all over Europe, and even in America, new theatrical techniques presumed a fluid perception among audiences, a way of seeing that simultaneously linked motion and sight and sound. Such revolutionary modern productions as Debussy's opera *Pelléas et Mélisande*, Maeterlinck's symbolist play *The Blue Bird*, Max Reinhardt's Oriental pantomime *Sumurun* (which were brought to New York in 1908, 1910, and 1912 respectively), not to speak of the Salomés and Gertrude Hoffman's Russian Ballet, required an imaginative response difficult for Americans. Yet some Americans were trying to keep up. That Diaghilev's Ballets Russes occupied an important outpost on this theatrical frontier—perhaps *the* most important—was known to anyone interested in the modern stage; and interested souls there now were. By 1914, America boasted amateur drama leagues all around the country, with a combined membership of at least thirty thousand. These members would feel duty-bound to see the Russian company; thousands more would flock to vaudeville to see its American equivalent—and Denishawn offered enough Russianized elements to be sometimes mistaken for the Russian Ballet.

In fact, Denishawn was held over by popular demand two more weeks at the Palace, while the Ballets Russes did not at first excite the public. The "name" dancers of Diaghilev's company, Nijinsky, Karsavina, Ida Rubinstein, were not appearing in America because of European wartime complications. But the Ballets Russes's glory eventually made itself felt without these stars, through the sheer abundance of theatrical ideas, as one after another of Fokine's ballets unfolded before the public, as the weird and vibrant colors of Diaghilev's artist-designers, Léon Bakst, Alexandre Benois, and Natalie Gontcharova, astonished everyone, and as the new lead dancers, Lydia Sokolova, Flora Revalles, Adolph Bolm, and the young Léonide Massine, gained a following of their own. Moreover, there were in America several newspaper arts critics, among them Carl Van Vechten and James Huneker in New York and Henry Taylor Parker (known as HTP) in Boston—superbly educated, open-minded men—who were able to interpret just what was revolutionary in the Ballets Russes's kind of theater. All of these men

had seen the company abroad since its 1909 Paris début; they had
followed the repertory and taken the trouble to learn about Russian
ballet, so different from the haphazard and off-color American art of
the same name. All three men were music critics, trained to hear the
musical logic in the complicated Stravinsky, Ravel, and Debussy
scores of the ballets. Therefore they instinctively reached for the
formal structure in the dancing.

It was there, in spite of Fokine's efforts to camouflage it in an
illusion of spontaneity. For these critics, the very source of the public's
unease—the absence of featured dancers—provided the occasion to examine the core of the Russians' art, its use of the ensemble. Van
Vechten brilliantly pointed out that Fokine had subdivided the corps
de ballet, not into traditional unison blocs, but into myriad smaller
units which he then animated kaleidoscopically—as Richard Strauss
had done with the elements of the orchestra. "Pictorial intricacy," Van
Vechten termed it. Both he and Parker saw that the moving patterns
of the dance complemented rather than reflected the patterns in music
and décor, that dance was independent of the other elements, even
while all were blended in the moment of performance. Parker singled
out the one ballet in the repertory by Nijinsky, *L'Après-midi d'un
Faune*, as an even starker experiment than Fokine's, since Nijinsky
appeared to have isolated the components of dance and then reinfused
pure motion into the flat archaic surface shapes he had chosen to work
with. To these critics the Ballets Russes brought not only impeccable
modernity in music and décor but also the revelation that ballet was
an artistic language, with a fund of traditions which these modern
Russians had absorbed, questioned, and now transcended. If the old
classical Russian Ballet, the grand tradition constructed in Russia in
the nineteenth century by the French-born ballet master Marius
Petipa, had allowed in Parker's words, "little room for the play of the
spirit," it had provided the dancers with indispensable skills. "The
alertness, the patience, the dexterity, the endless quest for exactitude
of the old virtuosities have their uses in the new freedoms," wrote
Parker in a moment of uncanny American insight into the Russians'
dance achievement.

These fine critics waged a lonely battle; while most American
audiences tolerated and even admired the Russians, few saw what
about them was different from, say, the Denishawn Company. Ted
Shawn didn't see either, or chose to say he didn't. His avowed ambition
in 1916 was to provide an instant base for dance in America—the
equivalent of the Russians' training, but more appropriately demo-

cratic. He said he found the Russians decadent, and the Diaghilev company's appearance not ballet's renaissance but its swan song. Shawn probably saw the company in New York with his wife, since Ruth St. Denis was listed among the celebrities in the Century Theater audience, "watching with professional interest." After their New York seasons, Shawn's and Diaghilev's companies set out simultaneously on tour—the Ballets Russes toward the West, then back up and around to New York; Denishawn on the Orpheum Circuit in almost the opposite circle, down the East Coast and then westward. They actually intersected in Pittsburgh when Denishawn played the Orpheum March 20–25 and the Ballets Russes gave a concert March 23, 1916.

Reviewers in many cities besides Pittsburgh lumped the two companies together. Denishawn, they agreed, offered more gentility and variety, while the Russians' special talent was sensuality. Both were, of course, slightly dangerous. In fact, the general countrywide reaction was almost the same as nine years before, when the wave of Salomés had hit. Denishawn and the Ballets Russes revived the American public's dumfounded gape in the face of the "optic intoxication" of this modern dance, which awakened "all our latent and barbaric sensibilities." Reviewers shook their critical heads: what had proved subversive in the imitation Salomés, Schéhérazades, and all the ragtime dances was now labelled high art in the Denishawn and Russian Ballet spectacles. Sometimes a reviewer, such as this one in St. Louis, offered whole lists of what he implied were hypocrisies, without daring to criticize:

> Through all of that new artistic movement which generally presents itself as cubism, futurism, Max Reinhardt scenery, frank sex plays, symbolistic poetry and not least the art of dancing as diversely shown by Isadora Duncan, Ruth St. Denis and the Russians, there is a strong reach out for new truths.

By 1916, because of the cognoscenti's artistic expertise on the one hand and the general public's resignation on the other, all of dance was seen from the Russian perspective. Therefore a vital connection between America's own "classic" dance and the theatrical forms it had come from was lost. Ruth St. Denis' *Radha*, ten years before, had been an extension of David Belasco's theater—itself a magnification of old-style melodrama. In *Radha* St. Denis had unified not the arts but the elements of theater she knew best—cloth and light and music and gesture—and afterward she continued her explorations in *Egypta* and *O-Mika*, assured of some understanding from Belasco's public. But now, compared to the efficient and self-aware stylistic essays of Fokine and Nijinsky, St. Denis' dances seemed plump, dreamy, almost lackadaisical. By 1916 critics were praising St. Denis not for herself but for her prefiguring Nijinsky before he arrived. Moreover, the Denishawn repertory under Shawn contained none of that luxurious spread-out time and resonant charm of St. Denis; Shawn had subdivided her art into a collection of small numbers. He copied the Russians; he borrowed their themes and their policy of mixed programs.

However, what the Russians intended as a medley of precise historical fantasies, Shawn saw as a travelogue, something like an expanded version of his Edison film *Dance of the Ages*. He even arranged his programs chronologically. After the Nature idylls he placed the Indian, Egyptian, and Japanese, amplified by new additions of the Hawaiian and Javanese, and then the modern numbers, the Fokine and Nijinsky imitations (Shawn's *Columbine*, a pointe solo, after Fokine's *Carnaval*; his *Baseball Dance*, inspired by Nijinsky's *Jeux*, about tennis) and the ballroom routines. As for the imposing Ruth St. Denis, she, now caught in a lightweight repertory, also grew imitative. To her old standbys she had added a Loie Fuller—type solo, *The Spirit of the Sea*, which framed her in yards of floating, undulating green drapery, and a dance-drama, *The Peacock*, whose Beardsley-esque theme was fixed up with a new Ballets Russes plot about kings, courtesans, poison rings, and human-to-peacock transmogrifications.

St. Denis' most glorious moment in the new repertory was her modern solo *Impromptu*, a spoof of all the amateur "classic" dancers. According to photographs of the dance, St. Denis skipped about, holding her tunic in delicate fingers and mugging at a wilted rose. Audience after audience was delighted—astonished—that the great Ruth St. Denis revealed an Irish wit in a "classic" number. But this was natural, she always told reporters. From one point of view she was still a Belasco actress, an extravagant theatrical soul like the great ones of the 1890s who planned their repertories to show off their own rich personalities. Now in 1916 that era had gone. A new spirit on the stage had bred a new kind of performer; Nijinsky was its consummation, or the dramatic soprano Mary Garden—both chameleon talents brilliantly transformed by their roles and unimaginable outside of them. St. Denis, however, as Radha, a peacock, or a comedienne, was always herself.

. . .

If the Russians' technique and culture had superseded Ruth St. Denis' kind of performing, Shawn, now the chief artistic influence on the Denishawn repertory, must provide an American alternative. In pure dance terms he was unable. His own training, a smattering of ballet, Delsarte, and ragtime-ballroom, gave him no resources to work out an idea within the logical limitations of a dance. He didn't have the concept—a dance—in anything like the Russians' formal sense of it. Obviously his evening of thirty-three dance vignettes had a certain visual impact. But even American critics noticed the "incongruities that bewildered" in the repertory—inexplicable pirouettes in the middle of Egyptian friezes. It wasn't merely Shawn's provincial origins that prevented his grasping the idea of choreography, of stylistic unity—after all, Isadora Duncan had emerged from this country's random training one of the most consistent and logical dance minds of her day. From the beginning, Duncan understood dance forms so wholly and so instinctively that she could integrate what she learned from many eras into her own dance motions. Even Ruth St. Denis was able to add on numerous Oriental gestures to *her* basic concept of a dance.

Shawn lacked that basic concept. He always hoped he was a choreographer, but he was obviously something else—a producer, a popularizer. He picked up what was in the air, what he saw in popular graphics, photography, and other dance entertainment. Anything that crossed his mind he could put on the stage, with no qualms about its quality or its brevity. And his talent answered the needs of a new American public, uneasy about its own culturally blank past. Bliss Carman and Richard Hovey had satisfied them in poetry; now Denishawn in dance offered a survey of the artistic past and present: everything the Russians gave you and more—echoes of Duncan, Pavlova, St. Denis—all watered down to suit the Denishawn mode of primitive-genteel.

"The reader who thinks the color has been drained out of the world and that grace and rhythm are forgotten arts," said a glowing review in a Reading, Pennsylvania, paper, "has only to see Miss St. Denis and her company of dancers. Allah be praised! These wonderful people at least have not failed the hungry." The reviewer then went on to describe whole sections of the concert in language he thought appropriate:

> The nature rhythms were exquisite. They were created
> and taught by Mr. Shawn. First, "Will o' the Wisp," with
> flitting white figures which might easily have been all mist.

And then "Dawn," with enchanting wraiths, "shaking their milk-white feet in a ring." Presently they took on rosy tints, like the hours preceding the coming of the sun god, and then came Apollo (Mr. Shawn) who looked his most splendid in the golden light of early day.

A slender, bright blue figure, representing a dragon-fly, was followed by three maidens blowing bubbles.

Mr. Shawn, as a fine figure of a harvester, with a lovely slim young woman gleaner were presently overtaken by showers, more slender fluttering nymphs. Then the rainbow and after that a sunset torch dance, which stung the senses with its reds.

Last came the crescent moon, a slim creature, too, all moonlight and veils, with a sinister bat crossing her beauty.

If the Denishawn Nature Rhythms plus Russian-style exotica seemed an impossible jumble, so did everything around it on the urban scene. Ragtime had caused a great shake-up of styles—anything was likely to be juxtaposed with anything. Although ragtime dancing was supposed to be half-dead by 1916, the spirit of the genre lived on. Composers and lyricists simply moved over to the Ziegfeld-type revues that had mushroomed on Broadway—and more artistic dance was so much more grist for their mill. They had a recent memory of Anna Pavlova's month-long stint in a version of *The Sleeping Beauty* at the Hippodrome variety shows, plus Isadora's impassioned re-appearance with her German student-refugees, in addition to the Ballets Russes and Denishawn's much publicized presences. Moreover, Nijinsky himself finally arrived from Europe in April 1916 to rejoin his company. The 1916 Ziegfeld Follies featured a whole scene of the "Blushing Ballet" with a "Suggestion of Spectre de la Rose," and a "Travesty of Schéhérazade"—in which black comedian Bert Williams "did" Nijinsky, and Fanny Brice sang the song "Nijinsky" (music by Dave Stamper). The Passing Show of 1916 had dreamed up a Greek-style "Olympic" Ballet with two rival female stars, Mme. Swirsanska and Ma-Belle, both on pointe; and Ziegfeld's Century Girl, the last revue of the season, trumped the others with "Waldorf Dryginsky and the Ballets Looses." Audiences who themselves resembled Pavlova, Isadora, Vernon Castle, or Irene in matters of dress passed on alternate evenings from the serious to the burlesque, which were now hard to tell apart. Theodore Kosloff, formerly under Gertrude Hoffman's umbrella, was playing "two-a-day" vaudeville with Vera Maslova and assorted

Russian dancers in a piece called "Ecstasie d'Amour" (at the opening, three dancers were discovered center stage covered by a scarf), and Gertrude Hoffman herself had returned to vaudeville in one of her serious burlesques, this time of Max Reinhardt's *Sumurun*.

By now American culture had weathered nearly eight years of exotic dancing. Style after dance style had appeared at the forefront of the new urban sophistication, especially on the East Coast. In those pre-war years, New York was taking its place as a culture center with its own New World elegance—ragtime and tango, Ziegfeld revues, Rector's (the restaurant), and Murray's Egyptian Palace—plus a wide range of gorgeous imported entertainment. But what did dance mean to the rest of the country by then? Had the tours of the Salomés, Loie Fuller, Isadora, Pavlova, Ruth St. Denis, the Castles, Denishawn, and the Ballets Russes penetrated the imaginations of average Americans? Could the ideals of smaller cities and towns absorb the exotica, or were most Americans still stubbornly rejecting it?

By 1916 dance meant something very substantial to Americans, but it wasn't theatrical dance; rather, it was a countercurrent, closer to the health and exercise spirit of the Ralstoners, of Theodore Roosevelt, of the eugenicists and the old dress reformers. Most Americans, when it came to dance, still clung to the vague, unexamined Greek statue styles that had first inspired Ted Shawn. To this way of thinking, dance was an important but indefinable presence—not an art, not a profession, but a cloudy idea. There were no terms in ordinary language to discuss it. But physical-culture enthusiasts—the women who made their families take the fresh air, the men who did exercises—connected artistic dance to an ideal state of the body and therefore of the soul: to the way a soul might look if photographed in heaven. Dance was part of the nostalgia of this time, part of its pastoral longings, part of that impulse to find a freer, simpler relation to the physical world in the midst of overwhelming rush to industrialize. And a mythological-type dance was pictured not only in people's minds but in the popular graphics they saw around them—in drawings, posters, cartoons, rotogravure photos, and moving pictures.

The pervasiveness of dance images in the teens is partly traceable to the work of American art-photographers around the turn of the century and after, who explored dance qualities. In 1903, the German-American photographer Alfred Stieglitz began his revolutionary art publication *Camera Work*, and in 1905 he founded Gallery 291, at

291 Fifth Avenue. Both magazine and gallery became the nucleus for a group of photographers working in the Pictorial mode—so named because of the soft-focus, "painterly" atmosphere of their pictures and the allegorical or symbolist subject matter. Over the next ten years, many of these men and women used dancers in their pictures, both known ones and amateurs, to convey a spirit intrinsic to their idea of photography—a spirit of motion, mystery, and veiled sensuality, a fascination with the human figure and new ways of perceiving it in a space. Arnold Genthe was the most prolific dance photographer; he recorded Isadora Duncan and her students, Pavlova, Denishawn, even smaller "classic" schools and companies (the Noyes School, the Marion Morgan Dancers); Baron Adolf de Meyer took the splendid light-etched photographs of Nijinsky and the Ballets Russes in Europe and continued to photograph that company, Denishawn, and other dancers after he came to America in 1914; in addition, Edward Steichen, Edward Weston, Anne Brigman, George Seeley, Clarence White—all made pictures of dancers.

The Pictorialists' dance photographs do not differ markedly from the rest of their work. Dancers were ideal subjects because they came equipped with a gestural precision desirable in any subject—the dancer had the power to enhance the life, the mobility, that was being captured raw on the photographer's plate. To photographers, dance represented the essence of their own modern aesthetic—their new understanding of motion as an environment. All of the Pictorialists' work can be said to be about motion—and stillness. Most of these artists were infatuated with light and moving surfaces, with buoyant space, with textures and subtle tones. And most used the human figure in an ideal state of nudity or aesthetic dress to depict the life-element in the composition. Of course they borrowed ideas of poses from the Impressionists, from Japanese prints, from Whistler, Sargent, and the Pre-Raphaelites. But their best work also reveals a shared understanding of gesture, an innate sense of the body's rhythms. Clarence White, for instance, created a coherent and spare vision of life in his small home town of Newark, Ohio, through his arrangements of the serene, sometimes dour women in his photos, alone or in pairs, with unexpected excesses of light on their skins and their surroundings. White could capture the peak of a twisting motion in one of his (usually female) subjects, or direct a source of light exactly to the emotional axis of exposed back or chestbone, or upturned face. He also collaborated with Edward Steichen on a series of nudes, some torsos, in close-up, each one expressive of a subtle, whole-body gesture.

At the same time, Anne Brigman in California was posing thin nudes in atmospheric landscapes to create a kinetic exchange between figure and Nature. Almost all of the Pictorialists delighted in pagan themes— "The Pipes of Pan," "The Hamadryads"—human figures emerging from a dappled surrounding, or receding into it, humans reposing in a rich world of shifting texture and chiaroscuro.

While the Pictorialists did not create a new artistic style for the world, their work did reflect key modes in the dream life of this country. Perhaps because photography was a pioneer art without obligations to America's artistic reputation, photographers were freer than painters to draw on popular obsessions—the most compelling of which was health reform. The physical self-consciousness of the age gave artists a license to imagine the visual ideal for human figures. In America, all modern artists—not just photographers—were supposed to be fighting stodgy bourgeois thought, just as health reformers fought sedentary bodies and meat-and-potatoes habits. Reformers' convictions about the body's need of light and moving air found a visual equivalent in the work of most photographers and some painters. What better vehicle than the human figure to express this spirit of the new? Robert Henri, the painter, was fond of saying that every American should be compelled by law to stand up nude in a public square one hour per year: that would correct the country's aesthetics. The proof that most of the photographers felt aesthetically connected to the health movement can be found in the themes in their photographs that also appear in physical culture and Delsarte manuals of the time. One of Clarence White's pictures—"What Shall I Say?"—shows a young girl reposing at a desk, holding a pen, and leaning slightly away from her empty writing paper, exactly like a standard vignette (found in Delsarte and oratory manuals) for school and church pageants. Amateur photographers depended much more than a professional like White on these formulas, and "What Shall I Say"'s (a convenient study, with light, desk, and white-gowned girl symbolizing that ideal state of reverie) appeared widely in amateur shows and photography publications.

Critics of the time rejoiced that photography was teaching ordinary people about composition in painting—and extending Americans' working definition of what art was. Artistic photographs were not only viewed like paintings, they were produced by thousands of amateurs with portable Kodaks (invented in 1888), who belonged to camera clubs all around the country, who tramped through woods and fields looking for aesthetic settings, who persuaded their families to get up at four in the morning to pose nude or draped in the dawn light. This kind of process was not the deluxe art-collecting of Stanford White and the 1890s gentlemen, but rather an active way of perceiving one's own world—even if the perceiving took a sentimental and artificial form, as in the pictures from a 1909 *Photography Annual* entitled: "The Joy of Youth," "What Shall I Say?" "Sun & Shadow," "The Wood Faëry," "The Return of the Prodigal," "Enchantment," "Sea and Sky," "My Sunshine."

Of course, the pictures with people in them required meaningful arrangements of the sitters, and discussions about posing were carried on endlessly in photography publications. One catalogue told the reader that "the sudden suspension of motion which is so admirably seen in statues is yet another means of obtaining animation in the model—as in the well-known photograph 'A Daughter of Niobe.'" It is sentences like these, buried in the most matter-of-fact contexts, that suggest the presence of a very broad popular understanding of gesture, pose, and momentum at this time—an understanding beyond the vague utopian hopes of the health reformers, perhaps a hold-over of the precise Delsarte discipline which equated gestures and states of mind. The thought about photographic posing recalls critic HTP's insight into Pavlova's art in a Boston *Evening Transcript* review of 1915: "She gave the impression of fluid motion arrested for an instant to expand in static beauty."

If there was such an implicit sense of physical, almost pantomimic language in this country, it was never applied to the one area where its logic was needed: dance. Any natural responsiveness to the elements of dance—gesture, rhythm, the body in space and time—slipped away or coarsened as dance grew more fashionable. Exactly what went on three-dimensionally on a dance stage was rarely talked over, since to most Americans "classic" dance now looked very much like pictures, photographs, of itself. Dance to most Americans then was a look, a style, not an art of motion. The look was either praised or condemned, depending on who was seeing it, since dance was caught up in larger questions within the culture. When the critic Hutchins Hapgood attacked a conservative colleague in the pages of *Camera Work*, he used a celebrated child dancer, little Virginia Myers, as his emblem of an endangered life force. He gave no clue about what she did while dancing; he merely wanted to warn his readers that in America, that life force in this little dancer would soon be crushed by "uninspired authority." Actually, by the teens the life force had escaped and multiplied in its unanalyzed state. Even though the original Pictorialists' enthusiasm had died by then and new and vigorous Abstractionists (Paul Strand, Paul Haviland) had brought a harder, clearer look to photography, soft-focus nostalgic photography survived in practically all popular magazine graphics. In 1916 *Vanity Fair* was running monthly aesthetic-dance-photography features; one, a spread of little Virginia Myers; another, a series of shadowy pictures of Isadora Duncan's makeshift school in Rye, New York; another a photo essay called "The Toy Balloon as an Aid to Terpsichore," in which dancers posed with translucent spheres that symbolized light. The sight of such idealized dancer-creatures cavorting in light and air was now so satisfying to everyone that it was slightly clichéd. Frederick Lewis Allen caught that note in his 1915 *Vanity Fair* sketch about "schools of rhythm, hygiene, physical culture and correlated arts prancing among the sand dunes." He wrote about posing his wife in a chilly dawn on the rocks at the beach. He told her to "lash herself about" and "express the rhythm of the waves," so he could make a picture called either "Andromeda Unbound" or "Narcissus, A Study," and sell it.

By the time Denishawn opened again in the summer of 1916, idyllic dance was such a constant presence that prosperous families in the West and Midwest could think of sending their daughters away to learn to look like that. The school was reputed to be a series of Pictorial photos come to life—and in fact a Denishawn feature appeared that summer in the Sunday rotogravure section of several cities' newspapers: pictures of Shawn in leopard skin, St. Denis and the girls in filmy things, posed on a wet and rocky beach as "The Sea-King and His Captors," "Discovering the Drowned Sailor," "Mocking the Spirit of the Storm." Other pictures, pamphlets, announcements, and descriptions emphasized the idyll of the setting: soft-focus California with its coasts, its mountains, its eucalyptus trees (which already called up aesthetic dance visions). Girls who could not venture into the ragtime dens of New York or Chicago had this alternative; they could learn grace, health, and self-expression at Denishawn without endangering their morals. Here was the true School of Rhythm, Hygiene, Physical Culture, and Correlated Arts; here was the feminine version of the Strenuous Life; here a dress reformer's dream—with school uniforms consisting of flesh-colored silk-jersey bathing tunics called "fleshings." "Is not a girl privileged to receive her training in such a paradise—this aesthetic school surrounded by bowers of vines and shrubs?" said one letter to a Los Angeles newspaper.

Besides the training, Denishawn's second summer offered participation in a grand project: the first open-air dance pageant in the massive Hearst Greek amphitheatre of Berkeley, California, on July 29, 1916. To direct a school in Los Angeles, then stage a pageant in San Francisco, then re-stage it in San Diego and again in Long Beach, required masterful organizing and publicity skills. Shawn had them. A newspaper advertisement announced the event at Shrine Auditorium, in Long Beach, September 1916:

> Ruth St. Denis, Ted Shawn & Co. of 100 dancers in the most gorgeous and magnificent dance pageant ever produced, depicting the life and afterlife of Egypt, Greece and India during the mythological period.
>
> Three tremendous features: 100 trained exponents of ancient Terpsichorean art. A specially constructed stage and stage-setting of ancient, elaborate, luxurious magnificence. A specially selected and trained orchestra of over 40 pieces. Perfect in detail and technicality. Absolutely correct historically. Wonderful in beauty of design and construction. Instructive from every point of view.

The pageant *was* a glorious construction with vast fluctuations of scale built in. At the very opening, fifty girls in green veils symbolizing the Nile River poured down the ramp, spread over the stage and out, leaving two tiny figures dressed in rough cloth and turbans—Ruth St. Denis and Ted Shawn—to begin the pageant with a plastique duet, "Tillers of the Soil." Afterward, the rise of Egypt was presented in gorgeous, populous scenes of armies and court divertissements; Egypt's fall was symbolized by the Queen staggering under her yoke; and finally Egypt's soul was judged in the Hall of Judgment. The scene then shifted to ancient Greece and a triptych of Grecian ladies at toilette, youths studying philosophy, and in the center, dancers with musical instruments. After a Pyrrhic dance and a Bacchic feast which became "an orgy and a complete abasement," according to one newspaper, the story of Orpheus and Eurydice was unfolded in the gloomy kingdom of Hades. The third and final Indian section offered scenes of daily life by the Ganges River, a widow's rite of suttee on her husband's funeral pyre, her transformation after death into the inevitable nautch girl, cobra-snake charmer, and then the yogi—which led to the finale, a vision of Nirvana. Reviews waxed eloquent about the colors: blue-clad Egyptian judges against other figures' black and yellow wings; Ruth St. Denis' Greek Spring Dance in a gauzy, rose-colored costume; the spots of topaz, yellow, and bronze among the crowds by the Ganges.

The Denishawn School and pageant owed their success that summer of 1916 to their timeliness: they were not unique, but the apotheosis of something countrywide. For a brief time in the mid-teens the country was "masque-mad and pageant-crazy." Every community had its small or large open-air "classic" dance school, which produced the pageants in parks, on lawns, on football fields. The Noyes School of Rhythmic Expression, for example, begun in Boston and New York, started branch schools in many parts of the country to spread the teachings of its founder, Florence Fleming Noyes, a former small-time actress, like Ruth St. Denis, with some extra physical-culture training. The Noyes School had aims like Denishawn's: "To approach the student through his elemental nature, correcting perverted ideals and clearing the way for natural growth . . . so that Art becomes the centre of education where it is dedicated to the service of practical living."

But Denishawn, unlike those other schools, meant its Art to serve not merely practical living but show business too. The Denishawn pageant outclassed all other pageants because it shrewdly blended modern exotic allure and old-time guaranteed entertainment. Its modern features were its hot and vibrant colors à la Léon Bakst and Paul Poiret, its musical tone-wash score on the Strauss model (written by a German composer, Walter Meyrowitz), and its Fokine confetti-like crowds of extras. But it also harked back to early Ruth St. Denis, to Belasco and his crowd scenes, and even further back to the Palisades Park *Egypt Through the Centuries* that had so thrilled Ruth as a child. The Denishawn pageant's main raison d'être was its traditional American grand scale—the biggest, the richest, the most exotic, the most daring orgy of theatrical sensations assembled for the edification of the curious. This pageant was not Ted Shawn's or even Ruth St. Denis' artistic statement; it was Denishawn's bid for ultimate popularity, it was an all-purpose entertainment product. In fact, it was designed to be dismantled and condensed for a fall and winter vaudeville tour. The pageant was also designed to be a publicity machine for the Denishawn School—and it succeeded. Each of the "100 trained exponents" of Terpsichore was a girl from a community somewhere in America, many were socially prominent in that community, and the society pages of newspapers always printed the adventurous doings of home-town daughters. Denishawn and dancing were news. A number of the young ladies who participated in the pageant were specialists in this sort of thing: a Miss Doris Hazlett sought at Denishawn "another phase in the art of interpretation" that she had encountered at a drama school in San Francisco, pursued at the Noyes School in Boston, and re-discovered at Denishawn, which had become, in one short year, the dance Mecca of America.

At any other interpretive school, Doris Hazlett would have learned deportment, then returned to her mid-America town. At Denishawn she had the chance to go on. Denishawn's real achievement was not its commercial success but the consistent training which that permitted. Inside the idyllic mist with which Shawn had purposely surrounded his school, he began, however haphazardly, to put down roots in America for acknowledged dance techniques. He wanted to acquaint his students with whatever body of knowledge was implied by The Dance—even though he didn't really grasp it himself. A Denishawn student was required to read widely in dance history, hear arts lectures, learn an aesthetic craft (such as photography), besides attending a daily dance class, practicing an hour, and occasionally working alone with Miss St. Denis—so that dance was now enshrined in a sort of academy, albeit a confused academy, which continued to pay lip service to an unacademic idea of free impulse. This was Shawn's credo, stated in the May 1916 New York *Dramatic Mirror*:

> We propose to gather the techniques of all types, Greek, ballet, Oriental, national; to have on hand all sorts of fabrics, all sorts of colors. We will have music in variety. . . . By assembling the techniques of all the world's dance, the pupil will naturally gravitate to his own.

This natural-drift theory of training—which still echoed Mary Perry King's slow-motion statue theories—was Ted Shawn's conscientious attempt to answer the Russians. Their "arduous and irksome requirements," said a Denishawn pamphlet, did not suit the present spirit of American youth. If Denishawn was to be a truly American school, thought Shawn, it must avoid the "imitation" part of learning that stifled individuals. However, with more and more techniques function-tioning in the classroom, Ted Shawn's theories and the school's practice inevitably began to diverge somewhat. Dance training, which requires a sort of imitation, was happening there.

At the end of its second summer, new staff kept the Denishawn school going while Shawn, St. Denis, and a company of eleven crossed and re-crossed the country again on a thirty-six-week Orpheum tour featuring its famous pageant in miniature. Meanwhile, new professional material was being produced at the school, dancers who would raise the performance level on the country's dance stages, and one or two who would become choreographers. To start with, Denishawn represented the possibility to perform. If the Salomés, goddesses, Greeks, and Russians on the concert and vaudeville circuits had failed to stir the entire public, they had touched a few girls and even some boys with a whole and magical vision of dance. For every group of young socialites in pursuit of the fashionable "interpretive art," there was one young person who came to Denishawn to become what he or she had seen on the stage. Denishawn was actually two schools with two different ideals—amateur versus professional, life versus theater.

But as the school grew, its professional activities began to draw more and more on its amateur population. The lower-priced vaudeville circuits were clamoring for more aesthetic dance; silent movies were demanding young people with dance training—and Denishawn was right in the middle of the activity. The California of Pan and the Hamadryads was becoming the California of Hollywood and movies. Both Denishawn and Hollywood were magnets to a kind of young American dreaming person who craved exotica. In 1916, a war was going on in Europe, and America was about to enter in. But Los Angeles, from the other direction, was sending its own compelling signals into the atmosphere. Denishawn—Hollywood—moving pictures—dancing—it was all mixed up together in a vision of new and monumental glamour.

CHAPTER 8
Hollywood

The story of American movies is miraculous enough to be told again and again. In the late nineties Thomas Edison invented a camera that captured motion; movie peep shows appeared at carnivals and expositions; working-class people began to crowd the urban storefronts to see one-reelers; the rest of the population scorned the movies and the dark little places where they were shown. Meanwhile the small film studios in New York off to one side and unobserved were turning out thousands of shorts and inventing story-telling techniques, so that when the movies as an industry emerged into the light—literally, since by the mid-teens half the studios were moving to southern California—they constituted a whole new branch of theater. They commanded a language of their own that both recalled and transformed the theater. They stretched theatrical perspectives to vast distances and shrank them to astonishing intimacies. And they gave birth to a new kind of silent, pantomimic, rhythmic acting, an art that was as new as dancing.

Popular theater, though, was the first source of movies, as it was of dance. This happened naturally: the trick shots of trains, horses, dancers, and other things that moved were expanded just so people would have reason to sit longer, and the theater provided the plots. Directors and actors were recruited from vaudeville and epic drama. America had no art-theater, so the movies took over the kind of popular theater everyone knew, the melodramatic plots, realistic characters, and swift action. In a sense, movies prolonged the life of the nineteenth-century theater, yet at the same time they took it forward, streamlined, expanded, modernized it. All the elements of the stage were re-thought in screen terms, and in the absence of sound, new visual details were found to tell the story.

Just how were the timing, space, and gestures of the stage transformed into their movie equivalents? What other elements were absorbed into movie language? These processes have never been thoroughly examined—but there are clues, one of them the evolution of "classic" dance. Dance, a new art in this country, accomplished the same thing as movies: it fused inherited theatrical gestures plus other kinds of behavior into a new, wordless, plastic language. Both arts in America stood at the frontier of theater; they were the equivalent in this country of Europe's New Theater with its re-discovery of poetry, pantomime, and the play of space and light on the stage. The theories of Gordon Craig on stagecraft, Constantin Stanislavsky on acting, and Maurice Maeterlinck on theatrical fantasy influenced American

movies and filtered into American dance. But American pioneers of
both movies and dance worked from instincts more than from theories.
Both film and dance in America were built on their creators' deep
sense of rhythmic continuity, and their feel for how theater could be
enriched by other impulses in America—the obsession with Nature,
the Delsarte fad, even ragtime. It was natural for movies and "classic"
dance to resemble each other, for they were new at the same time: Isadora Duncan first danced to serious music around 1901; Edwin Porter
filmed the first close-up in *The Great Train Robbery* in 1903; Ruth
St. Denis conceived *Radha* in 1905; in 1908 D. W. Griffith made his
first movie at the Biograph Studios. Both arts caught on at a rapid
rate; by the early teens neither could be called a gimmick any longer,
even by people who mistrusted them.

In California in the teens, dance and movies were especially close.
They looked alike; they favored the same antique costumes and
mannerisms, and they shared some performers. Both arts, condemned
for a long time as lower-class and vulgar, began with an openness, an
"anything is possible" air—something like the euphoria that marked
the experiments of the inventor-wizards of the time: Thomas Edison,
Alexander Graham Bell, Luther Burbank. It was clear to everyone:
movies were part of that day's technological miracles.

Dance was technology too, a re-thinking of the human anatomy
in terms of modern rhythms. This was not generally realized in the
United States until Martha Graham began to use boldly mechanistic
language in the twenties. Ruth St. Denis, out of vagueness in her basic
self-perception, never spoke about dance technique; Isadora Duncan
refrained from direct technical language because she believed metaphor and rhapsody should be the language of an art.

The great early movie directors spoke in metaphor too—they
said motion on the screen should be like the wind in the grasses or
the waves on the ocean—but they also talked about klieg lights and
filters and dollies and pans. This country's dance had no language of
craft, it had no French vocabulary like ballet or any sort of terms—
which was probably one cause of the different fates of American
movies and dancing. Movies in the teens in fact almost swallowed
dance up—but that was also the result of the artists' attitudes in each
of these media. The directors, actors, and cameramen who shaped the
first films—people like D. W. Griffith, Charlie Chaplin, Mack Sennett,
Mary Pickford, Billy Bitzer—were constantly fascinated by the elements of composition: how the camera could move, what a face in

close-up could say, how the lighting could change a scene, how an army could sweep across the screen. Any borrowing from dogmas, other arts, or the New Theater took second place to the urgency of the basic material of movies.

In dance, Ruth St. Denis was just as fascinated by the new expressive range of her body, her stage persona, her sets, and her lighting—the material of theatrical dance. But then she gave way to Ted Shawn—and he was only a borrower of dogmas and artistic pretentions. His visions of dances sprang from his opinions and commercial instincts rather than from the elements of his art.

In Hollywood in the mid-teens, Ted Shawn offered up dance to the movies. He was not the only one: the two other Los Angeles schools of dancing, Theodore Kosloff's ballet school (he was Gertrude Hoffman's Russian leading man) and the Celeste School of Ernest Belcher (he was a dance mime from London music halls) fed movies in a similar way. No dance school managed to get across a systematic idea of dancing, a coherent body of information to be built upon; and Shawn perhaps failed most of all, since he claimed Denishawn was the American equivalent of the Russian Ballet. Diaghilev's Ballets Russes was discovering new facets of the dance medium with every new production; Denishawn, though it made such productions, offered classes in every style, gave scenes to movies, established nothing as the core of American dance.

Movies on the other hand did gather together a coherent body of common expertise. Directors watched each other and learned. Under the guise of the old theatrical plots, the leftover Victorian morals, the exaggerated tenderness and cruelty of the characters, movies evolved a modern, fluid, movement-conscious, and peculiarly American language. It included dancing. Dance scenes in movies could control rhythm and pace, and allude to emblematic modern states of mind: the restlessness of ragtime, the serenity of "classic" dance, the pagan splendor of the danse Orientale. The usefulness of dance in silent movies guaranteed it a place in the nation's consciousness, but took away its identity. Movies made dance a presence, a mood, instead of a choreographic art with rules. The blame lay as much with certain movie directors as with Shawn and his dancer colleagues, directors with a brilliant feel for motion who used dance to their own ends. Dancing to them was distilled action, pure motion, the essence of that excitement which made the movies absolutely new and caused fevers in the mass audience.

. . .

The giant of silent film was D. W. Griffith, a stage actor who came to the Biograph Studios in 1908 for extra money, was given a script to shoot, and soon revealed himself, for reasons no one quite understood, the ideal person to take over directing the studio's several one-reelers a week. His imagination flowered in this new medium, he tried out techniques just barely invented, and he seemed to understand on the spot what new strategies could intensify the drama: close-ups, cuts within a scene, expressive lighting, characters' foreground and background movement instead of flat stagelike entrances and exits from the sides of the screen. Of course, American theater of those days was anything but flat—David Belasco and his colleagues had generated astonishing amounts of motion within the proscenium's boundaries: using actors, scenery, crowds, and massive music and lighting effects.

Griffith brought all that theatrical weaponry to the movies—as Ruth St. Denis did to dance. Griffith had toured with Nance O'Neil and Julia Marlowe, played Shakespeare and melodrama, and written a play himself; he understood rhythms like Belasco's and Belasco's staging: his private dramas played out against the movement of the crowd. But Griffith also brought some extra-theatrical concerns to movies similar to those the first dancers brought to their art. He loved literature as Isadora Duncan did, especially the Romantic poets Tennyson, Keats, Poe—and most of all he loved Walt Whitman. Griffith was a Whitmanesque soul like Isadora: he thrived on fresh air, action, and love of his fellow man, alias his audience. Like Whitman and like Isadora, Griffith's convictions were wedded to his physical self—his gusts of feeling determined the form of this new art of movies without previous guidelines from inside it. He made his art out of his senses and his deepest convictions, as they had theirs. On the screen he translated the passion of a story, the élan, into a cadenced flow just as Whitman had poured his physicality into the vicissitudes of words and Isadora had shaped her body around the dynamics of music.

The American health and open-air movement of the time supported this experimental physicality; Griffith's own senses had been educated by it. He was a physical-culture man; he believed in Theodore Roosevelt's idea of fitness and in exercise fetishes. He could have been a Ralstoner with his theories—"a man should sweat at least once a day to stay healthy," he liked to say. Obviously Griffith's American delight in health and Nature fed his visual sense just as it had Isadora's and that of such Pictorial photographers as Edward Steichen, Clarence White, Anne Brigman. Griffith reproduced their effects, whether consciously or unconsciously, in his films. He was the one who took the movies out of the studios into the outdoors where there was light and air. He filmed his actors in woods, in meadows; he caught the light on grasses and aureoles of light in girls' hair. In 1910 he was one of the first directors to try out California as a location, and there he discovered desert weather; he plunged his actors into high winds and sandstorms, capturing the resonance for his age of a human figure in Nature, which photographers and dancers also understood. On the other hand Griffith was just as richly aware of rooms, closed spaces, corners, closets, and all interiors; these two extremes of environment marked his breadth as an artist of motion and space, of the changing symbolism of space, the stylization of space around an actor.

His grasp of space shows up in a film like *The Avenging Conscience* (1915), the story of a young man (Henry Walthall) struggling between love for a girl (Blanche Sweet) and a desire to kill his uncle who opposes the match. The scenes between the young man and his uncle are pictured in one closed and darkened office while the scenes with the girl happen outdoors in fields, by streams, on paths by flower hedges; Griffith even poses the two against archaic stone benches and fountains—the domain of the "classic" dance. The characters' states of mind are portrayed through the indoor and outdoor landscapes around them. And when the story of the movie ends happily (the murder was all a dream) Griffith summarizes in a little coda of dancing, with children in Greek garb peeking out from trees like cherubimic hamadryads, and one little boy dressed as Pan playing the pipes.

Griffith's relation to dance went beyond shared imagery; he had a keen sense of it as both a theatrical and a social art and of the place it played in people's lives. Dance scenes appear in many of the 400-odd shorts he made for the Biograph company from 1908 to 1913. Also in these early films he began to invent his characters' pantomimic language, which for the girls included impromptu dancing and . skipping about. Some of his shorts took dance as a main subject and examined its human repercussions—something newspapers and novels of the time loved to do. *Oil and Water* (1912) starred Blanche Sweet as a dancer torn between career and home, and showed a dance performance which reminded the critic Vachel Lindsay of Isadora Duncan. Also in 1912, Griffith decided he needed a resident dance expert, so he lured a young dancer, Gertrude Bambrick, away from Gertrude Hoffman's Ballets Russes spectacle when it came through Los Angeles. Miss Bambrick's first task on joining Griffith was to teach *him* to dance, and ragtime dancing became his favorite recreation. Next she was put to work on the dance scenes in *The Mothering Heart* (1912): "If nothing else it will teach café managers in the interior how to run a café," said Griffith. She had a bigger project in 1912. In the four-reel feature *Judith of Bethulia*, she led the Assyrian dancing girls in two long Orientale dances she had arranged.

Judith of Bethulia, released in 1913, was the very first American feature film, and a landmark. Although Griffith had known the script of the popular stage play by Thomas Bailey Aldrich, he mounted his *Judith* completely in film terms—with the help of dance. The actors were the ensemble of very young people who had now worked with Griffith for four years and absorbed his monumental vision of what silent acting could mean: "We've gone beyond Babel, beyond words," he told them. "We've found a universal language—a power that can make men brothers and end war forever. Remember that. Remember that when you stand in front of a camera."

Griffith, often accused of anachronisms and of being mired in the nineteenth century, did depend mostly on old theatrical plots. But he knew more clearly than Belasco or any theater director that those old stories were parables, and within their bounds he changed the medium of acting into a craft that was as stylized as dance, and as different as dance was from old-style stage acting. Moreover, Griffith knew *how* his style of acting was different; he saw that actors who came to him from the theater used "quick broad gestures," whereas he wanted them to find a slower, more musical motion. He was trying to develop "realism" in pictures and "the values of deliberation and repose." Realism to Griffith meant abolishing the static, pompous individual acting of bad theater in favor of lifelikeness, continuity, and the surprising rhythms of human emotions. He had a vision of ensemble acting like that of the new schools of European theater, of Eleonora Duse's company or the Moscow Art Theater.

Griffith's *Judith of Bethulia* was the first completely American version of this new theatrical style—American because in the very progression of gestures it mixed the humble, the grand, the comic, and because its characters maintained a kind of fond distance from this material. None of the actors was really grown up; their gestures seemed like play-acting and so lightened the tragic legend of Judith of the Bible, who must kill the Persian king, Holofernes, to save her people. All the acting was a collage of current attitudes: some theatrical gestures, plus Salomé-dancing, Delsarte-posing, Ballets Russes impersonations, along with the latest fashionable mannerisms. The mixture made it American.

Judith (Blanche Sweet) prays to her Hebrew god, or anoints herself with ashes in the grand manner of Sarah Bernhardt or Mrs. Leslie Carter, yet she is so young the gestures look softened and not so serious—playful. In the seduction scene, wearing a shimmering sheath and peacock feathers, Judith rounds a shoulder and edges out of the tent like any young lady at a Tango Tea. Blanche Sweet's Judith is a keen portrait of a young girl in a crisis trying on grown-up ways to move and act. All the characters are "playing" with more serious and "artistic" models. Opposite her Henry Walthall plays a sensuous king on the Ballets Russes model, while his eunuch, an actor named Jaquel Lanot, is madly miming the attitudes of a Russian Ballet slave, just like Mikhail Mordkin, Theodore or Alexis Kosloff (or Nijinsky, who hadn't yet been seen in America) in *Schéhérazade*. Lanot's favorite pose, or Griffith's, is a decorative one of listening, with head cocked, foot pointed back, arms thrust down, and palms flexed.

And in among the pantomime close-ups we see several ensemble scenes of Assyrian dancing led by Gertrude Bambrick—an orgy of Salomé-Radha snake-charmer motions. The mime and the dancing blend rhythmically with the story's narrative sweep—the martial Persians in chariots galloping through the dust toward the doomed Bethulia, the weakened Bethulians crowding the city streets in a plea for water. Dance and mime marked pauses in the narrative and provided just the "deliberation and repose" Griffith was after. Moreover, the dancing rituals thickened the atmosphere, and the dancelike clothing, Biblical drapes, and Persian finery commented perfectly on the new fluid manners and costumes that were part of modern-day society.

Most of Griffith's feature films after *Judith* included a social dance scene or a glimpse of theater dance in the course of the story. And impromptu dancing was more than ever a keynote of his girl-characters' self-revelations to their audience. His actresses found ways of "dancing" for every part—even the fussy heroine of *True Heart Susie* (1920), played by Lillian Gish, skips about jerkily to show her happiness. Dance training was crucial to Griffith's whole idea of acting—and in fact, most of his actresses were dancers already. Blanche Sweet, born in 1896, came to Biograph in 1908 from Gertrude Hoffman's company of dancers, although she had begun in straight theater at age four with Chauncey Olcott and then turned to dance. Miss Sweet still considered herself a dancer in those first years of movies, sometimes taking time off from Griffith to tour with Gertrude Hoffman—and since Blanche Sweet appeared both in Hoffman's first burlesque of Salomé and the "Spring Song" and in the first Biograph shorts, that means she was present at the American births of both dance and movies.

The other early actresses brought similar dancing-acting experience from a theater that expected all of its players, even the youngest children, to be physically agile, to sing, dance, speak monologues, and play to the ensemble. The Gish girls, Lillian and Dorothy, born in 1896 and 1898, danced Highland flings in Sarah Bernhardt's company and danced, sang, spoke, whatever was required, in many other companies. Mary Pickford, born in 1893, was a child ingenue on the touring circuit for ten years, then starred in David Belasco's *The Warrens of Virginia* on Broadway just before she came to Griffith.

Mae Marsh, born in 1895, was the only one of Griffith's first actresses who didn't come from the theater but learned everything from Griffith himself. But Mae Marsh was the one who in 1921 wrote a book on film acting which reveals just how close were the dynamics of early dance and movies. She talks in the book about finding "character business," fresh ways to sit, walk, gesture, dance, that will reveal the essence of the role. She discusses the constant rhythmic awareness of silent screen actors; how close-ups, for instance, were played with more pause and restraint than the more numerous three-quarter shots. These concerns are part of all good acting, but they were the core of early film art—and also the kind of dance that was invented here. To find new rhythmic gestures for character roles was Ruth St. Denis' motive when she made up *Radha* and *The Cobras*, and it would remain the motive for the modern dancers who followed her. Miss Ruth, like Mae Marsh, was also a specialist in slowing down; by taking direct control of the pace inside of her own body she had made herself into a close-up of a Belasco play. Dance and movies, using different emphases, different equipment, but the same skills, were exploring theatrical time and theatrical behavior at the same moment.

. . .

In terms of the movies' growth, 1915 was the perfect time for Ruth St. Denis to arrive in Los Angeles with a dance school. D. W. Griffith responded to Denishawn's arrival by sending seven of his actresses including the Gish sisters over for lessons twice a week (said the New York *Dramatic Mirror*, May 13, 1916), and the connection between the school and Griffith's studio grew. Griffith himself went to watch Denishawn classes; that is where he first saw the young Carol Dempster, who became his star of the late teens and twenties. Meanwhile, other studios besides Griffith's made good use of Denishawn. The movies, which in ten years had become America's fifth-largest industry, boasted a new young population who had found their occupation almost by chance. Training routines didn't exist—after all, the first movie players hadn't ever seen a movie when they began to act in them. A theater background was usually a help, but it could also get in the way. Dance was thought to be the better preparation: "A good dancer frequently makes a good screen actor," said director Rex Ingram (about Rudolfo di Valentino, fresh from New York's ballrooms). "Why? Because he has both poise and repose and I don't know any better start than there." For this reason Denishawn was a key institution in Los Angeles, in the way Ted Shawn had dreamed of in 1910 when he first set up shop in that city. Now, finally, his school was vital to the movie world and to movie actors' training. Denishawn advertised special classes in the photoplay magazines, proposing to teach "the science of the human body as an expressive instrument." The ads of 1916 claimed that Denishawn produced dances "especially created to film well" and cited the stars who had already studied at the school:

Lillian & Dorothy	Bessie Eyton
Gish	Blanche Sweet
Signe Auen	Vivian Martin
Mary Alden	Mae Murray
Roszika Dolly	Louise Huff
Ina Claire	Gladys Brockwell
Mabel Normand	Florence Vidor
Enid Markey	Ann Little
Louise Glaum	Carmel Myers

Marjorie Daw   Virginia Corbin
and   and
the little Fox kiddies,   Gertie Messenger

Denishawn was fully mobilized for the first time in spring, 1916, when D. W. Griffith created his epic *Intolerance* about four different civilizations, and populated Babylon, the most magnificent of these, with festive, Fokine-like crowds. Griffith's Babylon represented the kind of ritualistic culture that all art and fashion adored in those years, especially American fashion, which was trying to shake off the stylistic traces of the Puritans. In Babylon, dancing was part of life; dancing was in fact the focus of the movie's most awesome scene— the long pan down the gigantic Babylonian steps where rows of dancers were celebrating the city's victory with hieroglyphic motions. Most of the dancers were Denishawners, although some were pick-up youngsters recruited to swell the ranks. Ruth St. Denis and Shawn coached the scenes; Griffith's Gertrude Bambrick led the performers on the screen.

It is striking how closely Griffith's Babylon matched the look of Orientale discovered simultaneously in America by such figures as Ruth St. Denis and in Europe by people like Paul Poiret, and echoed and elaborated by Gertrude Hoffman in vaudeville and by the various Russian dancers on the concert stage. Babylon with its great towers also prefigured the mammoth Manhattan skyline of the twenties, and the gorgeous air of revelry that took over that city in its heyday. However, if Griffith's visual sense was modern and cosmopolitan in tone, his view of dancing was American, like Ted Shawn's. He valued dance not for its choreographic patterns but for the rhythmic and sensual mood it evoked on the screen, a mood that carried an un- bearable freshness for Americans. To his vast dance sequences Griffith added close-ups in *Intolerance* of the "Babylonian Virgins of the Sacred Fire"; these emerged as a kind of adagio movement to the whole. According to history, certain Babylonian girls gave themselves ritualistically to men who came to the Temple of Ishtar to worship; they were pictured in *Intolerance* in beautiful slow-motion shots, sculpted in light and shadow and incense smoke.

The wonderful vivacity of the whole Babylonian episode arose from Griffith's profound imaginative belief in his own metaphor. That these Virgins really had existed was important to him, but his Virgins were clearly American girls dressed up in antique array, meeting the camera with unobstructed innocence and sweetness. This appeal matched Denishawn's; the pseudo-antique ceremonies served as frame for the revelation of the grave good will, the clean and unknowing sensuality, of the American girl. The Sacred Virgin sequences gave the audience repose in a bath of atmosphere and a long satisfying exchange with the performers, a precious glimpse of their inner beings, intimate but not pornographic. Lillian Gish described Griffith's intentions in her 1969 book *The Movies, Mr. Griffith and Me:*

> Mr. Griffith wanted to show these young Virgins in costumes that would be seductive yet in no way offensive. All the young girls were dressed in floating chiffons and photographed in motion, not dancing but moving rhythmically and sensually to music. Some of the scenes were shot through veiling or fountain sprays to add to the erotic yet poetic effect.

Intolerance, though it wasn't as popular as Griffith's famous 1915 epic, *Birth of a Nation,* highlighted an era of grand antique spectacles whose premieres in big cities cost two dollars a seat—as much as theater openings. All of these, movies like Thomas Ince's *Civilization,* Cecil B. DeMille's *Joan the Woman* (with Geraldine Farrar), and Fox Studio's *Daughter of the Gods* (starring Annette Kellerman), included scenes of dancing girls and dancing orgies. They corresponded to the live pageants that seized the country's imagination at the same time—of which Denishawn's 1916 *Egypt, Greece and India* was the prime example. In the same way that Denishawn's pageant echoed the spectacle-extravaganzas of the 1890s, movie spectacles also called forth old theatrical grandeur. The Vamp, for instance, was film's rediscovery of the grand actress, for whom a full spectacle was required. Movie vamps were the heirs of Sarah Bernhardt and Mrs. Carter; Theda Bara at Fox in 1916–1917 remade a number of these actresses' star roles for the screen— *Cleopatra, Under Two Flags* (a Belasco hit of 1902), *Camille, Du Barry.* Louise Glaum was the Vamp at Triangle Studios; she played in *The Idolators,* and for *Sex* (1917), she borrowed a peacock costume from Ruth St. Denis. *Sex* was one of the many spectacles that featured scenes with Denishawn dancers. (Some others were: *The Lily and the Rose,* 1915; *The Victoria Cross,* 1916; *A Little Princess, Conscience, The Legion of Death, Joan the Woman, Cleopatra,* all in 1917; *Hidden Pearls, Wild Youth, Bound in Morocco,* 1918; *Pettigrew's Girls* and *Backstage,* 1919.)

Denishawn had a special relationship with several of the casting offices—notably the Lasky Studio's, where Cecil B. DeMille was director. DeMille's obsessions with flashing back from modern to barbaric times (in *Male and Female*, 1919; *Adam's Rib*, 1920; *Manslaughter*, 1920, to name a few) provided work for dancers from Denishawn and from Kosloff's and Belcher's schools. Girls from the schools would appear at the studio, singly, in pairs, or in groups when a call came for dancers. They would work for the day and receive their five or ten dollars for a solo. Among these schools Denishawn, perhaps because it said it was a way of life and not just a school, and because it had Ruth St. Denis, was the best known throughout the country. Not only did movie actresses come to it, it sent several girls into movie careers: notably Carol Dempster, the baby of the first Denishawn touring company. Margaret Loomis, also a performing Denishawner, became a Lasky Studio leading lady who starred opposite the Japanese hero Sessue Hayakawa in films like *The Beggar Prince,* as well as in the films *The Bottle Imp, Money Money Money, Turn to the Right, The Brat* (with Alla Nazimova), *The Fighting Chance, The Sins of St. Anthony.*

Denishawn belonged both inside and outside this new Hollywood world, which, viewed by normal America, was a dangerous society of young people living like modern-day pagans—and the majority of them were girls. Girls shared houses, four to a house. Unchaperoned, they went to beaches; they went out driving with young men. If they couldn't find work as actresses or extras they learned editing, casting, costuming, but the dream was always to act. Runaway girls were not a new phenomenon in America, but in those years there were thousands of them heading for Hollywood. *Photoplay* magazine wrote articles warning them to bring money to live on, a year's worth at least, and not to hope. Denishawn drew girls too, but it promised, at least on paper, seclusion, some chaperonage, and the beneficial pursuit of Art. Denishawn was an institution valued in Hollywood because serious movie people longed for just this kind of respectability. Not only did Denishawn stand for order, decorum, and traditional girlhood, it was an artistic beacon in the midst of the movies' supposedly unbridled rush to vulgarity. Denishawn became useful in official Hollywood's constant campaign to prove its respectability to the rest of the country, a desire that found full expression in the years of World War I.

. . .

No community contributed as many patriotic gestures as Hollywood. Nowhere were more events staged to benefit the Red Cross, save the French Orphans, bolster Our Boys overseas—and Denishawn was a front-line participant along with the movies' most conscientious souls. Ted Shawn became an officer at nearby Camp Kearney, from where he supervised the school's activities while cutting a dashing figure in his uniform. (He also gave dance lessons to enlisted men and effulgent interviews to newspapers about the dancing armies of ancient Greece: "Terpsichore more Deadly than Mars" ran a typical Shawn interview headline.) At Camp Kearney, Denishawn girls entertained the soldiers; so did movie actresses. Mary Pickford, Charlie Chaplin, and other stars went on stump tours to sell Liberty Bonds; so did Ruth St. Denis. In Hollywood, Denishawn girls mingled in the parades and tableaux with the young movie starlets; in 1918, for instance, at a "Society Circus" on Douglas Fairbanks' fifteen-acre estate, St. Denis and the girls of her Red Cross Auxiliary led off an afternoon that finished with a boxing match between Fairbanks and Charlie Chaplin—"four rounds, for blood." Among the Lasky Studio events of 1918 was a "Folks at Home" benefit carnival with the following program:

> Clara Kimball Young in a feature act
> Vesta Vestoff in a modern dance
> The Mack Sennett Girls performing a stunt in conventional
>   (for them) attire
> Fatty Arbuckle in a "Swat the Kaiser" number
> The Denishawn Dancers in a Hawaiian release, "Wigglesville"

At another occasion St. Denis presented her Japanese sketch *O-Mika* right before a "Sweetheart of the Allies" gala—a Ziegfeld-style display of solo movie stars each costumed as an Allied country, with Mary Pickford bringing up the rear as a radiant and inevitable "America's Sweetheart."

Mary Pickford, the small valiant person with the Botticelli face, who from 1910 to 1930 defined the financial and spiritual parameters of stardom and practically invented a female acting style for her generation, became in the war years Hollywood's first citizen and patriot. Besides her countless Liberty Bond tours across the country, she galvanized Los Angeles itself with public appearances at charity teas and luncheons, by knitting parties for soldiers' socks, etc. She and her husband, Douglas Fairbanks, were thoroughly aware of their roles as informal ambassadors of the film industry, and of the dignified behavior expected of them in wartime. The "Debutante's Letter" of October 1918 in the Los Angeles *Times* reports:

> Miss Eleanor Martin, San Francisco's grande dame, has at last succumbed, at least tentatively, to the charms of the picture queens. When Mary Pickford poured tea at a Red Cross benefit up there, Miss Martin actually graced the event, but she stayed only a few minutes and was gently non-committal.

What is astonishing in this scene of Mary Pickford confronting the social lioness is that Mary, who was indeed earning $350,000 a picture by 1919 and had joined D. W. Griffith, Charlie Chaplin, and her husband Fairbanks to form United Artists, was only twenty-five years old. Most of her colleagues, veterans of the pre-Hollywood one- and two-reelers, were even younger. Of course older directors, producers, financial wizards, and mothers lived in Hollywood, but its featured population was strikingly young.

This suggests another reason why Denishawn was so favored by the Hollywood elite—Ruth St. Denis, its figurehead, provided a link for the young actresses and for the whole industry to its theatrical origins. She was a beloved figure in Hollywood. There was always some question about whether movie people were part of the old entertainment brotherhood, but here was Ruth St. Denis among them, a trouper in the old style, almost a dowager entertainer. She reminded the young movie people of the salty actresses of their childhood touring days, outrageous personae of ethereal glamour and earthy humor. Lillian Gish remembers she was in awe of Miss Ruth, of her peacocks (gifts of Ted Shawn), her sultry wide-brimmed hats, and her incongruous put-on Irish brogue. Miss Ruth never abandoned her taste for off-the-cuff vaudeville quips, which she dispensed along with her elegant poses and inspirational lectures on The Dance. Around 1918–1919 she publicly began to recall her theatrical origins "right next to the soil." "I started out doing seven performances a day in a Museum which exhibited queer things preserved in alcohol—I'm proud of it too," she told a reporter from the New York *Dramatic Mirror* (March 15, 1919). Her easy informality with audiences had grown; she knew exactly what to do, even with an audience of soldiers who didn't understand irony in dance recitals. A report from Camp Kearney, August 1918:

> She danced at night, and from the trees hundreds of lanterns swung, that flung over her the kind of light that goes with dreams. She came creeping through the grass in a flaming, filmy red slip of a costume, with her hair swathed in a red bandeau for the Hindu Snake dance, and appreciation of Art in its most seductive form ran riot in our thoughts. But—when she did a grotesque, ragtime impromptu dance that would have brought roars of laughter if George M. or one of the Ziegfeld girls had done it, no one laughed. She tried it once, she tried it twice then she complained right out loud to her audience; "Oh dear, I never can make anyone laugh. I'd just like to do something funny once." Such a charming, commonplace, plaintive little remark made everyone smile.

In 1919 Miss Ruth was forty years old. She was one of the inventors of "atmosphere" in dance and in movies—the atmosphere that had brought the whole American theater so much further into fluidity and exoticism. Newspapers all over the country were constantly spreading rumors that Ruth St. Denis had agreed to appear in this or that feature film; but she never did make a movie in those first years in Los Angeles (her only movie project on her own was to direct the dance scenes in Rupert Hughes's *The Bitterness of Sweets*). Her abstinence was probably the result of a sound theatrical instinct. That she would actually go on performing for another forty years did not change her status in Hollywood. There she was a senior performer. And she was revered as such not only by the young actresses who took lessons from her but also by the young Denishawn dancers who were beginning their own solo careers. To them especially, Ruth St. Denis had served as inspiration, as goddess; probably most of the Denishawn girls were there because they had once seen her *Radha* in their local concert hall or vaudeville theater.

By the end of the war there were little Ruth St. Denises all over, not just in amateur pageants but on Broadway, on vaudeville stages, all through the movies. Ted Shawn had manufactured many of them through the Denishawn "individual diagnosis" system that gave away, or rather sold, Nautches and Cobras and O-Mikas right and left, according to the personality of the young dancer. The Denishawn style had infiltrated all kinds of new theater displays and seemingly dissolved into them. But the Denishawn institution was meanwhile producing the dancers of the next generation, a different kind of girl with a different relation to theater. Some of these girls would find the way to take dance back into its own realm, and teach it again how to speak in its own language.

PART III

MARTHA GRAHAM

CHAPTER 9
California Children

What happened at Denishawn from the beginning prefigured what happened all over America in the twenties: absolutely ordinary middle-class girls became performers, in theater, movies, and dance. Of the Denishawn students who joined the first touring company of 1915, almost all came from backgrounds the opposite of Miss Ruth's and Isadora Duncan's. They didn't dance to earn a living; they didn't dance to defy conventions—dancing was there; they simply took the imaginative leap from lessons to a career (at least a temporary one).

California itself inspired its girls to enter show business: their own state represented daring, fluidity, undress in movies, and in dance they themselves were the ideal—even in vaudeville, even on Broadway far away from home. "Terpsichore is becoming the patron saint of Los Angeles," said the Los Angeles *Examiner* as early as June 1917, citing five big California dance acts in vaudeville, all but one on the top Orpheum Circuit: Theodore Kosloff's school had produced a troupe; a former teacher of gym and aesthetic drills had started the Marion Morgan Dancers; another aesthetic type named Helen Moeller directed an act; Brother St. Denis (who had helped manage his sister) had split from her and Shawn with *his* group of "Denishawn Dancers" in addition to the regular, very popular Denishawn Dancers of Denishawn. The companies were made of students just barely turned professional, so quickly had the demand arisen for this kind of dancing. Most of Shawn's and St. Denis' first performers were California girls, the kind who wouldn't have come near the theater if they hadn't lived right next door to it. Florence Andrews, for instance, went to Denishawn from her Los Angeles high school at age sixteen against her family's wishes; later she took the name Florence O'Denishawn to keep her banker-father's name untainted. (As Florence O'Denishawn she went on to star in the Ziegfeld Follies of 1921—a stroke of publicity that must have pleased Ted Shawn.) Margaret Loomis' father owned the elegant Hotel Angelus where Shawn had once demonstrated the tango; when Shawn reappeared in California with St. Denis and a school, Margaret gave up her debutante life to join him. On the first Denishawn tour, Miss Loomis declined money from her family and refused the invitations along the way from her father's hotel-owner colleagues, just to experience life on a showgirl's meager salary. In 1916 the Los Angeles *Times* reported she was writing a book on the subject. (Instead of finishing the book she became a Lasky Studio movie star.)

Something had happened to American girls to make them fall in love with the idea of performing—and dance, theater, and movie production had so burgeoned that performing was possible for them to do. The urge to run away to the theater was probably kin to young Americans' longing for low life that was creating in New York a Greenwich Village. But it changed the nature of acting and entertainment. Twenty years before in the 1890s ballet girls and chorines were, socially speaking, unclean creatures of another race. Now class lines were blurred; the girl on the screen or even in vaudeville could be the girl next door. There was little Mary Hay, for instance, daughter of a brigadier general, who haunted Denishawn and D. W. Griffith in the *Intolerance* era; Griffith told her to go get some experience with Flo Ziegfeld, and she emerged a comic ingenue of the 1919 Follies ("a pug-nosed youngster who dances like a doll, daughter of a General"); then she married screen actor Richard Barthelmess and played small movie parts. Marion Davies, the youngest, most devilish member of a well-to-do Irish family in New York, left home to be a Ziegfeld dancer and then a star of the silent screen.

Earlier these girls would have dragged their families off to Europe, like Daisy Miller in Henry James's novel, or to summer resorts; now they escaped alone to movies or dance, where their natural audacity was valued. In California the second wave of ingenues who followed the seasoned Pickfords, Gishes, et al. was mostly made of girls from absolutely non-theatrical milieux who had apprenticed on their own by imitating all the movies they saw. A division happened in one generation; Americans born in the 1890s saw no movies until they were almost grown; those born after 1900 saw movies once, twice, three times a week. The movies featured young actors—for the simple reason that only young faces stayed fresh under the harsh klieg lights used on movie sets. Therefore millions of very young Americans saw themselves as protagonists; that is probably one of the reasons they took things into their own hands in the teens and twenties and created the Era of Flaming Youth. Their field of vision had been drastically enlarged.

Colleen Moore was a girl like thousands of girls in America, the daughter of a Tampa, Florida, businessman; she was wild about the movies and desperately wished to be in Hollywood—until in 1917 a political connection of her uncle's actually got her a contract with Griffith's studio. Arriving in Hollywood at age fifteen with her grandmother in tow, she discovered that four of the six young ingenues on the lot were "payoffs" like herself. Of course they lasted only if they were smart and willing to work—but by 1917 there was something clear to work for, a style, a persona, a craft of performing. Colleen Moore became one of the outstanding soubrettes of the time (and one of those who came to Denishawn for extra training). What she had missed in theatrical experience she had absorbed by watching countless movies with ingenue heroines. It was a measure of D. W. Griffith's genius that he had created a girl character so easy to imitate, a modern version of that earlier elemental American heroine, the singing and dancing Lotta Crabtree, trouper of the Gold Coast, who left a string of progeny behind her all through vaudeville, theater, musicals, movies (Eva Tanguay, Minnie Maddern Fiske, Elsie Janis, Mary Pickford, Dorothy Gish, Constance Talmadge)—girls who projected this country's special qualities of health and high spirits and rhythmic wit. Of course a host of other characters young and old abounded in movies then, but the ingenue was always there; even the great silent comics, Chaplin, Keaton, and Harold Lloyd played to an ingenue co-star. By the time Colleen Moore was installed in Hollywood, in the late teens, the ingenue had become such a stock character that directors could issue formula commands to any lively girl: "Get that 'Poppa, what is beer?' look on your face!" they would shout, quoting from an old vaudeville skit about a father and a baby in a bar.

Ruth St. Denis herself was a descendant of the ingenue-soubrette, tempered with equal parts of the grand actress and the operatic diva. Now, though, the extreme youth of the new Denishawners who inherited her roles put the dancer squarely back with the ingenue—especially since some movie ingenues wore costumes of barbaric finery just like dancers. Performing conventions in dance were now as strong as in movies, and the second wave of Denishawn girls, like movie actresses, could come from anywhere and pick these up. They were sent by gym teachers who saw their talent, by dancing teachers who themselves had graduated from Denishawn, by benefactors who spotted them in charity performances. Or they came themselves from middle America; willful daughters of bankers and lawyers, they brought full wardrobes in trunks—and sometimes their mothers.

If they stayed on they could find work no matter what class they came from, because dancers were needed in movie scenes, in vaudeville, in the splendid live prologues in new movie palaces. It was not origins but competence that counted, quick reflexes and a will to deliver oneself to the rhythms of a scene or the pace of a dance. In the movies the ingenue would last another two generations, because the movies kept on entertaining their audience. New, wittier versions of her appeared in the twenties—the splendid Clara Bow, Marion Davies, Janet Gaynor, Bessie Love—and in the thirties she became the screwball comedienne. But dance was at a point where the Art would begin to disdain the Entertainment, and the ingenue was challenged to her very bones. It was none other than Ruth St. Denis who decided dancing must leave vaudeville and become pure; and it was a Denishawn student, Martha Graham, different from the other girls who came there, who began to transform the ingenue into something else, something more humbly serving of the dance. By the end of the twenties Martha Graham would abolish the dancing ingenue altogether.

Ruth St. Denis and Isadora Duncan had in their separate ways begun a tradition; neither had matched up physically or psychically with the kinds of dancing that went on in their time, so they had each imagined a new kind. Now Martha Graham didn't fit into Denishawn, although she stayed and worked there a long time. The convictions she brought from her pre-Denishawn life—which were different ones entirely from Ruth St. Denis'—plus her very different body, eventually caused things around her to shift a good deal before she left Denishawn and California. Martha Graham came from a tradition of vigorous thought; she arrived in dance already educated in literary values and mental coherence. Moreover, physically she was not the American Greek goddess disguised in Orientale, nor was she an ingenue-coquette. She was a California girl who didn't look like one. She was small, with a long torso, short legs, and a longish, serious face—and she was completely grown up. When she first got to Denishawn for a summer course in 1916, she was twenty-two, nearer in age to Mary Pickford and the senior actresses than to the Denishawn company and the second-generation movie ingenues in their teens.

Nothing in her background pointed Martha Graham to theater; she was the least likely person to bloom at Denishawn except for certain hidden qualities: a fanatic ambition, an immense personal vanity, and the kind of mind that could grasp the *forms* of dance or of any art. This last trait in Martha Graham is a difficult one to trace back—difficult in anyone's history. Perhaps it comes of a childhood where everything makes hierarchical sense. In Allegheny, Pennsylvania, where Martha Graham grew up, she belonged to that closed, upper-middle-class world that contains itself in school, church, and family. Perhaps she would have stayed in it if the Grahams hadn't moved to California in 1908, to Santa Barbara, an ideal climate for the asthma condition of the second daughter, Mary. All three Graham girls were well bred and dutiful in Allegheny; so were they too in Santa

Barbara, except that the oldest, Martha, age fourteen, experienced California as a sudden expansion of space and light. She remembers running and running on a cliff above the Pacific. The weather had a clarity, the evenings were light with a hint of desert; the town boasted magnificent oak groves, old Spanish missions, and the sea. And if the environment was new, so was the social system. In Allegheny, Martha Graham could always be placed in a design of cousins, grandparents, family; she in turn could place anyone in the town by sight. In Santa Barbara very few families had such roots: pioneering and restlessness were closer to the surface of everyone's story; nearly every family was uprooted.

The Grahams set down impressive surface roots in their new town. They bought a fine wooden house on De La Vina, one of the main streets, and lived well in it, even though Dr. George Greenfield Graham, a dedicated psychiatrist in the pre-Freudian tradition, stayed in Pennsylvania with his private practice and visited his family only on long vacations. The Grahams were much respected within the society around the Santa Barbara High School; the parents volunteered at school events; Martha was a top student and acted as chairman or editor of various enterprises. Gradually, though, the unique character of the region began to impinge on this small, guarded, "purposeful" eldest daughter. Santa Barbara was really two towns, one ordinary and one elegant. There were lots of things to dream about for the ordinary citizens. All around in the hills and by the beach were the houses of the very rich who wintered in southern California—Carnegies, Rockefellers, Astors. The great Potter Hotel on the beach with its Palm Room and fine ragtime bands catered to those rich people. As if that wasn't diversion enough, in 1910 a movie studio, The Flying A, moved into downtown with its seventy-five horses and its blond, Mary Pickford–like ingenue Mary Miles Minter (later notorious in the murder case of director William Desmond Taylor).

Movies were an inescapable part of almost all young Californians' lives, and the wave of movie enthusiasm hit just as Martha Graham was finishing high school. Her graduating class, in fact, voted to give a motion picture machine to the school as the class gift. To have moved to California at the precise time when movies became the common experience of everyone in the country meant that one had joined a chosen race just in time. Americans watched story after story set in California; Californians watched their own landscape made magical and their own history and legends turned into symbols. Old and new California were all mixed up together. Film after film celebrated Ra-

mona, Girl of the Missions, after the best-selling 1884 novel by Helen
Hunt Jackson, plus numbers of other Indian and Spanish maidens as
befitted the deserts and tropical vegetation of the background. In high
school Martha Graham adopted California's past for herself—a culture
older, sweeter, and yet more savage than Protestant America's. She
tried it out in at least one short story published in the school yearbook,
"Inez and the Wildflower," about a Spanish maiden, a villain, an old
woman, and a padre, told in the vigorous, high-literary language of
popular novels and silent movie titles: "Have ready the horses; tonight
I shall not fail!"

Martha Graham clearly harbored a theatrical streak in her nature,
but she didn't meet up with the workings of theater until Santa
Barbara High School, where one extraordinary firebrand teacher taught
English—Jane Carroll Byrd, red-haired and Irish. It was she who produced all the drama and oversaw the senior play, which in Martha's
year was *Prunella*, a light-hearted Symbolist comedy by Laurence
Housman and Granville Barker, two leaders of England's New Theater
movement.

Even though the play had charmed Broadway two years before
and would soon become a movie starring the very popular ingenue
Marguerite Clark, it was still a daring choice for a high school, since
it belonged to theater avant-garde. Its story was the one beloved of
that time, of the artist against the stodgy world. The heroine, Prunella,
a fanciful girl, is lured away, and rightly, from the home of her three
proper aunts by a quixotic Pierrot. Martha Graham played the part
of Privacy, one of the aunts. Ironic as it may seem in the light of her
later flamboyant roles on the dance stage, at this point Martha Graham
—in her graduation yearbook picture, a serious young lady with dark
eyes, hair drawn back in a madonna-like bun, a delicate long face composed above a smooth white collar—matched the character named Privacy, the "timid yet loving aunt." However, the importance of the
senior play to Martha Graham's story is not its retrospectively mistaken
casting of her but its introduction of barefoot "classic" dancing into
the school—interludes in the play staged by a high-school graduate
of the year before, Hope Weston, who had gone on to the Cumnock
School of Expression in Los Angeles. One can assume that it was in
rehearsals and in talks with Hope Weston that Martha Graham first
thought of dancing, though she might have caught the dream earlier
that same year when her father took her to see a performance of Ruth
St. Denis' in Los Angeles.

The serious, scholarly Martha Graham upset all expectations

about herself by entering the Cumnock School of Expression after high school, not Vassar, where her father had hoped to send her. Cumnock was artistic but a few shades more socially all right than Denishawn, because it contained nothing of show business; it was the oldest school of expression in the West, founded in 1893 "in the belief that art and life are one and the same thing." Between October 1913 when Martha Graham registered and June 1917 when she graduated, she took courses in literature and drama, art appreciation, physical training, and special work such as story telling. Her subjects in her final year were:

Literary Interpretation	Pedagogy
Private Work	Practice Teaching
Shakespeare	Voice
Robert Browning	History of Art
Dramatic Art	Physical Training
Public Speaking	

Such a program of learning set Martha Graham apart from almost everyone else at Denishawn, where she went to stay after finishing Cumnock. She had been inaugurated formally into the beauties of Art, Literature, and the Theater and had by-passed all the popular artistic and theatrical currents that had brought her predecessors to dance—Delsarte, dress reform, physical culture, melodrama, skirt dancing, Walt Whitman, David Belasco. In fact she had missed all of American popular culture, except what she might have absorbed in the movies. The elitest nature of her family and an education pretending to be European, like that of so many private academies in this country, had deprived her of instincts inherited by most American theater artists.

This was a drawback in dance, and yet through her disciplined education she was able to bring something to dance that no one in America had yet brought to it—a mind that could analyze the history of an art. This analytical gift was of no use at first at Denishawn, whose dances were constructed from instincts—Miss Ruth's imaginative ones and Ted Shawn's commercial—so Martha Graham just followed along for a time. Eventually in her best work she would combine the vigorous thinking she had learned young, with a dancer's instincts she worked hard to acquire, though in 1917 she was woefully lacking in these instincts and in the experience that brings them out. Here she was, a graduate of a school of expression, armed with many theories but no real experience in the theater. The proof of Martha Graham's intelligence is how unerringly she pursued the experience she needed and how thoroughly she identified herself with Denishawn's often shallow activities before she challenged them. One wonders not how Martha Graham would codify almost single-handedly the ungainly body of "classic" dance she inherited from Denishawn, but why it was dance she chose instead of drama or literature.

California is probably the answer; its unique native imagery, now amplified in movies, had claimed her for its own, and *it* saw an interpretive dancer as the most serious object of beauty in its culture. Martha Graham was a girl in a time and place that examined "The Girl" from every angle, in every costume, inside of every antique myth, through movies and through dancing. Her education at Cumnock may have pointed her to Europe and the East Coast; it may have ignored movies, which still carried the taint of lower-class entertainment in some circles, but it could not ignore dancing. Dance, thanks to Isadora Duncan, Gordon Craig, Serge Diaghilev, and the public-relations gifts of Ted Shawn, who connected himself with all of these others, had won its place in Theater, the New Theater that was increasingly part of America's anxious hopes to become a culture. Dance was where the serious European theater and the not-quite-serious California movie industry seemed to merge, although the serious part always got more credit. "Dance," said the self-conscious California-watchers in 1917, "has put Los Angeles on the artistic map," as if the movies had no claim to that. Martha Graham absorbed some of the lavish theatricality of movies through being a Californian, though consciously she belonged to a newer, narrower approach to Art among Americans. One assumes it was the unconscious, movie-formed California in her nature that responded to the theatrical part of Denishawn, and Denishawn gave her later dances their sure dramatic pace, if it failed to give them humor.

Martha Graham's "un-Denishawn" seriousness about dancing was bequeathed to her from two unlikely sources, her father and her nurse. Dr. Graham was an unusual alienist (the term of that day for a medical psychiatrist) who had trained himself to "read" his patients' physical behavior. "Movement never lies," he used to tell his daughter when she was young, and his pride in this facet of his professional skill stayed with her. One of Dr. Graham's former mental patients, an Irish-Catholic girl named Lizzie, came to live with the Grahams as nurse and governess when Martha was a baby and stayed all her life.

In addition to bestowing on the Graham girls all the tenderness and love that the conventional Mrs. Graham never quite offered, Lizzie must have taught the Presbyterian Martha about that other religion, about Catholic rituals and the Blessed Virgin. Possibly a half-conscious longing for these holy mysteries that weren't actually hers caused Martha's instant enchantment with Ruth St. Denis in the 1912 Los Angeles concert. At any rate these two opposite strains in her nature— the clear grasp of people's normal and abnormal physical actions from her father, the secret vicarious religious experience from her nurse who counted as mother—emerged in Martha Graham's mature dances. Now at Denishawn her initial seriousness about dancing increased after her glamorous and formidable father died in the summer of her first year at Cumnock; she would need to look hard at herself now since he wasn't there to see her.

Martha Graham's new self was a dancer, a result of Cumnock training and of a 1916 summer course at Denishawn. Her first newspaper review appeared in the Santa Barbara *News Press* on March 30, 1917, part of a description of Mrs. Robert McGowan's charity ball in wealthy Montecito:

> The artistic feature of the evening was a Santa Barbara girl, Martha Graham. She is a student at the Cumnock School and was a dancing pupil of Ruth St. Denis for a month last summer. In a Javanese dance she is lithe and graceful and her makeup was remarkably true to the type of the little brown women of Java. In her encore dance she posed as a woman of the East with a water jar, doing very deft work in the handling of her drapery. Her arm movements were particularly good . . . Mr. Lippett played for her numbers.

At Denishawn, where Martha Graham went to stay some time in the summer or fall of 1917, she would continue to study the techniques of Oriental dancing, the handling of drapery and the like. However, in her own eyes she was entering not a simple dancing school, not even a business linked to movies and vaudeville, but something grander, a domain of Art. Denishawn had managed to make itself the Artistic Salon of Los Angeles. It had moved to bigger quarters in the Eagle Rock suburb of that city. A lavish new home had been built for Miss Ruth and Shawn (which burned down shortly after it went up) and a special new theater for dance.

"It was just bound to come," said the Los Angeles *Times*, August 1917:

> a dance theater from whose classic shades will never resound the loud badinage and vulgar slapstick of the "vodvil" team, nor yet the nasal slang of George M. Cohan nor yet again the unaesthetic click of the motion picture projection machine.

An informal performance for an elite public was planned every week as well as a children's matinée. All sorts of luminaries were reputed to gather at Denishawn—painters, writers, composers, film celebrities, barons and baronesses, Swami Parmanader, Countess Sada Sckorska, plus all the dancers. Some artists even moved in; a young sculptor from Tacoma, Washington, Allan Clark, devised a studio on Denishawn's roof copied from the one in his favorite book, Rodin's autobiography. There the dancers walked about freely "while he caught their unconscious moments of grace" (Tacoma *Star*, April 21, 1918). It seemed Denishawn wanted to reproduce artistic conditions in *fin-de-siècle* Paris, while at the same time cheerfully providing chorines for movie scenes and wild ancient orgies. Only in Hollywood could an institution say it was both things—a haven for Art and a flourishing entertainment business—and be taken at its word.

As for the students inside, they saw the school as whatever they chose, according to the world they came from. A Denishawn girl like Ann Douglas had grown up in carnivals along the West Coast, where her father exhibited and lectured about a chimpanzee. While still a teenager in Oregon, she was chosen by her Denishawn-trained dancing teacher to replace a girl in a Denishawn vaudeville act. The act was passing through, the girl got sick, so young Miss Douglas joined up and came with the act to the school in Los Angeles. She stayed, although she felt free to come and go. Life was high-spirited, work was everywhere; she was tough, professional, young, and well-formed, and valuable to Shawn and St. Denis. Martha Graham on the other hand arrived as a student in awe of the institution Denishawn. The theatrical dance she studied there was not a natural part of her but rather a new religion with the school as its sacred center. As to dancing, Martha Graham took Miss Ruth at her word. An interview Martha gave while on tour in 1921 reveals her intense devotion to the Denishawn ideal and also her curious obsession about youthfulness, which remained throughout her career:

Women in their middle years find in the dance the spirit of youth which they had felt slipping away. You see when you enter Denishawn you seem to leave the whole busy worryful world behind, much as you would on entering a convent. . . . Everyone there has just one great passion, the passion to create beauty. The atmosphere is infectious. You simply can't stay in Denishawn and not catch that spirit. It is not like a treatment of an hour or two a day. It is there all the time. You live in it.

No matter what each student ultimately wanted from Denishawn, it is undeniable that there she could get a wider range of dance training than anywhere else in the country. The course catalogue for the summer of 1918, for example, announced the following curriculum:

Basic technical work building up a dance vocabulary.
Dramatic gesture based on the system of François Delsarte.
Oriental technique—East Indian, Arabic, Siamese, etc.—
     under the personal direction of Ruth St. Denis.
Egyptian and other hieratic dancing also by Miss St. Denis.
Ballet work by teachers trained in the French, Italian
     and Russian schools.
Greek dancing, nature and esthetic dancing.
Creative dancing, principles and practice.
Visualization of pure music themes, dancing Bach fugues
     and inventions.
Plastique movements—learning the decorative use of the
     body, the study of body line.
Piano lessons by Louis Horst, musical director.
French lessons included in each full summer course.
There is a Denishawn Red Cross Auxiliary where the girls
     learn to "do their bit."
Geisha dancing taught by a native Japanese lady formerly
     a geisha teacher in Tokio.
Lessons in craft-work—designing and making of costumes,
     jewelry, properties and decorative background.

One cannot tell certain crucial things from a printed curriculum: whether these myriad courses connected to each other in the students' minds and bodies; whether the "basic technical work" to build "a dance vocabulary" was a wise system or a haphazard one; and whether the ballet mentioned in the catalogue was sound or merely on the surface. Martha Graham has said she received very good ballet training at Denishawn. However, the only person listed as a ballet teacher in that summer course of 1918 was Doris Humphrey, a girl slightly younger than Martha Graham who had just come to Denishawn from Oak Park, Illinois, to study as well as teach. In the twenties Doris Humphrey became the other serious dancer and choreographer to rival Martha Graham, so it is useful to compare them as they arrived at Denishawn.

Doris Humphrey came from a world Martha Graham never knew, a world of child performers, like that of Ruth St. Denis. Born in 1895, Doris grew up in a Chicago hotel which her parents managed and was given lessons in every kind of dance that existed in Chicago: clog, character, ballroom, aesthetic, interpretive—and ballet, first from an older Viennese dancing mistress, then from Andreas Pavley and Serge Oukrainsky, two Russian dancer-teachers, even before they started their ballet school in association with the Chicago Opera. While Doris, the only child, was still a teenager, her father lost his job and so she went to work. In 1913, when Martha Graham was editing her high-school yearbook, Doris was dancing a potpourri of Spanish dances: a Yama Yama (a Broadway eccentric number), and such on the Santa Fe Railroad circuit (the same that got Ted Shawn to New York) with her mother as accompanist; while Martha was pursuing Art at Cumnock, Doris was teaching Oak Park's little girls in her own dancing school. Teaching took up a number of her best years, and Doris arrived at Denishawn in 1918, in the same senior age bracket as Martha Graham. She was noticed instantly (she was beautiful), recruited to teach, and also asked by Ruth St. Denis to join a vaudeville Liberty Bond tour going out in the fall—so she gave her Illinois school to another girl and stayed with Denishawn.

Martha Graham was not asked on that tour; she remained at the school and taught for Shawn, who was still in the army. At this point many of the other students didn't expect Martha Graham to be a performer. But there was minor performing work for all Denishawners in those last war years, 1918–1919: not on the road, but in charity shows, in movie scenes and movie prologues, in small separate vaudeville acts. Even Martha Graham reputedly appeared in a Cecil B. DeMille movie of 1919, *Male and Female*, as a mermaid draped on the shore of a desert island.

. . .

At the end of the war the basic configuration of Denishawn changed; Ruth St. Denis' and Ted Shawn's artistic differences finally emerged, and they split, dividing Denishawn's best dancers between them. St. Denis went off to experiment on the Art of Dance, taking Doris Humphrey and others with her; Shawn, when he got out of the army in December 1918, took over the vaudeville and movie end of the business and brought Denishawn to its peak years of activity. Among those he took along was his protégée Martha Graham.

Vaudeville opened its doors wide to aesthetic dance. A new circuit was born in the West, Pantages, which aimed to match the Orpheum Circuit's class and still undersell it. Alexander Pantages, a western entrepreneur, was ready to gamble on the masses' desire for aesthetics —and he gambled well. Denishawn was one of the first classy head-liners he signed on, for reasons made public in newspaper interviews on the occasion: Pantages paid three times as much as Keith of Or-pheum, his theaters were all new-built and clean, and his popular-priced tickets permitted a whole new part of the population to see dance. Maxwell Armfield, an English designer of the new wave, was hired at $3,500 weekly to make scenery in the opulent post-Art-Nouveau style of Ziegfeld's Joseph Urban. Armfield designed the Denishawn productions: five mammoth ones went out in the euphoric early Pantages years of 1919–1921, all very lucrative. The touring company of one of them, *Julnar of the Sea*, netted $1,200 a week with neither Shawn nor St. Denis along as soloists. It was typical of the kind of productions Shawn was turning out. The Pantages an-nouncement of the act said:

> A dozen capable men and women dance to the fanci-ful episodes of an Arabian fable, from the dream couch of a prince down to the depths of the sea and back again to earth, where the handsome heir to the throne traces Julnar to a slave market.

Julnar bloomed with a gorgeousness of fabric and décor: there were two complete sets, a pale misty under-the-sea scene and a full exotic market with village walls and palm trees. The star, Julnar (Lillian Powell), wore a cape of seed pearls hand-sewn together in myriad strands. Another Denishawn act was a patchwork production of various waltzes, nautches, and garlands plastiques, starring a Lillian Gish–like ingenue named Marjorie Peterson and a troupe of young dancers. For himself Shawn made a Bacchus ballet, *Les Mystères Dionysiaques*, to ballet music from Massenet operas. Shawn's earlier creation, *The Zodiac*, was apparently still in circulation, though it was not as popular as the others. The *Musical Courier,* however, found it gorgeous (August 4, 1921):

> [It opened] on a partially darkened stage upon which dimly, vague figures began to move, figures in deep blue against the heaven's blue, now becoming more distinct and beginning to scintillate as the light caught the hundreds of bugles which outlined their classic line; all turning rhythmically and in orbit around a central figure concealed by an immense veil covering the entire stage, the central figure also turning. They were the planets turning around our sun, which in the process of their turning unwrapped the figure in the center, lifting from him the great silken veil and revealing a golden youth with a golden orb above the head in a golden light. Day came, night descended broodingly, a lovely moon, a tiny comet. . . .

In 1920 Shawn made his most original vaudeville spectacle, *Xochitl* (pronounced Zō′ chel). He made it for himself and for Martha Graham, whose unusual qualities he had begun to notice; to show these off he departed from Arabian and Babylonian fables and turned to legends of the New World—in this case the Aztecs. This Latin American source was not a discovery of Shawn's: the movies had used it first when Cecil B. DeMille made his popular Inca drama of 1915, *The Woman God Forgot,* starring Geraldine Farrar and dancer Theodore Kosloff. Shawn's spectacle was an old melodrama spiced up in the DeMille manner—the story of a maiden, Xochitl, who dances, Salome-like, for an emperor, then fights him off as he, frenzied from the effects of the alcoholic brew from the maguey plant, advances upon her, whereupon she, "with the usual feminine inconsistency," begs her father to spare his life. The story may have been a movie imitation, but the production was innovative—Shawn's effort to achieve a unity of stage elements. According to the *Pacific Coast Musical Review,* the music for *Xochitl* was specially composed by Homer Grunn, an authority on "American aboriginal melodies," and the scenery and costumes were by Mexican artist Francisco Cornejo, the expert on ancient Aztec, Toltec, and Mayan art. Amid the growing fascination in America with theater's anthropomorphic roots, *Xochitl* was perceived as a breakthrough. It was everywhere hailed as the "first native American ballet" because of its décor and a powerful new dynamic in its dancing, to which the word "virile" was attached. "This virile feeling in *Xochitl*," said the Tacoma *Ledger*, "is carried out in the strong, close-to-the-ground movements which characterize it." The act played all over the West during 1920 and 1921—up and down the coast, north as far as Victoria and Vancouver and east as far as Toronto.

Xochitl was crucial to Martha Graham's whole career. During her three years at Denishawn she had not only trained her body but released some of the secret energy of her personality into dance movements—energy that might have been buried. This production gave her a chance to experiment night after night with dynamics—that link between the visible dance shapes and the dancer's inner passion. The story, conceived to show off her special gift for ferocity, was no mere ravishing tableau with a vamp at the center, but a vigorous action-drama mounting to a peak of frenzy in Xochitl's hand-to-hand defense of her purity.

In a curious way, *Xochitl* was a throwback to David Belasco's old extravaganzas with the physical feats highlighting the drama: Mrs. Leslie Carter swinging from the bell-rope (*The Heart of Maryland*, 1896). In the same curious way, Martha Graham resembled those grand old rampaging actresses even more than did Ruth St. Denis, who had imitated them directly. And yet, Graham was also proud of *Xochitl*'s modern aesthetics, its awareness of progressive design that looked forward to the Art Deco of the 1920s. Graham at twenty-seven was finding her voice in *Xochitl* just as St. Denis at twenty-eight had found hers in *Radha*; its drama suited her temperament; its visual boldness satisfied her restless imagination. "I love this dance-drama and have every faith in it; it has brought the joy of life to me," she told her home-town newspaper when *Xochitl* came through Santa Barbara (October 25, 1920, Santa Barbara *News Press*). Not only had *Xochitl* released Graham's powers in performance, it had shown her a future source for her choreography—not Greek myths, not idyllic ones at least, nor Asian rituals, but rhythms of her own land, the savage American earth. As the Russian choreographers of Diaghilev's Ballets Russes had re-discovered their people's earliest barbaric rites—Fokine in his Polovtsian Dances from *Prince Igor*, Nijinsky in his *Sacre du Printemps*—so Martha Graham would discover the land of the Southwest and its cruel implacable culture. This discovery would complete her vision of herself as a Californian, a western artist, but the seeds of this were sown with *Xochitl*.

Denishawn's triumphant vaudeville years were short-lived. While

Shawn was producing his spectacles, Miss Ruth was working along other, more virtuous lines, and eventually the thrust of her work took over Denishawn and edged it into High Art echelons as a concert group. Deprived of her original dance-drama territory by Ted Shawn, who had embellished it beyond recognition, Ruth St. Denis needed new ground of her own. In 1919 she announced her retirement from vaudeville. She turned her back on movies, on pageants, even on fabrics, and decided to go all the way with Dance as Art, following the half-acknowledged lead of Isadora Duncan. And indeed, Miss Ruth's natural rival and sister pioneer had reappeared in California in the winter of 1917–1918 to remind everyone by her silent example that dance was an art, not a lesser branch of movies and vaudeville.

Los Angeles saw Isadora Duncan in at least one concert in December 1917 at the Mason Opera House, accompanied by the six girls who had grown up in her school and were now teenage dancers. This direct dose of Isadora's mature art changed Miss Ruth's view of herself and of Denishawn. And for the younger dancers like Martha Graham, barely arrived at Denishawn, Isadora's art suddenly became something real, something they would have to know about and absorb into their own aspirations. On the program were movements from two of the big symphonic works as well as the stark, formal dances of mourning Isadora had made for her two children, who died in 1913 —Schubert's *Ave Maria* and his *Slow March*. The "chorus" of dancers in both these works wore long, trailing one-piece robes conceived by the visionary of English theater Gordon Craig (Isadora's lover and father of her child Deirdre)—columns of fabric that transformed the actor or dancer into a presence of light and mass and motion. In both dances the center figure, Isadora, mimed a monologue of grief and hope, framed by her dancers in stark lines or encircled by them, bent over in grief or in unison assailing heaven. Her own figure onstage was alive with the burden of pity and profound musicality that made certain women performers so loved by audiences then—women like Eleonora Duse and Ellen Terry in drama, Mary Garden in opera, and Anna Pavlova in ballet.

But Isadora in her maturity now understood something about dance beyond the performing of it; she had grasped principles of ensemble composition without losing her soloist's sense of buoyancy and lyricism. Duncan dances were still compiled of the few fluid gestures and patterns that the young Isadora had culled from Delsarte and character dancing—but these were now amplified by her younger dancers as corps and by a wider dynamic range. Now Isadora could highlight her own monumental plastique against her former youthful style, recaptured in these young girls she had trained. They played the chorus of angels in the *Ave Maria* and she the grieving human woman. This dance is a masterpiece of restraint; it is Duncan style distilled into a nearly primitive iconography, and it reveals Isadora's understanding of the way her basic material was transformed in the separate dynamic spirit of each dance. In this dance she smoothed all her buoyancy into a low, intense swell of momentum; while the violins generated more and more melody, the dancers simply twisted slowly in place, opening their arms flat in all the amplitude of fabric that hung straight from their wrists. The musical crescendos are accented by a step common to early Duncan dances, a small hop with the leg swung to the side, transformed now by the robed dancers into a weighted catch in the melody line, a rhythmic moment like a sob.

Not all the later dances were so stately and mournful. Using her girls, Isadora could still show all the Dionysiac joy of her youth. In the Schubert *C-Major Symphony* she created a finale for corps of girls without a soloist, presenting them as Diana's huntresses—an image that seems to well out of the galloping restlessness of the music's motifs. A "chariot" of girls enters from the back wing, one leading the rest in a V formation, and weaves gradually back and forth to the front of the stage, all the girls bent fiercely forward as they come, then bent back with arms trailing as the melody opens out. In the middle of the dance there is a strong section in which each girl alone leaps across the stage and strikes a heroic pose with an imaginary drawn bow; there is a circle of running girls at center stage who leap again and again into the air in unison, with Isadora's peculiar Bacchante leaps. All of this, transparent, simple, repetitious at times, is still stylistically whole and profoundly musical—as is any great choreography. Once the dance is known, one cannot hear the music without imagining the dancing; one cannot see the dance without hearing the music.

This concert struck at the heart of Ruth St. Denis' artistic conscience. Was the art of dance passing her by? Isadora here presented not only a whole new dimension in the art—the ensemble patterns America hadn't seen yet in her work—but the force of her solo presence, stirring all the rampant emotions of this country as it prepared to enter World War I. On that American tour Isadora always ended a concert with her famous *Marseillaise*, an exhortatory solo with red cloak, which called America to rescue the civilization that was France.

Ruth St. Denis' immediate response to Duncan's concert was to make a *Marseillaise*-like dance for herself in 1918, *The Spirit of Democracy* or *The Triumph of the Allies*, which she took on her first Liberty Bond tour. It wasn't quite like Isadora's musical rendition of the spirit of romantic French painting and sculpture; instead it was a more one-dimensional drama, according to a newspaper in Kansas City:

> The scene opens with the brooding Democracy seated on a throne. She lifts her eyes, sees the horizon and rises to try her strength. Suddenly her attention is drawn to a sinister object. . . . Democracy is staggered by its first on-slaught, but gathers herself together and calls her allies.

Miss Ruth in fact looked impressive if not Wagnerian in a white robe, with her hair, which had been prematurely white for years but always hidden under various Oriental wigs, streaming out behind her "like a plume on a warrior's helmet." After this solo Miss Ruth continued to ruminate on Isadora's art; one night she had a revelation about the future of dance in which she explained to herself why Isadora often stopped still on stage when the music grew particularly complex. She doesn't have the skill, Miss Ruth thought. With enough Denishawn dancers, perhaps she herself could represent all the instruments in a symphony orchestra in dance patterns. At the end of her 1919 Liberty Bond tour (a solo tour with Margaret Loomis assisting), Miss Ruth borrowed a number of Denishawners and took them off to work in a secluded studio. Here was born the idea of concert music visualization and the Ruth St. Denis Concert Dancers, a new troupe that went out in January 1920 for more than a year's tour of concert houses all over America. This tour would re-establish Ruth St. Denis as a serious artist of the dance and one capable of meeting Isadora on her own ground.

Unfortunately the Denishawn idea of music visualization was nothing like Isadora's profoundly musical constructs. True, these new dances did contrast with Shawn's baroque and seething vaudeville dramas—they were light and airy; the girls wore little Greek chitons, and "the stage was a bower of green, with only a statue or two to relieve with a dash of whiteness. . . ." Choreographically, though, they were mostly a regression to the youthful sentiments of Delsarte recital pieces. Of the forty-four rotating pieces in the concert repertory, most of them were new sketches to short piano pieces of serious composers, choreographed by Miss Ruth and Doris Humphrey. The sketches explored girlish themes: *Why?* a duet to Schumann; *Little Banjo*, a duet; *Jugleress*, a solo.

Even the large ensemble works such as Humphrey's and St. Denis' "Soaring" to Schumann's "Fantaisie Stücke" or the Beethoven "Sonata Pathétique" projected a distinct girlishness. These dances offered not images but picture-ideas about the music: when the piano bass notes of the Schumann piece approached a dissonant crescendo the girls mimed a thunderstorm, hiding under the big silken veil that was the central prop in the dance; when the music switched to the major key the girls came out from under the veil to greet the sun. The thundering motifs in the Beethoven caused one girl to turn traitor and pursue the others around the stage. The audiences were indeed seeing motion, responsibly crafted to fit the musical structures, but it was surface craft, nothing like Isadora's ensemble pieces wherein the ebb and flow of music became a river of dancing and flashed forth inevitable shapes and actions—images. Isadora's pieces had combined and re-combined the "words" of her vocabulary—the gentle leaps with lifted chest, the signal turns with one arm raised, the side "attitude" sweeps around, the call to comrades-in-arms—in works that varied tremendously in mood. Denishawn's dances on the other hand took any convenient shape or gesture and put it to the music, with no real instinct for internal coherence or a family of gestures.

Still, dancing as pure abstraction (without drama), dancing as ensemble patterns—these were Isadora's advanced concepts that lodged themselves here in the twenties through Denishawn's cruder efforts. The Ruth St. Denis Concert Dancers hit the country at a time when self-consciousness about Art reached a peak. Some communities had built municipal auditoriums; they were prepared to operate these at a loss so the people could hear good music, see serious drama and pure dance. And those cities and towns that welcomed the new Denishawn concert company were eminently reassured about the intentions of Dance: "The artist-pupils of the famous dancer propose to present pure dance," said the Hartford, Connecticut, *Times*.

> These girls know the value of regular exercise, simple food, plain dignified clothing, fresh air and sunshine. They are none of them corseted and they wear low-heeled shoes. They are wholesome, happy girls who read well and think intelligently and they are ideal American types, far from affectation, bad clothes, stupid habits of mind. If there were more of this kind, the world would be a much better place.

It seemed as if St. Denis was leading a willing new audience back to dress-reform visions of purity, to her mother's dreams of natural health, to the American-Delsarte ideal of clean emotions innocently communicated. A backlash against the movies, against the sheer material gorgeousness of film and vaudeville spectacles, had occurred in the interior of America, and Denishawn, with its sensitive commercial antennae, responded. Ted Shawn dropped his vaudeville work and followed Miss Ruth; his answer to her foray into Art was to go deeper into Religion.

When the *Xochitl* tour came home, Shawn put together *his* small concert company of himself, Martha Graham, and two younger dancers to do *his* concert tour. The new repertory of music visualizations, backed by the old exotic vignettes and a piece of *Xochitl,* transmitted Denishawn's Isadora-dancing direct to Martha Graham—she was given roles that purported to knit music and dance intimately together. But the showpiece of this tour was another vaudeville act in a new guise, Shawn's Church Service in Dance. Six years before, when Shawn first dared to dance a sermon, the newspapers met him with chortles of delight:

IF TED SHAWN DANCES A SERMON WE WON'T NEED
THE OLD PEPPERMINT LOZENGE TO KEEP AWAKE

Undaunted as always, Shawn had expanded his sermon into a complete Pre-Raphaelite spectacle, with solo Doxology, 23rd Psalm, Anthem ("alternate moods of hope and despair"), Andante Religioso (stirringly danced by Martha Graham), Jubilate, and the Sermon, "Ye Shall Know the Truth . . . ," in which Shawn appeared (according to the San Francisco *Call & Post*)

> . . . in a ragged shawl of vampirish red, mottled with splotches of rust-brown. He was so ragged, so unkempt with his curly Dutch-cut hair . . . he impersonated a tortured soul who toppled with a "sickening thud" to the floor at the dramatic climax.
>
> At the same moment from the wings came a white light such as was used throughout the dramatization of Ben Hur; Shawn pulled himself to his feet, inflated his chest and set free from ignorance, walked off the stage into the heart of the hidden calcium. . . .

Shawn's tour wound up in New York with a matinée at the Apollo, December 2, 1921. Here then, under Shawn's aegis, Martha Graham made her first New York appearance, dancing all the styles and genres that Denishawn had produced, her *Xochitl*, the "Andante Religioso," a lively "Juba" (in blackface), a fiery "Argentine Tango," a "Malaguena" with Shawn as partner, and a Chinese sketch of a maiden "whose only symbol of happiness was a branch of cherry blossoms" (*Musical Courier*, July 1921). New York to Martha Graham offered a radically different atmosphere from California; it was tough, it was staccato, it was unashamedly intellectual, it received plays and actors direct from Europe—it was, in short, everything she had been educated for. Martha Graham felt the change like a primal shift in the weather.

As the twenties got under way, the art of dance was cleft by an invisible dividing line. Things *seemed* to go on as before. Shawn rented a suite in the Chatsworth Apartments on West 72nd Street and instantly opened Denishawn East. Ruth St. Denis appeared in New York for a public show of solidarity. At a gala occasion at the Metropolitan Opera she presented a silver loving cup to Anna Pavlova, flanked on the stage by Otto Kahn the arts patron, Robert Henri the American painter, Roshanara the English-born Hindu dancer, Alexis Kosloff the Russian ballet émigré, Vestoff the modern ballroom dancer, Ruth Page the American ballerina, and Ted Shawn.

> Pavlova appeared in a modern gardenia crepe, white gown without a jewel or trimming anywhere, her dark hair banded madonna-style. Ruth St. Denis was stunning with her gray hair, dark evening gown in jade and wide black hat. "Only a dancer could understand how great were the achievements of Pavlova to whom America owes much for the inspiration of beauty she has given," said Ruth St. Denis as they embraced.

Here were the dance luminaries of the century's early years, the Russians who had brought fresh color and design and ballet technique to the world, the Americans who had made a dance genre out of visions of antique civilizations. Looking on were the younger dancers, their students, notably Martha Graham. These glittering exotic figures were her heritage, but New York was her future. It was a massive clump of new sights and noises, of jagged pace and bold new buildings. It was crazy and restless and luminous. Ragtime dancing, tap dancing, the specialty numbers in follies and revues—each of these styles reflected a bit of the raw power that lay under the surface of New York life. Denishawn dancing did not.

But it was Martha Graham who would forge from her Denishawn legacy the dance of a new urban world, a mechanized yet painfully alive America. She had learned what she could from the Denishawn enterprise: some theater from Shawn's vaudeville creations, some art from St. Denis' music visualizations—and from a distant Isadora the idea of a mind behind the dance structures. Even so, she stayed with Denishawn for two more years, through a southern tour, a season in London, and another endless cross-country concert tour in 1922–1923, honing her performance skills and gaining a reputation as a soloist. Somewhere along the way she lost her beloved *Xochitl* to Ruth St. Denis' senior claims—Miss Ruth danced it with a languid air.

But Martha Graham had seen New York, the outpost of America's own progressive new arts and the only city in America that understood what the Russians had made out of their ballet. That knowledge was necessary to the growth of dance. In April 1923 an offer came for her from John Murray Anderson, designer and impresario, to dance in his chic Broadway revue, the Greenwich Village Follies. So Martha Graham, once a California small-town girl, now a minor exotic solo dancer, threw in her lot with the city.

CHAPTER 10
The Twenties

artha Graham was familiar to her audience when she opened on Broadway in the Greenwich Village Follies in September 1923; some had seen her in Denishawn concerts, others knew her by reputation (a portrait of her had appeared in a 1921 issue of *Vanity Fair,* as part of that magazine's regular photographic spreads on The Dance), and everyone knew her genre, the California-Denishawn brand of interpretive dance. She was surrounded on other New York stages by Denishawners like her who had brought California style to the East: Marjorie Peterson, former Denishawn vaudevillian, had played the Greenwich Village Follies the year before and then moved to musical comedies; Florence O'Denishawn was starring in the Music Box Revue in a number called "The Fisherman's Dream"; Margaret Severn, a child in the 1916 Denishawn pageant, was featured in the Hippodrome vaudeville; Lillian Powell, former star of *Julnar of the Sea,* was working in movie-palace prologues.

.Most New York revues included at least one aesthetic-interpretive dance number—and there were a host of revues. The first of these glorified, spiced-up vaudeville shows, the Ziegfeld Follies, invented in 1907, was still the brightest and the biggest, and Florenz Ziegfeld was still the king, but Ziegfeld's Broadway competitors were close on his heels. Earl Carroll's Vanities, George White's Scandals, Irving Berlin's Music Box Revue, the Schubert Brothers' Passing Show and Artists and Models, John Murray Anderson's Greenwich Village Follies (named after its place of origin but thoroughly mid-town), the Negro revues Shuffle Along, Chocolate Dandies, Dixie to Broadway, special one-time shows designed for star performers, Murray Anderson's "Jack and Jill" for Clifton Webb and Ann Pennington, Ziegfeld's "Kid Boots" for Eddie Cantor, not to speak of the often very similar musical comedy shows, all bloomed on the Great White Way in the early twenties.

Each revue promised a distinctive aura: Artists and Models offered the briefest costumes; George White's Scandals the most dancing vitality—White was a former dancer; the Greenwich Village Follies was the most compact, streamlined, witty, and moderne of the group. John Murray Anderson, also a former dancer, now a dandy impresario, gifted designer, and follower of all the European ideas about modern stagecraft, was the first to use draperies and draw-curtains in a musical show rather than heavy scenery like wings and drops. His costumes were "arty" rather than just lavish; his showgirls, as he himself said, were "types, and not merely off the production line." Murray Anderson insisted on a kind of marriage between the popular and the aesthetic. He mingled vaudeville turns, skits, and popular songs in his Follies: in the 1921 edition in among the poetic vignettes he staged the song that came to represent the whole decade—"Three o'Clock in the Morning." In the 1922 Follies he unveiled a new kind of number, the "ballet ballad" (this one called "The Nightingale and the Rose," after Oscar Wilde), which starred former Denishawner Marjorie Peterson. His 1923 ballet ballad was "The Garden of Kama," inspired by the Indian love lyrics of Laurence Hope. It featured Martha Graham as the Dancing Girl, opposite a Tiller in the Garden, a Maharajee, and a White Peacock—all of whose movements were choreographed by the Japanese-born, Swiss-trained interpretive dancer Michio Ito. The·Garden of Kama attracted a fair amount of attention in a collage of other vignettes that ranged among an Artist's Studio (with the chorines playing Colors in the Paintbox), a New York Pier, a Dancing Room of a Central Park West Apartment, the Chamber of Edgar Allan Poe, a Greenwich Village Barnyard, and a Spanish Fiesta. Martha Graham, besides holding the feature spot in the Garden of Kama, contributed her Denishawn Spanish dances to the Fiesta.

The Greenwich Village Follies, for all its modern aura, was typical in its dancing—four or five kinds in one show: chorus numbers, popular dance exhibitions (ragtime and Charlestons), musical comedy numbers, ethnic and aesthetic-interpretive. By 1923 stage dancing in New York, in both the revues and the musical shows, had arranged itself in categories vaguely understood by audiences. Martha Graham's ballet ballad in the Denishawn manner belonged to the slot called "art dancing" or, loosely, "ballet." The divisions were partly determined by a highly successful New York showman-teacher, Ned Wayburn, the Ted Shawn of the East Coast, who from his factorylike school on West 58th Street turned out chorus girls and specialty dancers, touring dance units, live movie prologues, Broadway choreography, and reams of advice. (By the twenties there were several fine ballet teachers in New York, among them Luigi Albertieri, Ivan Tarasov, and Michel Fokine, but Ned Wayburn represented the prevailing American attitude about ballet.)

Wayburn's "ballet" included anything foreign or impressionistic: "Toe, Classical, Character, Interpretive, Oriental, Folk and National (Spanish, Russian, Greek, Javanese, etc.)." This list covers the extent of Denishawn's activities; Wayburn recognized four other kinds of stage dancing in addition to ballet: "Musical Comedy, Tap & Step, Acrobatic, and Exhibition Ballroom." All pupils in Wayburn's school, whatever their shape, experience, or persuasion, began with a basic series of limbering exercises designed to be universal (if seen today they would look like thinly camouflaged Delsartean gymnastics of the nineties). Wayburn in fact was an updated version of the American dancing master who taught the kinds of drastically simplified drawing-room techniques Ruth St. Denis and Isadora Duncan had studied as children. Wayburn's eclectic tradition explains why he viewed classical ballet even as late as the twenties as just another genre. He even taught it in a form he called his Modernized American Ballet, and like Ted Shawn he made light of the troubling claims of the Russians that ballet must be studied from childhood. In a 1925 manual on stage dancing, Wayburn wrote this remark to his students:

> Pavlova, you know, was kept subordinate 12 years be-
> fore she was permitted to attempt a solo dance in public.
> Imagine our American girls submitting to such apprentice-
> ship. And fortunately you don't have to, for we've revolu-
> tionized all that.

Once limbered up by Wayburn's universals, Wayburn students could devote themselves to ballet, or to one or several more of the five kinds of stage dancing—and Wayburn's star pupils on Broadway stages were remarkably versatile in their specialty numbers. At one time or other, Mary Eaton, Lina Basquette, Gilda Gray, Ann Pennington, Fred and Adele Astaire, and Marilyn Miller all studied or worked with Wayburn. Gilda Gray, who is usually remembered for her shimmy in blackface in the 1922 Ziegfeld Follies, performed three other separate specialties in that year too: a musical comedy dance, a Hawaiian dance, and a "come along" character dance—and the next year she tackled an Egyptian and a Javanese. This trading off was not so different from a Denishawn dancer's eclecticism, except that Denishawn soloists did *not* do tap and step or musical comedy dancing. California dance, influenced by idyllic weather and the special requirements of movie scenes, was a different thing from most American dancing: it was mood dancing. New York dance was still largely live entertainment, revolving around the individual performers in the vaudeville-like revues and musicals. Skirt dancing, greatly spun out and elaborated, could still be discerned in revue numbers, along with jazz and ragtime styles. These formed the basis for most of the specialty numbers that weren't ballet ballads, and probably for some that were.

Skirt dancing, it must be remembered, was itself a mongrel child of the union of clog and ballet styles on the vaudeville stage, and musical comedy dancing was its direct descendant. The genre of musical comedy dance wasn't strictly skirt dancing plus jazz, but an American amalgam of these and much more, impossible to describe minute by minute with any coherence; yet by the twenties it was possible to comprehend it as one coherent look, one language, one set of ingredients that could be mixed in recognizable ways. Ned Wayburn—who, for all his pomposity, was considered one of the Broadway master arrangers—described musical comedy dancing as:

> an exaggerated form of Fancy Dancing, including the new popular but simple soft shoe dances, dainty soft pretty movements, with many effective attitudes of the body, all sorts of "kicking" or "fancy steps," touches of dainty ballet interspersed with bits of character work which could be anything —Bowery, Spanish, Dutch, Eccentric, Hawaiian, etc.

This seemingly nonsensical combination of everything was the American dance form of the time, and a fairly sophisticated one, with its own history, its own conventions, its standards of aesthetic craftsmanship, and a structure resembling a part of a musical structure: the dancer entered on a travelling step, performed the dance in sixty-four bars of music, and exited on a travelling step. The expert arrangers like Wayburn knew from long experience how to build climaxes into the routines, how to tease the rhythms, how to decorate the motifs—in short, how to anticipate and play with a certain kind of dance logic that was mostly invisible but enchanting to their audiences. And how could they not be effective, these twenties dance arrangers like Wayburn, Allen K. Foster, Sammy Lee, Teddy Royce, when they were setting dances to the songs and musical interludes of the great American show composers Jerome Kern, Victor Herbert, Irving Berlin, Cole Porter, Vincent Youmans, George Gershwin? Fred Astaire in his autobiography remembers Gershwin coaching him from the piano during rehearsal for a musical, on a step Gershwin had just imagined for *that* bar of music.

The Astaire brother and sister were superb musical comedy dancers; as children they had danced on the vaudeville circuits, and they had always used bits of Spanish, Dutch, whatever, mixed up in smooth, effortless-looking routines. They could handle flyaway rhythms like the misplaced accents in Gershwin's "Fascinatin' Rhythm," one of their signature numbers in the show *Lady Be Good*

(1924). And their famous playfulness onstage was not just a manner; it was a feature of musical comedy dance and it allowed ideas to be slotted in even as the dance was being created—ideas of the dancer or the arranger that could come from any other dance style or from actual offstage behavior. The Astaires' signature exit step, invented by Teddy Royce on the spur of the moment, was a runaround "Oom Pah Trot," a cross between a cakewalk and a Harlequin's escape.

The Astaires were primarily a comedy dance team; in the 1920s they didn't command a lyric strain—that entered the genre only when Fred alone began to work out the choreography of his movie musicals at the RKO studio in the 1930s. Some fragments of sweetness and "mysterioso" must have appeared here and there in twenties dancing, just as they did in the show songs of the period—only to crescendo in the thirties. But not until then did Astaire forge a style that consciously recognized the undercurrent of sadness in the twenties legend, the moral crises and the anesthetic dreams, all the dark beautiful stuff that impinged like shadows on the illuminated center of the decade's life. An underdeveloped lyric strain appeared to be the weakness of twenties musical comedy dancing. But this was the time when the young Astaire and other smart dance arrangers began to melt down those musical comedy poses, those kicks and asymmetric poses from the Charlestons and popular dances, into a style as precise as classical ballet, as moderne and asymmetrical as Cubist or Futurist painting, as rhythmically compelling as African tribal rites.

Compared to musical comedy, the ballet ballad (interpretive dance) was a pale style, born of America's shy attempt to join the sensualists of history through ancient ceremonies, Pre-Raphaelite visions, and the sweeter parts of the early Ballets Russes repertory. The internal dynamics and rhythms of interpretive dancing were undeveloped except by Isadora Duncan, and she did not have direct influence on twenties dance numbers. Ballet ballads seemed cut off from the spirit of burlesque all around in the revues—even from burlesques of themselves. Nevertheless, the public seemed to want the classy *poésie* of "The Garden of Kama" and "The Fisherman's Dream" done straight, without any humor.

And the aesthetic dancers themselves saw with the same blinders. When Martha Graham first began to make dances of her own she didn't think for a moment about jazz dancing, but continued right on in the classic-interpretive vein taught to her by Denishawn. She was both too close to jazz, which surrounded her on twenties stages and at twenties parties, and too far from it, since none of its raw material, no skirt dancing or jigs or character—no rhythmic dance at all—figured in her early experience. What Martha Graham actually sought from New York was not new ideas about dancing but closer contact with the serious theater. After all, it was a play at the Santa Barbara High School that had first given her the idea of dancing, and dance remained in her mind an expressive arm of the theater. The Cumnock School had propagated this idea; Denishawn gave her no reason to change her mind, nor did New York. In New York the intellectuals were all on a quest for the true modern theater, and so, inevitably, was the idealistic Denishawn soloist of the Greenwich Village Follies.

Nineteen twenty-three, the year Martha Graham arrived in New York, brought a windfall for serious theater-goers, since three of the legendary figures of European drama arrived in New York to perform: the great Italian actress Eleonora Duse played a long run of Ibsen and Italian plays in Italian at the Century Theater; Constantin Stanislavsky's Moscow Art Theater installed itself at Jolson's Theater with a repertory of Tolstoy, Gorky, Chekhov, Turgenev, and Dostoevsky in Russian; and the leading art-theater director in Germany, Max Reinhardt, was about to stage his Gothic pageant, *The Miracle,* with a cast of thousands. The search within the pre-war European theater for truth, religion, poetic essentials, and the drama of the masses was now to be carried on by the Americans—by such middle-class young people as Martha Graham, educated in the theater's ideals. In some ways those ideals were personified by Eleonora Duse. Graham went to see every performance of Duse's she could—usually matinées, since she was onstage herself every night in the Follies.

Duse had survived from another age of acting techniques, when tragediennes resembled operatic divas in their methods and their roles. She had stayed in Europe in the years when her rival Sarah Bernhardt toured triumphantly back and forth across America; she had come here only once in the 1890s and then with inadequate publicity. Now an old, slight, tragedy-worn woman with white hair, Duse was brought to America as a Holy Mother of the theater. Imaginative critics like Stark Young sat at her feet and learned about Golden Age acting, even while Young recognized that Duse's mysterious power stemmed from her negation of the very idea of acting. She was in herself tragic. She had never depended on the brilliant contrivances of her actress-competitors, their chantings, beseechings, and vivid painted masks. She wore very little makeup onstage. Her actions and her speech were

quiet, unmelodramatic in the conventional sense. Yet she could evoke
the glamour of Sarah Bernhardt, the loveliness and compassion of Ellen
Terry, the tragic weight of the mature Isadora Duncan. It seems she
was an infinitely musical actress, that she put a spell on her audience
which caused them to perceive her every nuance, her every impulse
to move, her every rhythmic shading.

The play of Duse's that stirred Martha Graham most was *Cosa
Sia*, by Gallerati Scotti in the style of Gabriele D'Annunzio—strongly
Italian fatalistic. It opens on a Sicilian mother praying beside her dying
child's bed, promising God she will give up everything, even her lover,
if her child lives. Of course the child lives and deserts his mother in
later acts, but the moment that struck Graham was in the first act,
when Duse wrapped her rosary around the arm of the child, lifted her
face, and said, "Dear God, give me the life of this child. I will do anything. I will accept anything." It seems that Martha Graham thought
of her childhood nurse, Lizzie, when she saw Duse play this sacrificing
mother—Lizzie, who had given her life to the Graham girls. Martha
had already examined her own psyche; she knew Lizzie was responsible for the part in her that wasn't American-Protestant, the part that
understood profound religious feeling and responded to the Roman
Catholic art of Eleonora Duse.

That religious response was central to Martha Graham's view of
herself as an artist. With her fierce and private temperament, she
needed a model like Duse to watch, one who believed the theater was
an elemental ceremony, and the performers somehow sacrificial. And
Graham was smart enough to see *how* Duse reached her audience so
profoundly. Duse could cause people to see her impulse to move before she showed the motion, so that her actions seemed impelled from
inside, tragic and inevitable. The figure of the woman heroine who
contained the drama in her person fascinated Martha Graham, just as
it once had fascinated Ruth St. Denis. Miss Ruth's impersonation of
the heroine as goddess had first attracted Martha to dance. Now, through
Duse's last tour in America (she died here of pneumonia), Martha
encountered the kind of theater that had caused American art-dance
to be born a generation before. The spectacle of this tragic heroine in-
stilled the same desires in Martha that it had in her predecessors—
Isadora and Miss Ruth; once again she wanted to be that heroine on
the stage in her own way, a way that matched her new generation.

Martha Graham possessed what Ruth St. Denis had not: a fully
conscious psyche. Perhaps because of her father's profession of psychia-
try, Martha saw theater and dance as abstracted equivalents of in-

dividual lives, and she gradually developed a modern, psychologi-
cal approach to her medium. She believed that dance through its basic
patterns could deliver a message of the pain or anger or glory in the
individual artist's mind. Martha's aim was to draw directly on her
own experience and her family's and make them universal. Indeed,
certain of her mature dances are uncanny portraits of a Gothic family of
sisters and shadowy mother-figures—*Deaths and Entrances*, about the
Brontë sisters; *Letter to the World*, about Emily Dickinson. The vitality
of both these works proves the authenticity of her private sources.
Later this method of creating grew much clearer to her. It might have
been Eleonora Duse's acting in the twenties that showed her for the
first time how a "public" drama (the mother's sacrifice in *Cosa Sia*)
could exactly equal a private one (her own nurse's sacrifice) and no
one need know. One is reminded of the American playwright who was
emerging at this time too, Eugene O'Neill, who was even more
consciously examining the psychology of an individual in the structure
of a play. In their different idioms, O'Neill and Graham were part
of the process, often self-conscious and confused, occasionally very
vital, by which the American theater in the twenties borrowed the
forms of the new European theater and translated them into New
World terms.

In the midst of the eclectic and witty play of surface design of Broadway revues and musical comedies and dramas, the American art-
theater modeled on the European was struggling to gain a foothold.
Small New York groups that began as drama leagues in the teens had
found the courage and the support by now to turn professional.
The Provincetown Players moved into two theaters in Greenwich Village, the Washington Square Players became the Theater Guild and
built a theater near Broadway in 1925, and in 1920 the Neighborhood
Playhouse on the Lower East Side went professional. All these groups
were dedicated to finding serious values in the theater. Their idea was
to foster American playwrights while at the same time offering the
public a repertory of good theatrical literature that was not American.
The Theater Guild especially dipped into the pool of modern European
art plays—German, French, English, Irish, and Slavic—which hadn't
been produced in America, and the Neighborhood Playhouse formed
what amounted to an abstract folk theater, inspired originally by the
immigrant populations surrounding it and their various native pageants
and rituals.

One cannot summarize a whole decade of plays; however, it is clear that memorable twenties art plays differed from past and present Broadway plays in the nature of their characters. They weren't about special glamorous melodramatic individuals but about ordinary folk. Their protagonists, when specific characters, represented a whole mass of people like them, people who suffered or celebrated in like manner. Sometimes the crowd itself was the hero of the play. The Theater Guild's *Liliom* (1921; by Ferenc Molnar) was an allegory about a carnival ostler and his girl; Ernst Toller's *Man and the Masses* (1924), also a Theater Guild production, was a tale of a worker rebelling. Audiences were especially interested in the theme of medieval pageants, of the folk-religious drama of peasant crowds who believed in miracles. About 1919 the Neighborhood Playhouse produced *Guibour,* a fourteenth-century French miracle play, directed by the famous diseuse Yvette Guilbert. The Theater Guild mounted Paul Claudel's *The Tidings Brought to Mary,* a religious peasant drama, in 1922. And Reinhardt's *The Miracle* (early 1924), which transformed the entire Century Theater into a Gothic church, trumped all medieval pageant plays.

When attempts were made to translate these folk rituals into an American idiom, it was found that America didn't really have any primitive drama, any ritual or miracle plays in its theatrical past. The painful revelation of such foreign companies as the Moscow Art Theater, according to critic Stark Young, was that they could draw on a "racial and popular life Americans weren't in touch with." The decade sought an American theater of the folk in such plays as Elmer Rice's *The Adding Machine* (1923), whose hero was not one of the peasants in a vast processional but one of the keys in a vast adding machine (constructed on the Theater Guild's stage by Lee Simonson), or the Neighborhood Playhouse's *Pinwheel* (1927), about an urban "Guy" and his "Jane," representing all guys and Janes, or Eugene O'Neill's *Dynamo* (1929), in which the hero worships the machine in the factory where he works.

What to worship was a troubling question in the American theater. The Lewisohn sisters of the Neighborhood Playhouse confronted it in their 1921 visualization of Walt Whitman's *Salut au Monde!*—a collage of religious ceremonies from all over the world, with real Turkish dervishes, real Moslem prayer-callers, real Jewish cantors. The sisters decided that America, with no folk religion of its own, was therefore the natural home of all religions—and all theaters. Some of the later Neighborhood Playhouse's productions appeared to be close-ups of parts of *Salut au Monde!: An Arab Fantasia* ("an impression of Arab life"); *The Little Clay Cart,* an adaptation of an old Hindu drama; *Kuan Yin,* modeled on Chinese theater; *The Dybbuk,* inspired by the Russian Habima Players—and these productions generated intense interest in the whole New York theatrical community. Committed theater people, Martha Graham among them, journeyed not only to the Lower East Side to see the Neighborhood Playhouse's folk dramas but also to the real folk theaters in lower New York, the Yiddish theater, the Sicilian, and the Chinese. Folk plays were seen as a tonic after Broadway because they restored "primitive" impulses to the stage; one critic found it "refreshing" that a son would murder his mother-in-law in a Sicilian melodrama.

Art-theater people adopted a certain attitude toward the main body of theater in the twenties. They were at war with the star system of Broadway, with its commercialism and its audience of so-called "transient comers" who didn't know the meaning of values in the theater. If the search for America's ritual folk roots was in vain (since there weren't any), the art-theater was still bent on finding universal values and theatrical essences—and no wonder it was forced to turn to European and ethnic sources. The real roots of American theater were not buried but all too visible in the "ten-twent-thirt" melodramas, *Uncle Tom's Cabin, Under the Gaslight, The Drunkard, Way Down East, The Old Homestead,* still touring somewhere in one or many of the American "regions." All of the acting and scenic conventions represented by melodrama were dismissed by the urban art-theater as part of the "threadbare patterns" of the popular commercial theater. But that theater made money. Intellectuals couldn't smile on their own crude and vigorous past in the popular productions of David Belasco, because even though Belasco belonged to another theatrical era, he was still cheerfully producing successful spectacles on Broadway. Not even his attendance had dropped, only the caliber of his audience. Likewise, vaudeville was a threat instead of a curiosity, because it was still the preferred entertainment of the majority of Americans. Art-theater people were obliged to reject the recent past if they wanted theater to be literature as it was in Europe, if they wanted to star the play rather than the player, most of all if they wanted the theater to *look* appropriately "moderne."

In the 1920s the look of things was of prime importance, even more so than the new serious or religious subject matter. After all, religion had been dramatized before. Belasco had staged a passion play in his youth (with Salmi Morse, 1879); he had also been inspired, as were the twenties, by the ritual Oriental theater. But Belasco's stage *looked* musty to modern eyes; it looked like a clutter of material objects, vases and silverware and period furniture. His costumes, said twenties moderns, were unimaginative duplications of clothes in whatever time and place the play was set—and they came from establishments that Alice Lewisohn haughtily named the "caravanseries"—the Broadway costumers. The most passionate enclave in this contemporary art-theater was its new generation of talented American designers, who were transforming the look of the stage—Norman Bel Geddes, Robert Edmond Jones, Lee Simonson, Aline Bernstein.

They believed a play was not a facsimile of real life but a magical transmutation of it, and this truth must be reflected in the sets and costumes. In the spirit of Gordon Craig and Max Reinhardt they strove to make costumes that were metaphors for clothes, and settings that were not real but elemental places. Anonymous fabrics and neutral environments, steps, arches, mounds, and arenas, were often employed, and light became an important feature in the new designs, planes of light, which gave depth to the constructions and an illusion of pulse even in still scenes. Ordinary plays in their overall design became stylized tableaux with words added—and some movement—of single protagonists or of whole crowds.

Ritual movement in the twenties was a new feature as important as the lighting. An allegory like the Theater Guild's *Man and the Masses* (1924) was worked out as a series of movement vignettes, "moving" pictures of asymmetrical crowds with arms reaching high, set against darkened forms of the set and etched in light, much like Fritz Lang's expressionist crowds in the movie *Metropolis* (Germany, 1927). The constant use of stylized movement for the actors placed a high value on skills of pantomime and dance. Michio Ito choreographed many of the Theater Guild's productions, and at the Neighborhood Playhouse the Festival Dancers acted as an integral part of the drama company, working out the play in movement terms alongside the designers and the director. The Neighborhood Playhouse even produced some of its own versions of the Ballets Russes repertory it had seen or read about, featuring its Festival Dancers (trained in music visualization and Duncan-like techniques). They simply took the music of *Petrushka, La Boutique Fantasque,* and *Chout* (which they called *Buffoon!*) and staged colorful animated dance tableaux in the spirit of the artistic folk drama that seemed to be cropping up all over the world.

Lying about among the productions of the 1920s art-theater

were clues for a young dancer as to what the serious, post-Denishawn dance of the future would look like. By the same token, the theater needed clues from dance. In the mid-twenties, the art-theater's work on new techniques and training claimed Martha Graham even before she began visibly to be influenced by it. After all, she was a top performer from the California art circuit with a repertory of Aztec, Spanish, Greek, and Japanese maidens, and offstage she was just as exotic, mysterious, and intense. Two new theater schools invited her to teach, which meant that she could leave the Greenwich Village Follies and involve herself with the serious drama. She accepted both offers. The first was the Dance and Dramatic Action wing of the Eastman School of Music in Rochester. George Eastman, the Rochester school's patron, had brought a young Russian disciple of Stanislavsky, Rouben Mamoulian, to direct the operas in the school, and Mamoulian insisted on the presence of dance in the department. He had once noticed Graham on a Denishawn tour that passed through Rochester, and several years later he asked her to join him along with Swedish modern dancer Ronny Gustafson to teach the actors and stage expressionistic dances for his operas. At the same time the indefatigable John Murray Anderson decided to start a school in New York to represent all the disciplines of the theater: Drama, Singing, Scenic and Costume Design, Playwriting, Pageantry, Fencing, and Dance. He said he wanted to make as much money as Ned Wayburn, whose school was a block away, so he made the dance department quite large, with real ballet taught by Adolph Bolm, former Ballets Russes soloist, and then by Léo Staats, ballet master of the Paris Opera; interpretive dance taught by Michio Ito and Martha Graham; tap and step and exhibition ballroom were offered too.

Martha Graham, now professionally associated with the theatrical crusaders of her day, began to make dances of her own as soon as she began teaching. From the first she was interested in being an intellectual, in exploring ideas through her medium rather than just genres. For her first concert on April 18, 1926, at the 48th Street Theater, lent to her at cost by the Greenwich Village Follies theater manager, she brought three students from the Eastman School. They performed trios she had made for them, and she danced her own solos. Many of these first dances were named after the short piano pieces they were set to, some modern, some from the Romantic era. But they were not music visualizations, they were essays in dance—always conscientiously

designed, with costumes and lighting by Graham herself. A dance, to
Martha Graham, meant a whole theatrical look or pattern, just as it
had to Ruth St. Denis, although Graham's dances resulted as much
from conscious and intense thought as from instinct; they weren't the
spontaneous visions of her mentor. Her dances were spare, direct statements, whereas Denishawn's had always been spilling over with veils
and beads and material. Denishawn dances were pictures of other
exotic cultures, but Graham's first dances were pictures of pictures, already one level removed from raw imagination, and they sometimes
referred in their content to other works of art, such as *From a 12th
Century Tapestry,* or *A Study in Lacquer,* or *Bas Relief,* works in the
1926 concert.

The conscious artifice of the bold patterns and colors was what
struck the reviewer of *The Dance* (July 1926) most about that first
concert:

The Blessed Damozel Comes Down
from Rochester

Clad in a heavy gold kimona, making patterns with
her body against a screen of brilliant lacquer—a romantic
twelfth century tapestry in bold colorings, a gold crown on
her head—a modern portrait after Beltran-Masses, lithe and
tigerish in her crisp silk gown of black and orange stripes,
and red poppies in her sleek black hair—Martha Graham
presents a series of pictures that fire the imagination and
make a hundred stories for every gesture. Shall we say her
dances are motion pictures for the sophisticated—motion
pictures without the bothersome banality of sub-titles and
the sugary narrative of the movie theatre? . . .

From the Eastman School of Music, Miss Graham
brought with her three young girls. The three soft childish
figures nude and silhouetted whitely against the black drop
curtain made charming cameos while Louis Horst played
Debussy. Again, as the playful characters of Goossens'
Marionette Show, their dancing was so frolicsome, so
spontaneous and unforced that they were called back for an
encore. I liked them best, however, as the three gopis in
their lovely draped batik costumes of melting colors and
their young faces brightened by the warm flowers in their
shining hair. . . .

Concealed, however, underneath Martha Graham's modernistic images was a vigorous dance exploration of the motivation of the images. One cannot know how conscious an exploration it was; certainly no one described it then, even those who found her concerts significant. American audiences didn't consciously follow trails of movement on a stage, and rarely did they look at a dance for kinetic continuity. But one can know today something about what Martha Graham did in her mid-twenties dances because the Eastman Kodak studios, connected to the Eastman School of Music through George Eastman the camera magnate, used one of them as test material for a new color-film process. Miraculously, a short silent color film exists of a dance of Graham's from 1926, *The Flute of Krishna*, featuring Graham's Rochester students: Evelyn Sabin as Radha, Robert Ross as Krishna; Thelma Biracree, Betty MacDonald, and Suzanne Vacenti as the Dancing Girls.

By a coincidence this filmed dance was Martha Graham's version of "Radha," the Hindu legend that so long ago inspired Ruth St. Denis and made *her* reputation; that she would touch the same material indicates that Graham thought of herself in connection with St. Denis. Graham's *Radha,* although costumed in batiked veils and harem pants that would have satisfied Denishawn, was not a tableau of a demigoddess but rather a dance picture, or tracing, of the mysterious forces of Krishna's influence. His flute, or his presence, troubles the Dancing Girls and they run from him. The dance is a stylized chase by Krishna, first of the Dancing Girls, then of Radha herself, and it is conceived as one nearly seamless whole. It had unmistakable affinities with Nijinsky's *L'Après-midi d'un Faune,* wherein the Faun troubles the serenity of nymphs in a glade.

Graham's dance is not as carefully friezelike in its designs as Nijinsky's 1912 work for the Ballets Russes, but it does accumulate a conscious intensity as it goes along. It is a construction: from the moment Krishna appears in the marketplace, the atmosphere begins to thicken; the stage is stirred until in a very subtle but distinct climax Krishna pins Radha from behind, not by holding her but by willing her, it seems, to become motionless *as if* he had caught her by the shoulders. The dance is a series of impulses passed from one dancer to another, impulses originating deep in their bodies and propelling them to move. There are no wrong moves: when a Dancing Girl evades Krishna's playful reach, her twist has already started her in the direction she will run. Swirls of momentum materialize that are obeyed by all the figures in the dance, and yet "plastique" still images

are not denied within the constant motion; the dance images are
retained by the audience because they are the climax of a statement
in movement—as if a knot of momentum comes untied. And the one
moment when the motion stops is seen as the peak of the dance.

The Flute of Krishna is too subtle to be a Denishawn dance; it
looks more like a ballet ballad in the John Murray Anderson vein, but
it has dance features more advanced than either of those genres. A
structure of underlying design and the illusion that each movement
impelled the next were new elements for an American choreographer
to have found. The similarities to Nijinsky's dance suggest that
Martha Graham must have been thinking in wider terms than
Denishawn's about how to make a dance, thinking about the Ballets
Russes and about Isadora Duncan. Martha Graham had grasped the
clarity of directions and places on the stage that Duncan knew from
the first, but she had also located a dense dance texture of her own,
one that was different from Isadora's.

Duncan dances proceeded from motion to motion by a frothiness
of atmosphere, as if movements were shaken out of one another by
some light-handed culinary process. Intensity in the dance dynamics
contrasted with the basic texture of Isadora's dances, and she always
dramatized intensity as strong force; she all but visualized the force.
For instance, in Isadora's The Furies (1906), part of the Gluck
Orpheus, the dancer, an inhabitant of a Dantesque hell, mimes lifting a gigantic rock. The whole mood thus acquires force. Isadora's
dances about slavery, like the Marche Slav, stem from this struggle
of the dancer's with almost visible forces (here, imaginary heavy
chains), and since Isadora remained consistent in her idea of how to
create a dance, one can see the force evoked again in a late dance like
the Scriabin Revolutionary Étude made in Russia, 1921. In the
dynamic first motif the dancer runs toward the audience, rises and
opens her arms to the sky, drops to earth with her arms over her head,
then slowly, painfully brings her head up again in a kneeling position,
dramatizing the profound struggle of a revolutionary against weariness
and hopelessness. Dramatic tension was used by Duncan only for certain modes, with certain music; more often, she used broad planes of
space without visible tension, a broad reach and buoyant travelling
steps to create the drama of motion.

But Martha Graham, even before she found her own dance
shapes, had found that her constant source of drama would be this
visible force, the illusion of which a dancer creates herself through
the opposition of muscles inside her body. By 1926 Graham had

found ways to generate this tension without Duncan's apologetic
references to outside forces. This internalized visualized force, if a
constant part of the dancer's impulses, could keep a dance completely
in the control of the dancer. Perhaps Graham absorbed her close
control of the dynamics from Duse's acting; perhaps it was a faculty
like perfect pitch in music—an instinctive grasp of the relation of
space to the muscular tension inside a body. Whatever its origins,
it was a skill beyond that of visualizing the music; it deployed the
lines of thrusts of motion, the unheard music of dance itself.

Martha Graham spent the late twenties in finding a style, a look
that would be hers and consciously separate from anything of Denishawn's. Over these years she thoroughly altered the shapes of her
dances, even the shapes of her dancers' bodies; and with the shapes,
the rhythmic density of the dances changed too. For all its clarity, the
1926 *Flute of Krishna* was a composition of curves and arabesque
sweeps, more Art Nouveau in flavor than Cubist. But Graham, having
begun to give concerts and to build a repertory, started visibly searching for a style by showing herself flagrantly open to several kinds of
influence.

And in the high twenties, influences were rife. The world was
caught in a style revolution whereby an iconoclastic way of seeing,
fashioned by the Cubist and Futurist painters before World War I,
now permeated the way one lived an ordinary day in the city of New
York. Posters and signs and clothes and skyscrapers and the insides of
restaurants and popular dancing acquired masslike forms that were
then jostled crazily and cut up and decorated with lines and pieces of
angles. The 1922 discovery of King Tutankhamen's tomb in Egypt
emphasized the trend toward geometry in design, and the 1925 Art
Deco Exhibition in Paris confirmed the new geometric configuration
of the world.

Nowhere was the effect more dramatically deployed than in the figure
of the fashionable woman of the 1920s, an international figure. She
was in general a result of Paul Poiret's and Isadora's and Fokine's
release of women's inflated *fin-de-siècle* figures into fluid compilations of
drapes and trailing stuffs, but a result that implied a creative leap
somewhere. The extra stylization belonged to the naïve belief that the
significant part of the universe was not Nature but things man-made.
Machines became toys for artists to put into pictures, collages, and all
designed objects. Artist-couturiers stopped assuming a woman's body

was a natural object upon which designs could be hung and pasted;
they started gleefully to re-design the body itself according to geometric
machinery.

By day it now wore a long thin tubular suit with skirt just below
the knees, and it carried discreet industrial accouterments, steel beads,
a fat metal umbrella. Its head was reduced and streamlined by a cloche
hat fitted low over the eyes. In the evening the head was a helmet of
short-bobbed, brilliantined hair that topped another tube, but evening
tubes were made of velvet or eau-de-nil satin or crepella. The evening
also added things that swung, long ropes of pearls, or designer
Madeleine Vionnet's bias-cut panels on the lower parts of dresses, which
hung still unless the woman moved, and then they swirled at the knees.
The stationary effect was of a sort of totem pole, or a clothespin doll
with the hair and face painted on, but when the woman moved she
was a propellor—and in fact, stiff propellor-scarves at the neck made
their appearance briefly in mid-decade. The long straight shape was
so simple, so perceivable at a glance, so organized that it could
lend itself to violent ornamentation, such as French painter Sonia
Delaunay's patchwork Cubist dresses and coats, or Vionnet's asymmetrical hem lengths. A sleek silhouette, a shining helmet-head, and up and
down the torso a wild array of geometry, or around the legs the ragged
lines of a broken hem.

But the most elemental high-fashion twenties look appeared on
the beach, the long torso triumphant. Both boys and girls wore sleek
jersey bathing suits with one or two horizontal stripes, skin gleaming
and a small cap of hair glued to the head, extended around the girls'
faces in a couple of spit curls. The boys and girls didn't deliberately
resemble each other so much as both looked like the machine parts
they were designed after. However, this device made a wittier scenario
for the woman; it upset everything she had been before by portraying
her as a mechanistic Amazon. The small-headed bathing-suited tube
with undershirt-top usually denied all evidence of a bosom, but
proudly displayed a full, muscled strength of neck and shoulders.
Power was furtively admired in a woman's body, since the industrial
objects the body imitated were powerful machines.

In no other era was the body itself so available to the popular
mind as the stuff of art, stuff to be molded or distorted for the sheer
play of design. The dance and fashion revolutions, the free use of the
human figure in photographs and movies, and its distortion in painting
and sculpture, had brought this on. Now that the human torso had
been designed on its own, the arms and legs no longer needed to stick

close to it, mermaid style; they could move freely, even wildly, in opposition to it. Twenties dance revelled consciously and unconsciously in the general alertness about how the body looked, and its new separation into parts. The most popular vernacular dance forms of the day, the Charleston and the black bottom, were both variations on the whole person as one long stick, with hinges, and potentially flyaway arms and perhaps legs. The Charleston, to a jerky syncopation, almost tied the knees together but let the feet twist crazily against the floor and the arms either flap in opposition or make Egyptian-type designs on top. In the black bottom the backside was identified as something that moved; the arms slapped the bobbing backside as if to push the whole person forward through the pelvis. In general the torso, like the geometric dresses that covered it, was seen to contain surprise pieces of itself that promised whimsical expression.

Unending variations on these popular dances were done in cabarets all through the civilized world of the 1920s. Meanwhile more self-conscious experiments of a "mechanistic" kind were under way in theatrical dance: the Swedish Ballet emerged as a hotbed of modernity and visited America in 1923 with a fantastic ballet, *The Skating Rink*, designed and costumed by the Cubist painter Fernand Léger to music by Arthur Honegger. In Austria young women such as Claire Bonroff and Margot Kulka were inventing "Futuristic dances," sometimes with masks; in Germany Rudolf von Laban had scientifically sliced up human movement and invented a language to describe the directions, forces, weights, and densities in dance, Labanotation—a page of which resembled a Cubist painting, with forms, letters, and symbols floating in it. Mary Wigman and her student Harald Kreutzberg were finding new kinds of angles the body could visualize, and new tensions it could show inside itself. But the center of experiments in the essential shapes of dance was also the center of design, fashion, and art—Paris. Here Diaghilev's Ballets Russes reigned supreme, turning out dance ideas all through the decade, ideas that were transparently related to the explosive new shapes in fashion, décor, and popular dancing, yet still clearly plotted on the grid of anatomical knowledge and precision of manners that was classical ballet.

Ever since the Russian Ballet had first appeared in Paris in 1909, with its bold sweeps of sinuous movement invented by Michel Fokine and its resplendent fabrics and colors conceived by Léon Bakst, it had given potent inspiration to the whole world of art and design. The inspiration never stopped coming; throughout the teens and twenties the Ballets Russes was always several steps ahead of popular ideas about costumes and bodies. First Nijinsky in 1912 had calmed the heady progression of Fokine's dances and organized it into frieze images of exact design, precise but mysteriously serene, in his Debussy ballet *L'Après-midi d'un Faune.* In that year he also made *Jeux,* about a trio of young people at lawn tennis, in which he used snatches of real offstage behavior. This, the first "sports ballet," already prefigured the intimate link in the 1920s between sports and design. In 1913 Nijinsky made still another kind of modern ballet of syncopated poses and frenzied attitudes, the Stravinsky *Sacre du Printemps.* Nijinsky's three ballets revealed a whole new repertory of choreographic tools, which he was never able to develop, since he gradually went insane during World War I.

The very young Léonide Massine emerged as Diaghilev's next choreographer with *Soleil de Nuit* in 1915, and in 1917 he completed a deliberately Cubist ballet, *Parade,* written by Cocteau, designed by Picasso, and danced to a bombastically witty score by Erik Satie. It was a ballet treatment of the favorite Cubist strategy of sleight-of-hand, during which a tiny street circus of three small acts, and a two-person horse, are dismissed by two oversized managers, each made out of a human body piled high with painted boxes at crazy angles. The three solos for the circus acts—Chinaman, American Girl, and Two Acrobats —were exercises in the various Cubist illusions about the human figure (see Braque, Léger, and Picasso, in that order, for guides to these solos, said an English critic). And in the course of designing the bodies, Massine sliced up and redesigned the movement too; his American Girl, for instance, performed ragtime steps, imitated Charlie Chaplin, rolled on the grass, chased a thief with a gun, and generally behaved in an animated and mechanistic manner in the course of her "variation."

In the midst of his trailblazing post-Cubist ballet essays on modernity, Diaghilev made the extraordinary decision in 1921 to revive the full three-act Tchaikovsky ballet *La Belle au Bois Dormant* (*Sleeping Beauty*) with sets and costumes by Bakst, perhaps in tribute to the gigantic patronage machinery of Imperial Russia that was gone now with the Russian Revolution, and in its passing left the Ballets Russes dancers forever exiles. Diaghilev wanted to remind his elegant public that his company had emerged from a gorgeous tradition of nineteenth-century pantomime spectacle, notwithstanding all of its outrageous experiments in new design. Once *The Sleeping Beauty* was completed and shown in a not very successful London season, Diaghilev, saddened, continued with moderne ballets, entrusting the productions of the mid-twenties to the sister of Nijinsky, Bronislava Nijinska, who became in a sense the natural extension of her brother. Three of her ballets of that time, *Les Noces* (1923), *Le Train Bleu* and *Les Biches* (both 1924), were powerful syntheses of theatrical ideas, real-life behavior, and classical ballet steps—and all displayed a vigor of attack and trenchant wit. Even *Les Noces*, a stark and severe stylization of primitive marriage rites of Russian peasants, elicited a relish in its audience, an amused and lively recognition of the right invention at the right time.

The other two ballets were satires of then modern society and high fashion, which was already a satire of itself. *Le Train Bleu* took place in that elemental twenties landscape, a Côte d'Azur beach; its characters were the Bright Boys and their Flappers, who during the ballet performed something like a musical comedy chorus number based on motions of swimming and diving. *Les Biches* presented an *outré* party, weaving into the musical structure the small desires, actions, and gestures of its population: a Hostess with a long rope of pearls and a cigarette holder, a "garçonne" beauty in a deep-blue velvet tunic, some girls in pink feathers, and three beautiful athletic boys. The scores of Milhaud (*Le Train Bleu*) and Poulenc (*Les Biches*) had absorbed ragtime and jazz into classical forms exactly as Nijinska must have included contemporary behavior in her choreography—contemporary behavior that ranged from salon manners to musical comedy dances.

The greatness of the Ballets Russes lay in its capacity to absorb all kinds of modern ideas and integrate them in a progression of graphic logic—guided by the common ballet training of every dancer and choreographer in Diaghilev's company, plus Diaghilev's own understanding of the points where his dances connected to their tradition and the points where they could be freely experimental. The Ballets Russes lasted and grew over the two generations of the moderne in this century, a feat that few single artists managed: partly because the early work of Vaslav Nijinsky was so concentrated and ahead of its time, it transcended the break in everyone's consciousness caused by World War I. Thus, when twenty-year-old George Balanchine began his career as the last of Diaghilev's choreographers, he could superimpose the irony of Massine and Nijinska onto his own Russian training in classical ballet and some modernist music visualization, thus continuing the whole Ballets Russes enterprise through his blend of its elements—an even more coherent modern style that was eccentrically but logically neo-classical.

All over Europe, culture partook of the Ballets Russes and Cubist conceptions of art as a hyper-civilized charade, an illusionary collage-catalogue of motions and poses, a reflection of the fantastical features of some entirely Moderne New World. In some ways America was that New World. America, seen through the wise and world-weary eyes of post-war Europe, was the impetus for the entire high-style phenomenon called the twenties. American cocktails were its drinks, American slang was its language, the American composers who had made melodic jazz out of ragtime and blues—Gershwin, Cole Porter, Duke Ellington—provided the atmosphere of all twenties scenes. And American dancing—popular and theatrical—decided the tone of the age, its suavity and its casualness as well as its craziness, its tremors up and down the torso, its jagged angles and syncopated rhythms. In fact, American musical comedies with dancing were the *dernier cri* of several European capitals: Fred and Adele Astaire played endless runs in London of two of their Gershwin shows, and they were extravagantly admired. To the English they represented, according to the London *Times* (Sidney Carroll), "the primal spirit of animal delight that could not restrain itself, the vitality that bursts its bonds in the Garden of Eden."

In Paris, 1925, the public adored another American show in a slightly different idiom. A tall gangly black dancer named Josephine Baker, a graduate of Sissle and Blake's Broadway revue Shuffle Along, now a performer in the Harlem-sprung La Revue Nègre, dazzled Paris in a free-form, flapping Charleston that embodied its wildest visions—just as Loie Fuller had embodied them two decades before at the Folies Bergères. Bringing real Harlem dancers to Paris was the idea of Fernand Léger, the Cubist painter and designer of ballets; he thought of it after writing a scenario for a Ballet Nègre and then realizing it already existed in New York. After Léger had conjured her up, the real Josephine became a further catalyst to the picture-making process at the time, especially the Cubist-influenced theatrical posters, which showed her tall sticklike figure jutting out at knees, elbows, and derrière (covered by a little skirt of bananas). In Paris or London in the high twenties, an audience could find itself one night watching the ultra-sophisticated works of the Russian Ballet and the next the ultra-primitive Charleston of Josephine or the dislocated rhythmic antics of Fred and Adele. Somehow it was all part of the same world. Styles, degrees of humor, and consciousness or unconsciousness were mixed and juggled and absorbed easily one into the other.

In New York, where so many twenties impulses originated, no such easy amalgam, no mixture of sheer play and serious refinement, was yet possible, at least in dance. F. Scott Fitzgerald made it possible in literature with such works of high seriousness *and* high style as *The Great Gatsby* and *Tender Is the Night*. But no one was able to take real American dancing from musical comedies, with its snippets of folk and drawing-room and vaudeville roots, and use it to make ballets about American life—simply because musical comedies had never been used for "serious" commentary. There was plenty of design around in the air—a Ziegfeld number like the famous "Rio Rita" was typical with its rows of tutued girls in checkered black and white, each girl with a toeshoe of each color—but the design wasn't connected with content, nor with the artistic process of paring down and selecting metaphors to stand for larger things. The "content" was all in the other kind of genre, the newer, non-indigenous ballet ballads, which in turn never attempted the wit of musical comedy.

By the late 1920s in New York the two kinds of dance—musical comedy and art-dance—were assumed to be separate and to carry separate cargoes—one all silliness and light-hearted rhythmic play, the other all heavy lyricism, perfume, and drama. There was no acknowledged cross-over until Fred Astaire put heavier sentiment into his shows and then his movies (probably starting consciously with *The Gay Divorce* on Broadway, 1932) and the young American Ballet of George Balanchine and Lincoln Kirstein put popular material into serious ballets. In the twenties the only way one of these kinds of dancing could absorb the badly needed qualities of the other was by seepage—usually unconscious. It happened in Martha Graham's case because of her inherent eye for pattern and design; it did not happen in the case of some of the other art-dancers who by 1926 and '27 were beginning to present themselves in small recitals.

These evenings, although they occurred in legitimate theaters, were almost a throwback to the Delsartean soirées of the nineties, soirées for the elite and committed. Graham herself always insisted on a Broadway house as a showcase for her prolific output of the late 1920s, of trios, solos, and finally ensemble dances, once or twice a year. Most concert recitalists, though, were content with Carnegie Hall, which saw nearly all the new art-dance activity of this time. The concert field appeared to be dominated by Californians, Russians, and

Orientals: there were ex-Denishawners Doris Niles and her sister
Cornelia, who put on traditionally three-pronged concerts combining
the Interpretive (*St. Joan, Dancing Waves, Wind Dance*), the
Classical (*Mme. Pompadour, Mme. Du Barry, Shepherdess*), and the
Character (*Japanese Cherry Tree, Turkish Intime*); there was the
Adolph Bolm Ballet, with Ruth Page or Vera Murova or Berenice
Holmes and sometimes the young Agnes George de Mille alternating
in short vignettes (de Mille introduced one of the first American
numbers then, her '49, about the Gold Rush); there was Michio Ito,
Japanese but trained in the Dalcroze School of Eurythmics (essentially
music visualization), who presented works entitled *Pavane, Saraband,
Nocturne,* or *Oriental Impressions;* there was Doris Humphrey, who
left Denishawn in 1929 with Charles Weidman to pursue her concert
work, sometimes exploring movement qualities, sometimes capturing
human foibles in dance terms. And of course there was the dance of
the previous generation, Denishawn itself, finishing up a decade of
popular success on the concert circuit, as well as the several adopted
daughters of Isadora Duncan performing under the Hurok aegis on
the concert circuit.

There was one prominent new dancer trained in New York,
Helen Tamiris, a product of the Neighborhood Playhouse and the
Michel Fokine school, also a veteran of the 1925 Music Box Revue.
She made some attempts to mingle jazz, serious dance, and even "le
sport"; in her 1927 concert she used a Gershwin score; she made
dances called *20th Century Bacchante* and *Prize Fight Studies.* However, not even Tamiris' solos carried a weight of tradition or worldliness; they were small studies, made by a young girl who was not yet a
significantly talented choreographer. Most of the concert activity
consisted of short genre studies or exercises. The dances were like
advanced ballet ballads detached from the more vulgar context of the
musical revues; they were self-conscious impressions, not of the present
or of the theatrical past, but of an imagined limbo in a poetic past or
present—the dance equivalents of the subject matter and settings of
twenties art plays.

However, art-dance in America didn't yet command a form such
as the acts and scenes of a play, and its activities in the late 1920s
were above all the attempt to find a form, some kind of form that
was not musical comedy, or ballet, or interpretive/classique, but a
new unknown modern art-dance form. Some version of modern art-
dance was going on in every country in Western Europe, but in most
other places it was connected to the ballet with its bulwark of tradi-

tions. The Russian companies—Diaghilev's, Pavlova's—had travelled everywhere and in the process had left enough awareness and cast-off personnel to enable new versions of themselves to emerge. The Russians occupied France and would eventually command the Paris Opera; they had occupied Britain often enough to generate a British ballet starting in the mid-twenties. Moreover, Britain with its healthy tradition of pantomime-spectacle saw the connections the Ballets Russes offered to its own theatrical past. *The Triumph of Neptune* (1927) was Diaghilev's and Balanchine's "English ballet," a summation of all the delightful features of the English penny pantomimes. Sweden, with its Futuristic ballet, subscribed to the Ballets Russes idea of modern classical dancing. Even Soviet Russia, where the Russian ballet schools still flourished, was grafting music visualizations and new ensemble ideas onto its accepted classical formations. Only Germany and America, because of unusual pressures in their cultures, distortions about the very nature of art, produced a kind of dance that claimed to be independent of the past. In Germany, the presence of the powerful modern art-theater guaranteed artistic dance a serious place that it couldn't claim in America. And because Germany was the other locus of modern dance activity that wasn't connected to ballet, the new generation of American art-dancers was very interested indeed in what was happening there.

Modern dance in Germany was linked to the pedagogical attention the Germans had always paid to the body—it was in Germany that gymnasiums, Turnverein societies, and physical culture originated— because Germany liked to imagine itself a reincarnation of the disciplined athleticism of ancient Greece. The features of the German modern dance emerged in the teens and early twenties, out of the national enthusiasm for Physik-Kultur, the memory of Isadora Duncan's triumphs in Berlin and Munich, and the teachings of Swiss-born Émile Jaques-Dalcroze. He believed music education must be integrated with movement. The systems of his student Rudolf von Laban, Hungarian scientist, mathematician, sculptor, and philosopher, who found out how to write dance down, describing and analyzing its various qualities, were also essential in the development of new German dance. There were links to the theater in all of these areas, especially through Laban, who had specific ideas about it. It was he who encouraged his student Mary Wigman to become a performer instead of a teacher, and he later inspired and collaborated with Kurt Jooss in England.

Mary Wigman, the acknowledged founder in Germany of modern dance, in turn taught Harald Kreutzberg, Gret Palucca, Hanya Holm—all of whom extended Laban's belief that there is such a thing as pure motion, and that a human body can have a relationship to it without intermediating factors like classical ballet technique or any other system of pre-determined steps and gestures. The Germans became theater dancers not because they were speaking through any known theatrical genre, but because each made himself, through fanatical self-discipline and mastery of the body, a precise performing instrument worthy of an audience. German dance substituted a cult of supreme self-discipline for theatrical tradition; it put forth a philosophy of the Physical distilled until it became the Spiritual.

The spiritual aura of The Body was present in other kinds of German art as well as in education, especially in a unique series of films made in Germany in the late twenties, the mountain films of Dr. Arnold Fanck, starring Leni Riefenstahl, former dancer, student of Mary Wigman, and protégée of Max Reinhardt—and great film-maker under the Nazis. The most famous of these were *Der Heilige Berg* (*The Holy Mountain*) of 1926, *Die Weisse Holle vom Piz Palu* (*The White Hell of Piz Palu*) of 1929, and *Das Blaue Licht* (*The Blue Light*), directed by Riefenstahl herself in 1932. The films were lyric hymns to Man's battles with Nature in its extreme and terrible forms —visually they told of the heavenly hallucination of this world of high mountains and physical fitness. Dance was like this in Mary Wigman's eyes; it too represented the conquest by a human will of the Nature inside the human body, and the state of spiritual ecstasy resulting from that conquest.

"[My students] must become hard, bitter and hungry," Mary Wigman told *Die Weltwoche* in 1926. "When I dance I must above all be hungry. This is the easiest way for me and my troupe to be overcome by ecstasy." The content of Wigman's dances reflected her fascination with physical and spiritual extremes; she made dances exploring trance motions, with endless turning or vibrating; she made studies of mysterious rituals like a Witch Dance, a Dance of Death— and yet she could also make intensely lyrical dances exploring single lyric gestures in concentrated fashion: *Sommertanz* was one of these. The only notable thing missing in Wigman's art was humor—and yet one can't blame her: conditions all over Germany were grim in the late 1920s, inflation was rife, and everyone was hungry. However, the saga of twenties dance everywhere leads to the conclusion that humor or wit in dance steps comes easiest when there is a tradition, a context already determined, as in the Ballets Russes productions, or even in American musical comedy dance. The task of forging context and steps together that was undertaken by the German and American art-dance left little room for any kind of teasing around the edges. Wigman's dance was the militant version of the usually playful twenties view of Woman as Amazon. She made this conceit into a serious social posture: "My students must give such an impression that every man should enthusiastically call out: 'I would not like to be married to any one of them!'" she said in the same 1926 interview in *Die Weltwoche*.

But the real content of Wigman's dances was not its social implications or its visual designs but rather its assumption that the human body could mirror spiritual states of being. Wigman's dance can be seen as the final flowering of François Delsarte's dreams of exact spiritual and physical equivalents; moreover, the Germans had found out how to *produce* the spiritual states through physical means (like starvation). There is a traceable succession from Delsarte down through German dance: Dalcroze, who taught Laban, who in turn taught Wigman, did indeed borrow large chunks of Delsarte for his movement theories (a famous Delsarte professor was teaching in Vienna while Dalcroze was studying music there around 1906).

America had its own Delsartean residues, which perhaps made the Germans when they came here more sympathetic to the younger American dancers. Mary Wigman didn't perform in America until 1931, but her student Harold Kreutzberg made an American tour in 1928 sponsored by Max Reinhardt, partnering the very elegant cabaret dancer Tilly Losch. Their repertory included Wigman-like explorations of haunted dance states: *Arabesque, Three Mad Furies, Waltzes* (to Richard Strauss, a haunted composer), *Gothic Dance, Horror, Revolt*. One can imagine the Futuristic look of these dances from the comments of the New York *Herald Tribune* (January 9, 1928); one can also see the awareness of styles that New York was acquiring:

> They represent a school which varies slightly from either the Russian or the so-called Modern or Impressionistic. The arms and particularly the hands are prominently used and the body is frequently made so bony and pliable that the spectator is reminded relentlessly of the contortionist and the acrobat.

The "so-called Modern or Impressionistic" American school—no one could ever give it just one name—cited by the *Herald Tribune* did in fact exist, however tenuously, when the Germans first arrived: Martha Graham had already composed forty-four dances and Doris Humphrey, nineteen. However, if only because of the extreme veneration by the American theater of all German forms, our dance was susceptible to Germany's and sometimes imitated it. To certain of American modern dancers, Germany supplied justifications that were lacking in the United States. Most of all it reiterated the Delsartean claim that movement qualities could be explored without a stylistic context or an intention to entertain.

Doris Humphrey, whose abstract mind had so easily embraced Ruth St. Denis' plan to "visualize the music," now turned to Germanic ideas of isolated qualities in dance and of spiritual equivalents. Her pre-1928 Denishawn dances had been papillons, spring dances, pavanes; following Kreutzberg's 1928 visit she produced *The Banshee* (April 1928), such exercises in silence as *Water Study* (October 1928) and *Speed* (March 1929), the intriguing ensemble work *Life of the Bee* (based on Maeterlinck's book; March 1929) with buzzing accompaniment, and *The Shakers* (January 1931), about the hallucinatory dancing of that American religious sect. Denishawn had thrown its graduates into the hands of German dance credos by undermining the school's training with the idea that dance is finally something you make up yourself, according to what you have sniffed out about the progression of Art. Germany provided firm and compelling philosophic underpinnings that Denishawn, namely Shawn, hadn't been able to provide even with all its talk of religion, eugenics, sex philosophy, Greek elitism, and Delsarte. The Germans and the Americans did have Delsarte in common: although their slants were different, the genealogy of both countries' art-dance can be traced directly back to this brilliant, mathematical, and visionary mid-nineteenth-century Frenchman.

Martha Graham in her rejection of Denishawn lushness and Denishawn's infernal mixtures was also thrown back on an earlier idea of pure objective Delsarte vignettes, depictions of moods and emotions. She was less tempted by the spiritual aspects of Delsarte than some of her colleagues. But many of Graham's late-twenties dances bore distinct relation to Delsartean abstractions, not quite camouflaged by their foreign titles and modern music: *Fragilité, Lugubre, Poème Ailé, Esquisse Antique, Ronde, Scherza,* from 1927; *Trouvères, Fragments, Resonances,* from 1928; *Four Insincerities,* from 1929. One of her 1930 dances, called *Project in Movement for a Divine Comedy,* was complained about by the *Herald Tribune* reviewer as being "dangerously close to a modernist's Delsarte." Martha Graham had discovered this idea for portraits of movement qualities before the Germans came. What she may have taken from the Germans was renewed justification for her own fanatic dedication to dancing that had started in 1917, and a proven example of the total discipline she required from her own performing group that she formed in 1929. But by the end of the decade her dances contained, in addition to some German rationale, at least a touch of Franco-Russian irony, and a healthy dose of American theatricality-in-spite-of-itself.

The reasons why Graham's dances were not merely genteel Delsarte entertainment or transposed schematic German dance had to do with her imagination, which at its American best was dramatically sensual, and saw things in theatrical tones and patterns. This is what Martha had taken from Miss Ruth and indirectly from Belasco. Years later in her autobiography St. Denis was still lamenting the fact that in all her career she never had "enough lighting, enough people, enough music with which to tell my story." Graham, who on the surface opposed Miss Ruth's dreams, who *seemed* to be paring down and stripping her dance-theater as furiously as were the Germans, was constitutionally unable to eliminate all the visual melodrama of the spectacle. Somehow in her best work she summoned a fullness of drama by means of the very sparseness and severity of her constructions. But Graham was always more connected in her own mind to the theater than her colleagues were: she was always looking not just for dance forms but for the dance equivalent to the modern art-theater—and many of her dances in the late twenties, just like the miracle plays of the Theater Guild and the Neighborhood Playhouse, examined the imagery of folk religions and European peasants.

Martha Graham in those years, aiming for a dance vocabulary and for a modern theatrical iconography, shared the interest of theater intellectuals in primitive religious art as a relevant source. In 1927 she made *Peasant Sketches*, a triptych composed of "Dance," "Berceuse," and "In the Church," to music by Vladimir Rebikov, Alexandre Tansman, and Tchaikovsky; in 1929 *Figure of a Saint* to Handel, *Resurrection* to Tibor Harsányi's music, and her first work for her larger group, *Vision of the Apocalypse*, to Herman Reutter's *Variations on Bach's Chorale "Komm' Süsser Tod"* (*Come Sweet Death*). Also in the style of the Theater Guild, Graham made political dances intended to abstract or iconize the feelings of the masses. In 1928 she made *Immigrant* in two sections, "Steerage" and "Strike," to music by Josip

Slavenski (*Suite aus dem Balken*), and *Poems of 1917* in two sections, "Song Behind the Lines," and "Dance of Death"—both visually recalling the Theater Guild's *Man and the Masses* of 1924.

In making these sorts of dances about real instances of war and death Martha Graham was partially deserting the pure abstraction of German dance and taking on content that usually belonged to theater. She was making dance allegories of "the one" representing "the many," the sorrows of one man containing the sorrows of all. The first section of *Poems of 1917*, "Song Behind the Lines," was about motherhood, "war-mad motherhood, a lullaby of empty arms, a bitter cry against the useless convention of war." Perhaps it was Martha's tribute to Isadora, who had died in Nice the year before, since it recalled Isadora's great themes of war and motherhood from dances like the *Ave Maria*, the *Marseillaise*, the César Franck *Rédemption*. Whether or not these dances were linked in theme to Isadora, in construction they were clear examples of Graham's own evolving style. The *New York Times* remarked (April 23, 1928) that *Poems of 1917* suggested "modern reproductions of ancient wood sculptures, and are deeply moving by their very sparseness." Graham's constant goal was to isolate the gesture, distill the movement down to the essence of its drama, and thereby find the lyric in modern terms.

By 1929 Martha Graham barely covered space in her dances. However, none of the lush swirl and dip from *The Flute of Krishna* three years before was gone; it was merely pressed back into the torso of the dancer, instilling her with power and intensity within, further compressed by the illusion of something stopping it from the outside. She was ruthless in her experimental reduction of the movement: in some dances she didn't move at all from one spot, such as the 1929 *Dance* which took its motto from Nietzsche, "Strong, Free, Joyous Action," and then proceeded to be technically immovable. Even so, intelligent critics could follow exactly what she was doing.

In a review of Graham's January 1929 concerts at the Booth Theater, John Martin, the new dance critic of the *New York Times* called her great, although with some reservations: "Bitter, intellectual, cold, if you will, her art is arresting, even aggressive, with a hard beauty as of sculptured steel." He noted the irony of the opening piece called "Dance—strong, free, joyous action," in which the dancer's feet remained planted in their "original stance." He questioned Miss Graham's "Oriental tendency toward staccato attack and slow recovery which was somewhat overworked."

But Martin revealed through his comments on nearly every

dance that he was just as interested in the pure movement qualities of the dances as were their choreographers; his column was essentially a monologue on compositional features of these short dances:

> Of the new numbers, "Insincerities," to music of Pro-
> kofieff, and "Two Variations from Sonatina," by Gretch-
> aninoff, were outstanding. The former is impudent and
> malignant in its comment on the four commonplace human
> qualities of petulance, remorse, politeness and vivacity. The
> variations, subtitled "Country Lane" and "City Street," re-
> spectively, reveal the dancer's command of plastic design.
> The charming, lyrical movement of the first part becomes
> strongly inhibited in the second, at the same time retaining
> the thematic characteristics. From the standpoint of move-
> ment alone, this was the high spot of the afternoon.

Following nearly a decade of eager experimentation, the critics, the dancers, the intellectuals, and perhaps even some of the general public possessed an endless capacity to look at small studies of "movement alone," or "plastic design," without reference to plot, spectacle, or even very much attention to qualities in the performance. The social context of the event, a gathering of intellectuals, was also an important feature: "A crowded house, containing almost every local dancer of prominence, was obviously delighted with the program. Louis Horst, as usual, assisted with first-rate accompaniments on the piano."

Louis Horst, visible in New York at the piano of every art-dance recital in the late twenties, was probably more of a deciding factor in this new kind of American dance than any other single figure. A pot-bellied, white-haired man with a long nose, Horst was born in Kansas City. He studied piano and violin while playing ragtime scores to silent movies until his mid-thirties, at which time he became music director of Denishawn. Obviously responsible for finding the modern composers (such as Homer Grunn—*Xochitl*) that Shawn and Miss Ruth commissioned to write their scores, Horst was a self-appointed crusader in the arts, interested in furthering the causes of American music and American dance. He also liked women, but he liked them especially if they burned with a pure fanatic flame for art, or if they were interested in his telling them they should.

Besides this extracurricular philosophy, he gave the Denishawn girls sound educations in music and in rhythm—and in Martha Graham's case, he was able to bring her to a musical and rhythmic competence rare in those who are not trained young. Horst left Denishawn in 1926 to study composing in Vienna, and the year after, when he came home to join Graham in her work, he brought immeasurable amounts of information about new European composers and European modern dance. It was Horst's advice that taught Graham to build a repertory on such bold and eclectic musical sources, and to attempt to parallel in dance the experiments of modern composers with melody as percussion and vice versa. The music that she used determined to a large extent the suppressed, staccato qualities she invented in movement, qualities that both constrained and intensified the lyric sense she began with and that she always infused into her dances, no matter how modern. Always it was Louis Horst who urged her on to a greater iconoclasm. One wonders whether she would have been gentler without Horst, whether it was he who made her so severe about cleansing the sweetness of her Denishawn past from her dances.

But by 1929 Martha Graham had found the core of this iconoclasm. A basic irony was at work on her stage: a contrast between the naïve American idea of dance as a light tripping over the grass—a return to the Golden Age in some idyllic grove or Utopia—and the actual bound, truncated, and drastically curtailed possibilities for Utopias in this modern world. The passionate force of this irony and the sorrow of it gave her dances a philosophic weight. The irony was the axis of her dances. But the aura of theatricality in the best of them arose from a paradox: even as the dances excluded all direct signs of humorous or lyric popular expression, they still reflected it on a high, removed plane. The playful, dynamic shapes of twenties life were not absent from Graham's stage, even in her most serious dances.

Lamentation (1930), a dance of mourning to piano music by Zoltán Kodály, presented the dancer in one long jersey tube that left only her feet and a part of her face showing. In a seated position she reels and turns in the planes of space above and around her, and folds of the material are wrenched into taut lines. The dance is a powerful one not only because it was rhythmically well-constructed but because it abstracted the densities, rhythms, and shapes of New York, 1930. The jersey pyramid recalled the grandeur of an Art Deco tower rising on its triangle base; a skyscraper reeling. The heavy stretch material resembled something of another property, stone or steel, rather as the piano melody resembled percussion. Moreover, since the industrial shape of Lamentation was actually a woman, the dance stood as a final fantasy on the fashionable woman-as-tube; the long tubular line of sheath-dress and sportsclothes was stretched in the costume to an extreme degree. The whole dance in a sense was built on Fashion's originally witty conception of a tube that is really a living torso, and so it won't stay still and remain a perfect tube. It juts out in different places.

By 1930 Martha Graham had designed a new body for her dance stage; it was a torso that made visible the mobility and power compressed in it. Her self-designed apprenticeship, her period of searching, was almost over, and by the thirties she would begin to open up her dances to more space and time, to broader dramatic ideas and her own obsessive themes. It was then that she began with her group of girls the intensive work on technique, not a technique of Denishawn gestures nor one of German-related trance dancing but one of actions in the modern American manner—suppressed actions with stopped resolutions, or actions reiterated with fanatical insistence. She caused her students to jump again and again, to jump-turn in great arcs, to fall swiftly backward in perfect control, to roll on the ground taut and held in at the stomach. Not only had she pictured Amazons on her stage, she had created them. She had taken, from twenties clothes and dancing, the allusions to power in women's arms, backs, and necks—and through dance work made them physically real. Then she added strong thighs for jumping power, and strong feet. In fact Graham fashioned a group of dancers like peasant women with working bodies—the ideal of the art-theater. For executing the movements, she gave girls the strength to hold themselves off balance, a visible strength in the lower torso, so they could jump and run stiffly and not give in to languishings or too sensual swoops.

In 1930 Martha Graham went with Louis Horst to teach in one of America's oldest frontier art schools, the Cornish School in Seattle (named for the intrepid Nellie Cornish, its founder). She supplanted a ballet teacher and began to show the students all over again the origin of the body's essential impulses. She instructed her students, young girls, to stand profile to profile and spit at one another, to find a convulsive power in the torso and stomach. By this time Graham radiated intensity from her person; she had become a Duse or an Isadora of her own day, a tragic heroine whose keynote was not sorrow but a mysterious rage. Students followed her like a Pied Piper. Three of the healthy, western country girls at the Cornish School joined her group later in New York in 1930, to mingle with others who were now her dancers: small, intense left-wing Jewish girls from immigrant families, some girls from the Lower East Side who had been her students at the Neighborhood Playhouse, along with one or two who stayed with her from John Murray Anderson's school.

On her way home from the Cornish School, Martha Graham returned to California, where her mother had remarried and where her nurse Lizzie was still living, then she and Louis Horst stayed on for a vacation in the mountain and desert country of New Mexico, the territory of the Sangre de Cristo Mountains. There she encountered the strange, savage Hispanic-Indian religious sect of the Penitentes. This sect engaged in processions through the mountains at certain times of the year, long trails of people flagellating themselves with ropes; it also made painted wooden icons of saints, the Santos. The Penitentes rites were the New World version of the European peasant ceremonies Graham had been using as material in her dances. They revealed to Graham her own pre-history, more vital than a borrowed one. Her encounter with this southwestern culture gave her a path to her great dance of 1931, *Primitive Mysteries*, which emerged as a lyric dream with an undercurrent of savage rites. Through New Mexico she re-discovered the West that had so dazzled her senses when she went with her family to California at the age of fourteen, and that was now restored to her after seven years in New York. The Penitente sect seemed to have been born out of the landscape of the Southwest, Martha Graham's own landscape by the grace of fate—the opposite of small-town Pennsylvania, where ordinarily she would have grown up. Moreover, the Penitentes were kin to the Aztecs as envisioned by Ted Shawn in Martha Graham's own dance-drama *Xochitl*. The West and the American frontier became a line of continuity to Graham the artist; they revealed her past to her and they would permeate her future.

Neither Penitentes nor Aztecs nor even California pioneers were literally present in the ensemble dance *Primitive Mysteries*, whose premiere was at New York's Craig Theater on February 2, 1931. Instead their aura was freely transposed into a dance whose subject was itself, a society of dancers and their priestess, Martha Graham, who leads them. Even though this was an organization like the German Mary Wigman's of modern novitiates of the Dance, its scent, its primal quality, was worlds away from the Germanic.

The three sections of the dance all start and end with a processional in silence from the wings at stage left, out to the center of the stage, the eighteen dancers in phalanx, four abreast, wearing plain dark blue dresses—and Martha Graham walking alone among them

in a white dress. In the program she is called the Virgin. The formations of dancers throughout the work become its breathing texture—
only two dancers detach themselves as individuals from time to time
to serve as handmaidens to the Virgin. In the first section, "Hymn to
the Virgin," four lines of four girls ranged about the stage take turns
framing the Virgin, their arms creating jagged Santos-like halos for
her head. She skims across the stage from group to group on the line
of a single flute melody. The simple, delicate, yet martial flute-and-
piano score was tailored to the dance by Louis Horst, so that each
group-pose falls on a strong brooding chord and the lone Virgin travels
on the solo flute song. (This was music visualization reversed; the music
mirrored the dance patterns instead of the other way around.) The section called "Crucifixus" places the Virgin in center stage as the dancers
circle her in single-file leaps set to dramatic staccato piano chords, big
slow leaps in a forward crouch, so that the foot of each dancer seems
to pass her mouth on the way through the leap. The third section,
"Hosanna," is one of small, staggered rhythms, in which waves of girls
move on little skips, archaic skips forward and back, and then around
in a circle that turns and then reverse-turns, like some strange keening
mountain dance. It looks a little like wild Indians attempting an
ordered Square Dance of the Pioneers.

The dancers in *Primitive Mysteries* are wild, but they have been
tamed just enough to fit the order of the dance. With its fierce sense
of form and reductive pattern, this work is nearer to the Russians'
musically influenced compositions on "primitive" themes than to the
Germans' impressionistic movement essays to percussion. It speaks
through its evolving formations, which are nakedly visible. It is as
formal a dance as Bronislava Nijinska's *Les Noces* about Russian peasant rites, and at the same time as evocative of other forms—its dancers
unexpectedly recall the corps of dancers in *Giselle,* the Wilis, who are
the Amazons of the Romantic ballet, and also the Bacchae of Greek
myth and drama, the bands of women who followed Dionysus. The
uncanny aura of *Primitive Mysteries* arises from the power projected
by the bonding of this female corps.

These are not conscious, friendly, American bonds among its
women, but mysterious and mythic ones that have cropped up before
in ballet history. The dance not only portrays them but implies they
have always existed, even in America. The ensemble in *Primitive
Mysteries*—in fact Martha Graham's group as a whole—was her re-
vitalization of the corps de ballet, an idea that hadn't exactly made
sense in America before. Graham was not the first to form a society of

women within her dance—Isadora, Ruth St. Denis, even Gertrude
Hoffman in vaudeville had used companies of girl pupils—but Graham
made this fact almost the central one. In dances like *Primitive Mysteries* the compelling quality of such a corps was revealed and named,
with a vengeance. Moreover, the dancers in *Primitive Mysteries* are
not girls but women, Amazons who obey the rites of a sect only they
know about—a sect infinitely fierce yet benign, something like Denishawn as Martha Graham experienced it, which revolved around the
figure of Ruth St. Denis. The corps of dancers groups and regroups
around the figure of the Virgin, who is an icon of all the maternal
ripeness of Isadora Duncan in her Primavera dances, of Ruth St.
Denis in her exotic rituals of the Orient, of Eleonora Duse in her
Mater Dolorosa plays.

Primitive Mysteries examines a matriarchy in all its dimensions:
it calls up a fragrant and faraway Catholic aura inside its dynamics,
which are essentially fierce, aggressive, and Protestant. It has united
these two worlds and shows their need of each other. It is about that
longing for the sensual in the Methodist child Ruth St. Denis, so
drawn to the finery and rituals of the stage, and in the Presbyterian
child Martha Graham, so intoxicated with the sun and jagged foliage
of California and with her first major dance role as savage Aztec princess. *Primitive Mysteries* can be seen as a strangely matured vision of
why its kind of dancing was born in America: because a certain part
of the population couldn't do without myths anymore, certain primal
myths Americans had never heard about—among them the myth of
the matriarchy and of a society of women. Some young women and
ultimately young men hallucinated dance into being, in the form of
its imaginary past. Then they taught it to other dancers so it had an
existence outside of their own bodies.

Martha Graham came along just when America was shyly accept-
ing the existence of this mysterious art that had been seen so long
as a domain of ballet girls' illicit behavior, of Salomé shamelessness and
ragtime violence. But even when it was wrapped up and packaged by
dancers like Ted Shawn to look like other phenomena in the culture,
dancing wasn't really yet understood. Graham could make a career for
herself, which was probably the most important one of its time of any
woman in theater or any of the arts, because that career was in dance,
and dance was undigested by America. She could tell the public anything she wanted to about this realm, because she was able to translate
dance into rhapsodic but also forceful and logical rhetoric. And aside
from speaking about dance, Graham made the dances themselves at-

tractive to the *minds* that encountered them: she gave them schemata, developments, recapitulations; she explained the irrational. Martha Graham was really two people who are rarely combined in one psyche: her childhood in a household of women, watched over by an Irish-Catholic nurse, had given her the intuitive, sensory world; her privileged education, strong in logic and moral distinctions, gave her the means to look at the other world, to colonize it. She was a different creature from the earlier dance creators, Isadora, Ruth St. Denis, and the others. They came to dancing as social outcasts—their families were poor and eccentric—and expanded inside it. Graham came as a favored daughter of the conventional world that opposed dancing, and unlike her predecessors she gave up something substantial to become a dancer—the full virtuous life of an American wife and active citizen.

The only way to assuage all the doubts and fears that resulted from abandoning one's patrimony was to capture dance and bring it back alive, even though it would be changed in the process. This Martha Graham did, paradoxically by abandoning the mass audience. As a young dancer Graham came into an idyll, that time before and even during World War I when the new arts of photography, movies, décor, and dance were drawing on a fresh and all-pervasive sense of an American lyric, which flowered furiously in those years. This was a mood attractive to a broad base of people yet still capable of subtle kinds of expression—as witness the silent movies of Griffith and other directors. Dancing in that mood contained special urgencies of its own, since it had emerged partly as a liberating force against women's peculiar ideological bind within the democracy. Ted Shawn brought it as close as he could to the commercial side of the American idyllic mode but he didn't destroy the underlying missions of its women founders—to give some kind of gift of themselves to their audiences and to allow all women to know this place of physical ease and musical motion. Martha Graham did destroy those missions in favor of her different obsessions.

Graham was haunted by the America she had abandoned, and by the residue of fear and sorrow left among American youth by World War I. This compelled her continually to explain or reveal to her audience why she was a dancer. Her subject matter was more than dancing, more than musical and rhythmical motion—it was self-justification—and eventually her art would suffer from that. As she gradually became the undisputed queen of the art-dance stage, she enacted again and again in dance her own break with the nurturing mission of American women. In a sense she returned to the dilemma of Catharine Esther Beecher's and Ruth Emma Dennis' generation:

where was the place of art in a virtuous American woman's life? Over the decades of her career a gallery of dance heroines was added by Martha Graham to the earlier Radhas and Egyptas and Salomés and all the Greek maidens of Isadora. These heroines were not exotic and fragrant mirages, but sturdily constructed psyches with ample, if violent, cause for action. Some of them—the Emily Dickinson figure in *Letter to the World* (1940), the Bride in *Appalachian Spring* (1944), the One Who Seeks in *Dark Meadow* (1946)—are full, complex, and alive in the manner of the women of *Primitive Mysteries,* wherein gentleness and sternness war with each other to make a high vivacity. Others of her heroines are more schematic representations of the violent act of disrupting a family—Medea in *Cave of the Heart* (1946), Jocasta in *Night Journey* (1947), Clytemnestra (1958), even Joan of Arc in *Seraphic Dialogue* (1955). They rage inside dances that are in some mysterious way hermetically sealed. They are never just dancers; they are never beings simply set in motion by music, as were Isadora's and Ruth St. Denis' dance heroines. Graham's heroines always bear the weight of their intellects.

Martha Graham's territory of innumerable dances and a self-sufficient dance technique is a vast but closed territory, since to create an art out of one's experience alone is ultimately a self-limiting act. If there had been other choreographers with Graham's gifts and her stature, her work might have seemed a more balanced part of the story of American dance. But as she built her repertory her own language seemed to shut out all other kinds. Even when an audience thinks it discerns traces of influence from other dance styles, the totality of Graham's theatrical idiom, its control of costumes, lights, and every impulse of the dance, makes the reference seem a mirage. Dance is not her main subject. It is only her servant.

Graham had achieved her autonomy by 1931. By that time, three giant figures who had invented the new twentieth-century dance were dead: Serge Diaghilev, Anna Pavlova, and Isadora Duncan. Their era ended with them, and their dance values nearly disappeared. Their colleagues Michel Fokine and Ruth St. Denis lived on in America like whales on the beach. During the twenties Martha Graham and *her* colleagues had rescued art-dance from vaudeville and movies and musical comedy and all the resonances of the American idyllic mode, but in so doing they closed the channels through which different kinds of dance could speak to one another—and these stayed closed for half a century. Modern dance dedicated itself to deep significance. It gave up lightness, it gave up a wealth of exotic color, it gave up a certain kind of theatrical wit and that age-old mobile exchange between a dancer and the dancer's rhythmical and musical material. No material in modern dance was neutral. The core of the art became an obsession with meaning and allegory as expressed in bodies. Modern dance excluded its own theatrical traditions of casual play, gratuitous liveliness, the spontaneous pretend, and the rainbow of genres that had formed it. But all these things survived in the public domain, where they had always lived, and they have continued to surface in American dance, if only by accident.

Bibliographic Essay
and
Index

Bibliographic Essay

The sources for this book were the thousands of newspaper clippings in the Denishawn and Louis Horst collections of memorabilia, in the Dance Collection of the Library of the Performing Arts, Lincoln Center; also the Drama Archives of that library. The existence of Lincoln Kirstein's 1940s dance magazine *Dance Index* helped my work, and so did Arlene Croce's *Ballet Review* as a source of information and a place to try out portions of this book. Ruth St. Denis' *An Unfinished Life* (New York, 1939) and Isadora Duncan's *My Life* (New York, 1927) provided chronological skeletons—both are fascinating and contain many more facts than are at first apparent—and Christina Schlundt's *The Professional Appearances of Ruth St. Denis and Ted Shawn* (New York, 1962) was a masterful guide. Three books provided ideological marking points: Lincoln Kirstein's *Dance: A Short History of Classic Theatrical Dancing* (New York, 1935 and 1974), Stella Mary Newton's *Health, Art and Reason: Dress Reformers of the Nineteenth Century* (London, 1974), and Arlene Croce's *The Fred Astaire & Ginger Rogers Book* (New York, 1972). The books by Constance Rourke on popular and folk culture inspired me—*Trumpets of Jubilee* (New York, 1927 and 1963), *The Roots of American Culture* (New York, 1942), and *American Humor* (New York, 1931 and 1959)—and reproductions in *Camera Work: A Critical Anthology*, edited by Jonathan Green (New York, 1973) and *De Meyer*, edited by Robert Brandau (New York, 1976), gave me a sense of the period's poses and gestures.

In addition:

The PROLOGUE emerged from Nicholas A. Vardac's book *Stage to Screen* (Cambridge, Massachusetts, 1949), *The San Francisco Stage*, by Edmond M. Gagey (Westport, Connecticut, 1970), Selma Jeanne Cohen's *Dance as a Theater Art* (New York, 1974), and the scrapbooks in Amelia Gilmore's house.

CHAPTER 1's information came from a collection of dress-reform and Delsarte manuals of the period; it also relied on Ann Douglas' extensive work on women's health in the nineteenth century (see "Fashionable Diseases: Women's Complaints and Their Treatment in Nineteenth-Century America," *Journal of Interdisciplinary History*, IV, 1973, 25–53) and on Suzanne Shelton's work on Ruth St. Denis' early life. *The Oven*

Birds, edited by Gail Parker (New York, 1972), was also a source. Anyone interested in Ruth St. Denis' philosophical origins should read Mary Baker Eddy's *Science and Health.*

CHAPTER 2 owes much to Douglas Gilbert's book *American Vaudeville; Its Life and Times* (New York, 1940), to Craig Timberlake's and William Winter's biographies of David Belasco, to Archie Binn's book *Minnie Maddern Fiske* (New York, 1955), to Gerda Taranow's study of Sarah Bernhardt, *The Art Within the Legend* (Princeton, New Jersey, 1972), to Constance Rourke's *Troupers of the Gold Coast, or the Rise of Lotta Crabtree* (New York, 1928), and to the collection of Ruth St. Denis' unpublished letters and other writings in the library at UCLA.

CHAPTER 3 has borrowed from past work of Frank Kermode and present work of Sally R. Sommers on Loie Fuller, from Loie Fuller's autobiography and from Maud Allan's, from Nesta MacDonald's work on Isadora Duncan, which was published in installments in *Dance Magazine* in 1978, from Francis Steegmuller's lovely book *Your Isadora* (New York, 1974), from the WPA records of San Francisco's theater and concert activity in the nineteenth century, from Ina Coolbrith's poetry and Robert Ingersoll's speeches—and from my dance classes with Julia Levien in Isadora Duncan technique, which taught me more than books.

FOR CHAPTER 4, I gained much material from Charles C. Baldwin's biography of Stanford White (New York, 1931; paperback, 1976), from Carl Van Vechten's dance reviews, from Palmer White's book *Paul Poiret* (New York, 1972), from Barbara Naomi Cohen's work on Gertrude Hoffman, from the *Vogue* magazines I read in the Condé Nast library. Lacking in the field is a serious book on Florenz Ziegfeld.

CHAPTER 5 relied on *They All Played Ragtime,* by Rudi Blesh and Harriet Janis (New York, 1971); the collected reviews of James Huneker and his *New Cosmopolis* (New York, 1915); on Irene Castle's autobiography, *Castles in the Air* (New York, 1958); on the Castles' feature movie of 1914, *Whirl of Life*; on many issues of *Vanity Fair*; and on the ragtime phonograph records I listened to. (Thanks to Music Masters, Joan Morris, William Bolcum, Max Morath for re-issues and revivals.)

For CHAPTER 6, I read Elbert Hubbard, Bliss Carman, Richard Hovey, Theodore Roosevelt, and Ted Shawn; also the manual of the Ralston Club. Ellen Moers' book *The Dandy: Brummel to Beerbohm* (New York, 1960) provided some clues, and here Benjamin B. Hampton's *History of the American Film Industry from Its Beginnings to 1931* was useful (New York, 1970).

CHAPTER 7 owes much to Nesta MacDonald's *Diaghilev Observed: By Critics in England and the United States 1911–1929* (New York,

1975), through which I found the Boston critic HTP's (Henry T. Parker) writings. The photographs of George Seeley, Gertrude Käsebier, Anne Brigman, Clarence White, Edward Steichen, Arnold Genthe, et al., were core material for this chapter, along with a book called *The Ideal Orator* (1904) and more *Vanity Fairs*.

CHAPTER 8 came out of the Museum of Modern Art's extensive festival of D. W. Griffith films in 1975, and Robert Henderson's, Anthony Slide's, Billy Bitzer's, Karl Brown's, and especially Lillian Gish's books on D. W. Griffith; Charles Higham's biography of Cecil B. De Mille; Mary Pickford's autobiography; and a little-known novel by Rupert Hughes, *Souls for Sale* (1921). Vachel Lindsay's *The Art of the Moving Picture* (reprinted, New York, 1970) was an aesthetic guide.

CHAPTER 9 borrowed from Colleen Moore's autobiography, *Silent Star* (New York, 1968), from Selma Jeanne Cohen's biography of Doris Humphrey, *An Artist First* (Connecticut, 1972), from Don McDonagh's biography of Martha Graham (New York, 1973), from a performance of Marion Rice and her company of Denishawn dancers (also those of Joyce Tristler's company), and from Julia Levien's and Hortense Kooluris' concerts with Gemze de Lappe and the Isadora Duncan Centenary Company.

CHAPTER 10's sources were Allen Churchill's *The Theatrical Twenties* (New York, 1975), Ned Wayburn's 1925 manual on stage dancing, Fred Astaire's autobiography, *Steps in Time* (New York, 1959), John Murray Anderson's autobiography, *Out Without My Rubbers* (New York, 1954), Lee Simonson's autobiographical book on stage design, *The Art of Scenic Design* (New York, 1950), Stark Young's essays and reviews, Alice Lewisohn Crowley's book *The Neighborhood Playhouse* (New York, 1959), Theresa Helburn's and Lawrence Langner's books on the Theater Guild, also more *Vogues* and *Vanity Fairs*, Don McDonagh's and Nesta MacDonald's chronologies, Walter Sorell's book on Mary Wigman, and an interview with Martha Graham.

Index

A NOTE ON THE TYPE

The text of this book was set on the Linotype in Fairfield, the first typeface from the hand of the distinguished American artist and engraver Rudolph Ruzicka. In its structure Fairfield displays the sober and sane qualities of a master craftsman whose talent was long dedicated to clarity. It is this trait that accounts for the trim grace and virility, the spirited design, and sensitive balance of this original face, first issued in 1940.

Rudolph Ruzicka was born in Bohemia in 1883 and came to America in 1894. He set up his own shop devoted to wood engraving and printing in New York in 1913, after a varied career as a wood engraver, in photo-engraving and bank-note printing plants, as an art director and a freelance artist. Mr. Ruzicka died at Hanover, New Hampshire, in 1978. He had designed and illustrated many books and had created a considerable list of individual prints—wood engravings, line engravings on copper, aquatints. W. A. Dwiggins wrote: "Until you see the things themselves you have no sense of the artist behind them. His outstanding quality, as artist and person, is *sanity*. Complete esthetic equipment, all managed by good sound judgment about ways and means, aims and purposes, utilities and 'functions'—and all this level-headed balance-mechanism added to the lively mental state that makes an artist an artist. Fortunate equipment in a disordered world . . ."

Composed by
Maryland Linotype Composition Co., Inc.,
Baltimore, Maryland.
Printed by
The Murray Printing Company,
Forge Village, Massachusetts.
Bound by
American Book—Stratford Press,
Saddle Brook, New Jersey.

This book was designed by
Holly McNeely.